THE BARLOW CLOWES AFFAIR

LAWRENCE LEVER

The
Barlow Clowes
Affair

MACMILLAN
LONDON

First published 1992 by
MACMILLAN LONDON LIMITED
Cavaye Place London SW10 9PG
and Basingstoke

Associated companies in Auckland, Delhi, Dublin, Gaborone,
Hamburg, Harare, Hong Kong, Johannesburg, Kuala Lumpur,
Lagos, Manzini, Melbourne, Mexico City, Nairobi, New York,
Singapore and Tokyo.

ISBN 0–333–51377 0

A CIP catalogue record for this book is available from
the British Library

Photytypeset by Intype, London
Printed by Billing and Sons Ltd, Worcester

To my parents, Esther and David Lever,
and my wife, Keren.

ACKNOWLEDGEMENTS

•

Many people gave generously of their time to help me research and write this book. Some of them wish to remain anonymous and I can only thank them for their kindness. Among those I can identify I would particularly like to thank Per Eric Hawthorne and Jacqui Webster. Our work together in producing a Channel 4 documentary on Barlow Clowes gave me tremendous support and impetus in writing this book. I would also like to thank the following people: John Bell, Andy Bowers, David Brewerton, Nikki Brokenshire, Meredith Chambers, Bernard Clark, Peter Clarke, the Reverend John Clowes, Adrian Collins, the late Barbara Conway, John Dyer, Geoffrey Farrington, Kathleen and Misha Fedouloff, Barbara Felby-Hollis, Antony Gold, Professor Jim Gower, Peter Hayes, Kate Jones, Anthony Julius, Richard Millett, David North, Gaynor Pengelly, David Pine, Geoffrey Pointon, Simon Preston, Ken Robinson, Dominique Searle, Julie Scott-Bayfield, Tim Trotter, Araminta Whitley, Bob Wilkinson and Clive Wolman. A special thank-you goes to Katie Owen and Roland Philipps of Macmillan for their patience and guidance throughout this project. Finally, I would like to thank my wife, Keren, for her invaluable advice and support.

The book was researched and written over a three-year period. It is based on interviews with approximately 150 people, the official reports of Sir Godfray Le Quesne and the Ombudsman into Barlow Clowes, transcripts of evidence given during the Barlow Clowes trial between July 1991 and January 1992, and a myriad of other published and unpublished documents. From this material I compiled a chronology covering most of the major events from Peter Clowes's birth in December 1942 through to his first arrest in June 1988. This formed the backbone of the book. I had three separate interviews with Peter Clowes (and for some of the time his wife Pamela) at his home in the latter half of 1988. Clowes later refused to co-operate in the preparation of this book.

Lawrence Lever
13 January 1992

CONTENTS

.

PROLOGUE: The Tail 1
1 Early Days: Pots and Pans 7
2 The Partnership 18
3 Robbing Peter to Pay Paul 25
4 A Narrow Escape 32
5 The Turning Point 40
6 The Advertising Campaign 47
7 A Litany of Warnings 55
8 Jewellery, Lies and the Department of Trade 63
9 The Time Bomb 75
10 Corporate Forays 98
11 The Man with the 'Von' in the Middle 107
12 Hello Gibraltar 115
13 A Dark Day in August 122
14 In the Kingdom of the Blind 133
15 The Farce Continues 140
16 The Hermes Fiddle 149
17 The Mole 163
18 Out of Control 168
19 The Secret Investigation 178
20 The Cover-Up Operation 184
21 Countdown to Disaster 192
22 The Fight for Compensation 212
23 Breathtaking Cheek 230
EPILOGUE: Is Anyone's Money Safe? 258
NOTES 268
PICTURE ACKNOWLEDGEMENTS 278

PROLOGUE

·

THE TAIL

·

It was the evening of Monday 13 June 1988 when Peter Clowes, head bowed, stepped out of a side door of the south London offices of accountants Ernst & Whinney. He hardly noticed the press photographers who snatched pictures of him as he was ushered into a waiting car. He was tired, desperate and on the verge of a nervous breakdown. Peter Clowes had just confessed.

He had admitted to some of his closest friends and business associates that he had systematically cheated and lied to them for years; that he had diverted almost £100 million of ordinary people's life-savings into planes, boats, jewellery companies and a series of other entities owned by him. Much of this money would never be recovered. On top of this, £37 million was missing, completely unaccounted for. It had taken two weeks of repeated questioning by investigators to break Clowes down.

As the car proceeded across Westminster Bridge, several other cars started up and took the same route. Unknown to him, Clowes was being followed.

The ideal number of policemen for a tailing operation is twelve per person being followed. On this occasion only seven policemen, from a specially trained surveillance squad, were following Clowes in a series of unmarked cars. At first they did not know where he was going, but soon it became clear that he was on his way to Euston Station. He was going home to Manchester. But the surveillance squad were taking no chances.

As Clowes went through the barrier at Euston and boarded the Manchester train, three plain-clothes police officers flashed their credentials at the ticket inspector and entered the train. The Serious Fraud Office in London had already made arrangements for a team to pick up Clowes's tail in Manchester. A drugs surveillance squad was allocated to the job. Every station where the Manchester train stopped *en route* was already covered by plain-clothes policemen in unmarked cars. Police officers at Barlow Clowes's Cheshire headquarters were frantically assembling sufficient evidence to arrest the company's chairman. In the meantime it was vital that he was not allowed to flee the country.

1

The collapse of Barlow Clowes had, in the space of a fortnight, become a major public scandal, one which had already triggered enormous embarrassment for the Government. While the weary Clowes was travelling home, questions were being asked in both Houses of Parliament as to why the Government had given him a licence to deal with the public.

Barlow Clowes had had its licence – from the Department of Trade and Industry – since October 1985. In theory the company took people's money and invested it in one of the safest forms of investments – British Government securities, known as 'gilts'. Barlow Clowes' offer of security of capital and a fixed income, made it particularly attractive to elderly investors. The reality had turned out to be shockingly different. And there were already headline stories in the press claiming that the Government had been warned years before of fraud at Barlow Clowes.

That same Monday afternoon Lord Young, head of the Department of Trade and Industry, had announced a public enquiry into his Department's handling of what had already become known as the 'Barlow Clowes affair'. 'Public concern has been expressed about the role of my department,' Lord Young told the House of Lords. 'I have decided that this should be examined objectively and independently.'

Meanwhile, in the House of Commons, Francis Maude, junior minister at the Department of Trade, was making an identical statement and being attacked by all sides of the House. Tony Blair, opposition spokesman on Trade and Industry, criticised the DTI for its 'years of incompetence and gullibility'. Fifteen thousand people, mainly retired and elderly, had entrusted their life-savings to Barlow Clowes. Some were threatening to kill themselves if they did not get their money back. The Government had to help the Barlow Clowes investors, Blair said. Allen McKay, Labour MP for Barnsley, said that he had just received a letter from one of his constituents whose home, retirement funds and car depended on his investment. When would he get his money back?

The plight of the investors did not trouble Clowes. His mind was working overtime on a series of rationalisations and justifications for his behaviour. It was anybody's fault but his. All he was trying to do was to get the investment returns which he had promised his customers. He could not do it from gilts so he had invested in other assets. If only the authorities had not closed him down investors would not have lost out. He was like a bank. If you asked Midland Bank to pay back all its customers at the same time it could not do it either. It was enemies in the City who, jealous of the amount of money he had raised from investors, had contrived to bring him down.

These and other explanations swirled around Clowes's mind as he arrived home that Monday evening. His house, on a hill just outside the village of Prestbury, had a splendid view of the surrounding fields from its massive living-room window. Centre House, Paddock Brow, Prestbury, had another distinctive feature: Clowes had bought it with money belonging to Barlow Clowes investors.

It was only a temporary home for Clowes, his wife Pamela, and two of their children. A top-class firm of local builders, Brown's of Wilmslow, was completely refurbishing the Clowes marital home, Swingate Cottage, near Macclesfield, at a cost of several hundred thousand pounds. Clowes had given Swingate to Pamela, 'in consideration of my natural love and affection on the occasion of Pamela's first pregnancy by me'. But there may have been another, more sinister, motivation. Swingate was just one of a number of homes which Clowes had given to his family in recent years. Perhaps he had seen the writing on the wall and had been looking to put his money into friendly hands, which would resist any subsequent attempts by investigators to retrieve it. At that stage, with a picture of massive fraud just emerging, no explanation could be discounted.

Centre House is located at the top of a narrow drive barely visible from the main road. At the bottom of the drive the drugs surveillance squad from Crewe, near Manchester, were camped out for the night. The Clowes job was not an easy one for the twelve-man team, who clearly had to avoid being spotted. It was not uncommon for them to bring spades and dig trenches in which to hide. 'It's bloody awful here,' one of the team radioed back to base, 'there's nowhere we can dig in.'

The next day brought news for which Graham Balchin, the Detective Superintendent in charge of the Clowes case at the Serious Fraud Office, had been waiting. Following a series of interviews with staff at Barlow Clowes's head office in Poynton, the police had assembled enough evidence to arrest Clowes. It was to be a holding charge. Clowes would be arrested for systematically shredding documents under the nose of two government inspectors who had been probing his business since the previous November. It amounted to a charge of perverting the course of justice but it was enough for the time being.

The interviews with Barlow Clowes staff were faxed to London. Balchin typed the necessary documents with his junior officer Detective Inspector Graham Watson. Just before midnight they obtained a warrant for Clowes's arrest. At 4 a.m. Watson and Balchin started the 200–mile drive to Manchester. The plan was to rendezvous with the surveillance squad at 8 a.m at Macclesfield police station and for Balchin to arrest Clowes at home later that day. It was Wednesday 15 June 1988.

Clowes had not been idle. Despite his ordeal in London, he had left his home the previous day to visit his secretary, the loyal Dorothy Wilson. The surveillance squad, who had tailed him to Wilson's home, watched Clowes leave and load a pile of documents into his car.

Clowes had also made a trip to Prestbury village to buy that day's newspapers. Many people who find themselves under constant attack in the national press try to cope with the unbearable strain which this exerts by not buying the papers. At the height of the Guinness affair, when former chairman Ernest Saunders was struggling for sanity, his family deliberately kept them away from him. Tony Berry, whose controversial dealings as chairman of Blue Arrow were exposed in the national media, stopped buying newspapers and watched fellow commuters reading about him as he travelled to work each day. But Clowes was different. Having persuaded himself that he was a wronged man, and seething with desire for retribution, he wanted to absorb everything that was said about him.

On the Wednesday morning of his intended arrest the surveillance squad were waiting for him to collect the papers from the local newsagent. Clowes had done this the previous day at around 8 a.m. and the squad hung around, rather than keep the rendezvous back at the police station with Balchin and Watson. They arrived at 8.10 a.m. and waited for the squad to arrive.

Clowes drove off to the village in his red Shogun. The surveillance team immediately followed him. They were under standing instructions to move in and arrest him immediately if they ever sensed they might lose him.

As Clowes sped down the road towards the village some of the junior members of the team became nervous. It was only a matter of an hour or so before his arrest and to lose him now would be disastrous. As Clowes was approaching the main village junction they decided to act. One unmarked police car overtook him and screeched to a halt, blocking the road, while the other stopped behind. Clowes was trapped by the village church. Bringing up the rear was a breathless pack of journalists and television crews who arrived on the scene too late to witness the actual arrest. Visibly shaken, Clowes was asked by one of the surveillance team to accompany them and was driven to Macclesfield police station. He looked blank and vacant as he arrived at the station and was put in a cell.

The press pack trundled back down the road to break the news of her husband's arrest to Pamela Clowes. The wife's reaction would be some consolation for missing the actual arrest.

At Macclesfield police station Balchin told Clowes that he had a warrant to search Centre House. Clowes did not want the house searched under the eyes of the national press so it was decided to drive to the house and wait nearby until the press had dispersed. Some of the surveillance team were still watching the house and would give the all-clear. With any luck the press would get the distraught wife's reaction and leave. However, Pamela Clowes, after receiving the news of her husband's arrest, had invited some of the pressmen in for a cup of tea.

'This was absolutely unnecessary. Peter had co-operated with everyone from the beginning and has acted with great honour and dignity,' she said. Pamela, who was publicly sticking by her husband despite privately cold-shouldering him, described the manner of his arrest as 'disgraceful'.

'I feel terribly upset and humiliated,' she told pressmen.

Balchin, Watson, Clowes and two other policemen crammed in a single unmarked police car waited patiently in the car park of a nearby private housing estate for the all-clear from the surveillance team. A busybody local resident told them to move on.

It was a hot sunny day and the police officers were becoming restless. Eventually the signal came and Clowes was taken back to Centre House to be reunited with his wife. A Manchester solicitor, Charles Buckley, was already at the house. A bankrupt and something of a maverick, Buckley had offered his services to Clowes a few days earlier. When she heard of her husband's arrest Pamela's first reaction had been to telephone Buckley.[1]

The house was searched, various documents were found and taken away. A large haul was found crammed into the boot of Pamela's red Mercedes. Clowes was driven back to London and interviewed on tape. He admitted shredding documents but claimed it was routine and not an attempt to escape detection. Balchin rang Assistant Commissioner John Tate and told him there was enough evidence to charge Clowes. He spent the night in a cell in Bishopsgate police station while Buckley and Pamela drank pink champagne in a London hotel.

Clowes, who started his working life selling pots and pans in his father's hardware shop, had become a national villain. In the space of eighteen years he had risen to become a man entrusted with almost £200 million of other people's money. He had fooled government departments and some of the country's top firms of lawyers, accountants, merchant bankers and financial advisers. Worst of all he had cheated 15,000 investors, most of whom were elderly or retired and had little financial expertise. They had invested their life-savings, their redundancy money, many of them living off the income. Former teachers, ex-civil servants, widows and disabled people who had received financial compensation for their disabilities. The result was the largest financial scandal of the century, one which would lead to two separate government enquiries, and eventually trigger an unprecedented £155–million government handout to the defrauded investors.

What kind of man is Peter Clowes? And how did he do it?

CHAPTER ONE

•

EARLY DAYS: POTS AND PANS

•

'My parents' one value in life, the one thing they passed on,
certainly to Peter, was that everything had a monetary price.'
The Reverend John Clowes, Peter Clowes's brother.

Peter Clowes was born on 8 December 1942 into a modest working-class family living in Flixton near Manchester. Number 8 Lawrence Road had been the Clowes family home for six years but, with the advent of war, was uncomfortably close to the Trafford Park industrial estate, where the Vickers factory made aircraft engines and which was a prime target for Luftwaffe bombers. Both Lawrence Road and nearby Derwent Road were regularly splintered with shrapnel and Eric Clowes, Peter's father, built an Anderson shelter in the back garden, where the family would huddle together during air raids.

Peter was the only natural child of Eric and Mary Clowes. The couple were unable to have any more and when Peter was three adopted another son, John. Eric and Mary Clowes had come from very poor backgrounds. Mary was born in the mill town of Todmorden near Manchester. 'My mother did split schooling, going to school in the mornings and working in the afternoons and leaving school completely at fourteen,' says John Clowes, now a vicar at Oakhill near Bath. 'She was one of a very large family, as my father was as well. Leaving school with nothing, with no qualifications, very very poor, and then working up to buying their own business.'

The Clowes business was running a hardware shop in Moss Side, a couple of miles from Manchester city centre. In those days Moss Side was a solid working-class area, with wide cobbled streets lined on either side with shops. Peter's parents moved from Flixton to live above the shop – Eric B. Clowes Hardware Dealer – at number 46 Ellesmere Street. The street's inhabitants were mainly tradesmen and, like the Cloweses, lived above their shops. At number 45 Elles-

mere Street was Harry Addis, a 'garment maker', while Arthur Bar-
nett, at number 74, was a blacksmith. Frank Boole at number 81 was
a packing-case maker and a tram cleaner, Albert Rhodes, lived at
number 35.[1]

Eric Clowes and his brother Bill had married two sisters, Mary
and Isabelle. Bill and Isabelle had a son and a daughter and for a
time all eight members of the Clowes family lived in cramped conditions above the Moss Side shop. Large tracts of Moss Side were
slum areas, already earmarked for demolition in the early 1950s. It
was adjacent to Hulme, another semi-slum area where the demolition
process had started in 1929. Both areas had been quite badly bombed
during the war and prefabricated houses lined the main road, Princess Parkway, which led through Moss Side, then Hulme, towards
the city centre.

During the 1950s the hardware business was run by Peter's parents alone. It thrived on selling heating fuel in the days before
central heating became commonplace. 'They sold more paraffin than
anything, it was built up on paraffin. They worked very hard,' says
John Clowes. 'My mother ran the shop in Moss Side. We helped as
boys, we all had jobs. My jobs were cleaning all the brassware on a
Friday evening, cleaning the cellars, washing the cellar steps, when
I was old enough serving in the shop, delivering firewood on a
Saturday. We sold a lot of coalbricks and peat, delivering them in a
little truck.'[2]

While Mary Clowes ran the shop, Eric would be out all day
selling his paraffin door to door in the working-class suburbs of south
Manchester. 'Peter on a Saturday helped my father on his rounds.
My father had a little trailer which he towed behind a truck which
held four hundred gallons of paraffin. They would sell that in the
day and sometimes they would come back half-way through the day
and load up again. During the winter they were very very busy,'
John Clowes says.

'We were brought up in the same way that my parents were
brought up. We never had pocket money. Everything you had you
earned. We never questioned it. My parents were given nothing in
their lives and neither were we.'

Both the Clowes brothers were bright. They passed their eleven-
plus examinations which entitled them to attend Chorlton Grammar
School, on Sandy Lane a mile and a half from their home. Peter
Clowes claims that he excelled at maths. However, school records
indicate that he did not get the O level. 'He was neither a scholar
nor a scoundrel,' says Ernie Gallagher, his mathematics teacher.

Clowes also took courses in commerce and economics and developed a passion for chess. 'Chess appealed to his mind, he had that sort of mind,' says John Clowes, who describes his brother as 'calculating'. But he had few if any friends and was regarded as a loner by his fellow pupils. 'He didn't seem to fit in', says Dave McEwen, who was at Chorlton Grammar at the same time as Clowes. 'I don't think he was very popular, he was harassed and picked on.' McEwen has memories of a short-trousered, short-legged and green-blazered Peter Clowes running as fast as he could in the fields behind the school chased by hordes of fellow pupils. The fields ran down to the local railway line and offered no escape. McEwen's memory does not stretch to recalling what happened next.

John, in contrast, founded the Christian Fellowship Society at Chorlton Grammar and from an early age wrote rather formal accounts of its activities in the *Arrow*, the school magazine, describing the society's 'lively' or 'stimulating' discussions which normally followed 'witty addresses' from visiting churchmen. 'I was going through my obnoxious phase,' says John Clowes.

Peter meanwhile may well have envied his younger brother his early recognition. The brothers were not close and Peter later bitterly regretted not having a university education as his brother had. Much later, when his collapsed empire had transformed him into a national figure, Peter spontaneously remarked of his brother, 'He can't steal my thunder now.'

After school every day the brothers were expected to help out in the hardware shop. 'I'm surprised we ever found time for studying,' says John Clowes. The brothers were paid wages – every Friday evening – not pocket money. But the Cloweses were generous with them, paying them far more in wages than other children received in pocket money. Peter saved his obsessively, even to the point of preferring a thrashing from his father when he had misbehaved rather than pay a 'fine' – which was the alternative form of punishment in the Clowes household. Eric Clowes, a weak man in most other respects, was responsible for administering discipline. This he did with a razer strop which hung at the top of the cellar steps underneath the shop in Moss Side. John Clowes remembers one occasion when he and Peter were offered the choice of a thrashing or a half-crown fine: John paid the fine; Peter took the thrashing.

Money was the dominant theme and value running through the Clowes household in Peter's early years, which was hardly surprising given the backgrounds of Peter's parents and that the family was surrounded by poverty. The Clowes hardware shop doubled as a pawnbroker's. 'A lot of people couldn't have lived without the book – the weekly credit in the shop,' says John Clowes. 'My mother would take goods from them and they would redeem them at the end of the week against coal and things that they needed.

'The one thing my parents couldn't see was anything that couldn't be measured in terms of money. "How much does it cost?" was their way of judging, their criterion. That was their one value in life, the one thing they passed on, certainly to Peter, that everything had a monetary price. That was the ethos with which we were both brought up. I'm not saying that my values were better than his but they certainly did not revolve around money – the acquisition of money.' John took refuge in religion while Peter absorbed the hardworking materialistic attitude embodied by his parents – and particularly by his mother.

Mary Clowes ran the shop and the home and was the dominant influence on the family. 'We had great respect for my mother, we had more contact with her. She was fair, hard and absolutely impossible to have any kind of disagreement with or discussion or debate. Absolutely single-minded in what she decided. Just like Peter.' She was also an honest woman, according to John Clowes. 'Any concept of dishonesty being used to reach one's goal was an anathema to my parents. It had to be achieved honestly.'

Work and school filled the formative years of the young Peter Clowes. He also spent a lot of time on his own in the attic of the Moss Side shop, playing with his model railway set, which he kept in immaculate condition. 'I remember him collecting matchsticks,' says John. 'I can see him with a Stanley knife, cutting the burned ends off and using them all to make fencing, to make buildings. It was a laborious job, painstaking, creating things out of these ruddy matchsticks – I wouldn't have the patience to do it – sitting for hours making things all by himself. Most of the things he did were completely by himself, solo activities, he wasn't a group person at all, not a team man.'

Another characteristic of the adolescent Peter Clowes was an absence of humour. He was a serious, intense child, below average height and introverted. John remembers just one occasion when his brother made the family laugh. Peter was around twelve at the time. It was early evening and, feeling a little ill, he had taken a couple of aspirins. He and his brother were bouncing up and down on the dining-room chairs when Peter's chair broke. Mary Clowes immediately accosted Peter, asking what he thought he had been playing

10

at. Clowes said that the extra weight of the aspirins had caused his chair to break.

His isolation and capacity for hard work appear to have paid dividends for Peter. He passed four O-levels and was one of the few pupils who skipped a year, going straight from the fourth year to the sixth. This put him in the top 5 per cent of a school which reckoned that overall its pupils were drawn from the top 10 per cent of the country. In the sixth form Peter wrote a couple of articles for the *Arrow* about adventures and adventurers. One, entitled 'The Frontier of Space', bore witness to a brief interest in astronomy. 'It did not last long,' says John. 'There was no money in stars.'

Peter's school magazine articles describe feats of achievement which required great persistence and resourcefulness: 'Today, in this modern age, Man has met his toughest obstacle yet – the conquest of space: the first trip to the moon . . . and back! Soon followed no doubt by the conquest of the planets Mars and Venus' reveals the theme of one. The other describes arduous North Pole expeditions, fighting against 'winds that could flatten buildings'. The idea of man struggling against the odds and coming out on top clearly appealed to him. There were other early indications of the future Peter Clowes; he was dogmatic to the point where it was hard to hold a proper discussion with him. John identifies this as a trait inherited from his mother. 'Peter never had any great political views, he had lots of his own views, about most things, he was almost impossible to argue with or debate with because he knew exactly, he'd worked it out. He was very difficult, he was a very bright person.'

Clowes was also very keen to get on and make money in the outside world; there was an outcry among the masters at Chorlton Grammar when he decided to abandon his A-levels after only one year in favour of working in the family hardware shop. He had been earmarked as obvious university material, but he was also a young man in a hurry. His parents welcomed him into the family business.

Around the same time, at the beginning of the 1960s, the Clowes family moved to Heaton Moor, a Mancunian suburb on the outskirts of the former cotton workers' town of Stockport. Number 33 Shaw Road is now 'Martin's on the Moor', an antique shop. The owner, Rex Martin, has preserved the last vestige of the Clowes family's presence in the area – a green tarpaulin awning bearing the name Clowes Brothers Hardware. Eric Clowes and his brother, with their wives and families, all lived above the shop.

Heaton Moor was a social leap upwards from Moss Side but a mish-mash of an area nevertheless. Many of the houses had been divided into bedsitters but the town also had its fair share of professionals, stockbrokers and solicitors who worked in Manchester town centre, four miles away. Shaw Road is a bleak, narrow road, whose shop-fronted houses reflect the past inconsistencies of Heaton Moor's character. The styles are mixed, some houses having bay windows while others have black and white mock Tudor strips running down their front. The move upwards did not make much difference to the lifestyle of the Cloweses. They never ate out – John recalls that he did not eat in a restaurant until he was eighteen – and worked long hours. Peter worked both behind the counter and out on the paraffin rounds. After a while he developed a local round of his own, effectively working for himself and paying for the stock, mainly paraffin, which he took from the shop. He and his cousin David sold paraffin door to door from the back of a Clowes Brothers van. David, like John, later became a vicar.

When he was just twenty-one Peter married the girl down the road. Patricia Slann, a thin girl who wore heavy glasses, lived at number 9 Shaw Road where her family ran a woollens shop. They married in St Mary's church, a towering black building behind the hardware shop. 'Pat Slann was a shopkeeper's daughter,' says John. 'Peter had a spell of religion, I think when he was looking for a girlfriend . . . and he met her at the church youth club; she was a local girl. It was just one of those awful marriages. There was no thought about it, they just drifted into it.'

It was around now that Peter developed a passion for rally driving, his only relief from the grinding work schedule he imposed on himself. In the evenings, the Clowes Brothers van would be exchanged for a Mini Coupé, which Peter had fitted up with large, flashy headlights, and drove fast around the Heaton Moor area. He joined the Stockport Motor Club and went on overnight and weekend rallies, with Patricia – a timid woman who wanted to settle down and raise a family – acting as his navigator.

Even when not taking part in rallies Peter was a fast driver. 'I drove with him until I got wise enough to know better,' says John. 'I wouldn't drive with him now. He drove like he lived. He couldn't drive slowly. It was a frightening experience to drive with him on just a normal road, on a normal journey from A to B. It frightened me to death. He would go very fast, but accurate, accurate.'

Peter Clowes had plans to build a business on his own and decided to work on the markets as well as selling paraffin and hardware, having first one stall and then several, selling anything that would make a profit. He was a shy, introverted type and working on the markets would have involved enormous effort for him to overcome his natural inclinations. Still he succeeded, his brother describing the market-stall operation as 'very lucrative'.

When Peter's parents retired he decided against taking on the shop himself. His vision of the future had long outstripped that of his parents and aunt and uncle. 'My parents, when they started the business and up until they retired, never changed their style of doing business,' says John. 'It was my brother who spotted, years before they did, supermarkets and the way business would develop, that the days of the corner shop were limited.

'My parents had their own wholesalers, they had the same ones for years; I remember them coming round, collar and tie, poor little chaps with suits, to get the weekly order. Peter could see that wasn't going to last, that one would buy in bulk. And it was true that those days did go. Anything Peter could sell in the markets, he would buy. But he wouldn't buy little bits to keep the store going; he would buy in bulk.'

The Shaw Road hardware shop was sold and Peter Clowes set up a new business selling turf. 'He was still doing the market stall, and I used to deliver turf for him during vacations,' says John. 'He sold the turf from a clapped-out lorry. There was a chap in Poynton who would cut it and Peter would load up the van and deliver it. There was a lot of money in that. So he started his own landscape gardening business because he could see there were property developments, people wanted lawns, new gardens . . . he employed at that time six or seven people, I was one of them during vacations. Peter would pay me generously – very, very generously. We would get paid at a local pub, on Friday evenings.'

The money he made from his various businesses allowed Clowes to buy the first proper home for himself and Patricia. 'Varykeno' was a detached cottage with a grey slate roof, parts of which were believed to date back to the seventeenth century. It was isolated at the end of an Ernocroft Lane, a private road on the edge of the village of Marple, leading to a large wood of the same name. 'It was out in the wilds, people did not want to live there,' says Paul Sieben, who installed central heating in Varykeno for Clowes. 'I considered it a bit strange myself. It was up a lonely track right at the top of a hill.'

It was around this time that Clowes met a woman who would change the course of his life completely. Elizabeth Barlow was a tall, straight-backed, confident lady with a passion for fast cars, money and high living. To the young Peter Clowes, who met her at the

Stockport Motor Club where she was one of the star attractions, she must have seemed glamorous and unattainable. Certainly she epitomised many things which had been absent from Clowes's upbringing. She came from a cultured, reasonably affluent family. 'My father was very educated and my grandfather owned a lot of property in Chester,' she says. 'Peter lacked education. He dropped his aitches and I used to kick him under the table.'

The two struck up a friendship, partly rooted in their mutual interest in rally-car driving. A local pharmaceutical company was sponsoring Barlow to race Formula V cars and she won several cups. In 1969, when she was sponsored to compete in the Tulip international car rally, she invited Peter Clowes to be her navigator and replacement driver. 'We came first in our class and fifteenth or sixteenth overall,' she says.

Friendship turned into a love affair and Barlow became Clowes's mistress. They made an improbable couple: she towered above the short, squat Clowes and her accent gave no hint of her northern origins while Clowes's was redolent of his. She seemed sophisticated and socially at ease. Clowes, possibly because he had no sisters and had attended a single-sex grammar school, was uncomfortable with women. But they were united by a love of fast cars and a passion for money.

Elizabeth Barlow was a sharp saleswoman. Despite training as a nurse and working for a time in Africa, she had become an insurance saleswoman and was brilliant and ruthless at her job. 'Elizabeth had a clever ability to walk into a roomful of strangers and interest them,' says one of Barlow's acquaintances. 'She was also the kind of lady-friend a man could talk business with. And she used virtually all her friends as selling points to get new business.' Barlow's success attracted Clowes and she persuaded him to join her at the organis-ation where she worked – International Life Insurance Company, a subsidiary of the soon-to-become notorious Investors Overseas Ser-vices (IOS). Clowes, abandoning the markets, selling turf and land-scape gardening, signed up as an 'inspector' – the IOS expression for an insurance salesman – in March 1970.

IOS had been built up by Bernard Cornfeld, who employed 25,000 salesmen in 100 different countries mainly to sell its Fund of Funds investment product. The Fund of Funds was a heavily pro-moted and highly dubious product, targeted mainly at the man in the street and with a charging structure weighted strongly in favour of IOS and its salesmen. It was originally set up to invest in funds operated by other fund management groups which were separate from IOS but it developed from this to investing the public's money in a series of companies or ventures, many of them highly speculative, in which Cornfeld or his associates had a commercial interest.

International Life had been set up in April 1963 as a way of sidestepping United Kingdom exchange control and other regulations which prevented IOS from selling the Fund of Funds door to door in Britain. Its product was the Dover Plan, a life insurance policy. The bulk of the Dover Plan's premiums found their way, via Luxembourg and other routes, into the Fund of Funds.

By the time Clowes joined International Life, both the company and the Dover Plan had been heavily criticised in the national press. The Dover Plan was ambiguous when it came to spelling out its charges. When the stock market fell and people who wanted to encash their Dover Plan policies discovered they had low surrender values, the high charges levied on the policies were exposed. Moreover, the terms of the Dover Plan meant that International Life could increase the charges on a policy even after it had been sold. 'IOS was very exciting. It was swashbuckling, very successful and patchy in terms of its business ethics,' says John Bird, who worked at IOS at the same time as Peter Clowes. 'I think Peter would have fitted into that ethos as many did, by the sheer ebullience of the organisation and feeling that he was part of something that was always going to be right.'

Although International Life and the Dover Plan had been fiercely attacked, the company itself, and the IOS ethos, focused on a completely different dimension to its business: the possibility of its salesmen making a fortune by selling IOS/International Life products. Nowhere was this better encapsulated than in the words of the master himself, Bernard Cornfeld: 'Do you sincerely want to be rich?' he would boom from the podium at IOS sales conventions and seminars. Clowes met Cornfeld once at an IOS sales convention at the Royal Albert Hall. Although he dismisses the occasion – 'Frankly I was not impressed' – so much of Clowes's future behaviour, his perspective and ultimately his lifestyle, emulates and mirrors Cornfeld's that his dismissal of the man is barely credible. IOS was Clowes's training ground. A few weeks after he joined, IOS announced that it would be holding a Millionaires Conference at the Grosvenor Square Hotel for all IOS salesmen whose sales had equalled or exceeded £1 million the previous year.[3] The company, its aspirations and values – suggested by an IOS dictum 'write the business first, fix the sweat later' – must have made a deep imprint on an impressionable Clowes anxious to get on in the world and make money. Later, when he had built his own business, Clowes would adapt Cornfeld's rhetorical question, asking people whom he wanted to join in his bold, fantastical schemes, 'Do you seriously want to be rich?'

'He talked about Cornfeld in reverential terms,' says James Wright, one man who was persuaded by Clowes. Wright also says that IOS's influence on Clowes extended beyond the reign of its founder Bernard Cornfeld to his successor Robert Vesco. According to Wright, he 'idolised' Vesco, who later embezzled £146 million from IOS and disappeared.[4]

Clowes arrived at International Life at the pinnacle of its success and of the wealth of its founder Bernard Cornfeld. The trappings of Cornfeld's wealth – the yachts, châteaux, castles, model agencies and private jets – were well known in the organisation. But much of his empire had been built on sand: IOS was using money raised from its recent public launch to support its share price artificially and to guarantee a series of loans to its directors. These included a $4.9 million guarantee on a loan to purchase a BAC 1–11 jet Cornfeld had recently ordered. Clowes had joined IOS too late to participate in Bernard Cornfeld's dream. It was already turning sour, and in January 1971, eleven months after Clowes's arrival, Cornfeld lost control of IOS. International Life went into liquidation – there were no more fortunes to be made. Clowes drove around in a white Volkswagen Beetle which cost him £750, and his bank statements contain no evidence that he made substantial sums at International Life.

In 1972 International Life was bought from the liquidators by Keyser Ullman, the fringe bank chaired at the time by Tory MP Edward du Cann, and changed its name to Cannon Assurance.

At International Life and then Cannon Assurance Elizabeth Barlow was a saleswoman who sold direct to the public. For a brief period Clowes too had been a salesman, selling the Dover Plan. Barlow remembers him as a good salesman although others say, probably more accurately, that selling was not Clowes's forte. His manner is awkward, he never looks people in the eye and he is not a fluent speaker or a good communicator. He tends to become too absorbed in detail when explaining things. He soon moved on to a different job within Cannon: to establish a network of financial intermediaries who would recommend Cannon's products to their clients. Clowes covered hundreds of miles in his Beetle, travelling as far north as Scotland and across to Anglesey in Wales, establishing contacts with the intermediaries. Some would later prove useful to him when he had his own products to sell.

Clowes was not popular with his own colleagues at Cannon. Paul Wood, who arrived at Cannon in the summer of 1972 to motivate the twelve-man salesforce, including Clowes and Barlow, describes Peter Clowes as 'a nasty arrogant little sod with an aggressive nature'.[5] Barlow, he considered, was a 'shrewd businesswoman, open and gregarious'. Clowes was a loner, Barlow a participator. 'He deliberately seemed to isolate himself,' says John Bird, a former Cannon salesman. 'He was insular, nasty, pompous, shrewd and introverted.'[6]

Barlow and Clowes shared an ambition to go beyond being mere employees of Cannon. The Manchester Yellow Pages from 1972 and 1973 reveal a curious state of affairs at Cannon involving both Elizabeth Barlow and Peter Clowes. The directory lists a business 'Barlowe & Clowes' as insurance brokers operating out of Cannon's offices at 7 Charlotte Street, in the centre of Manchester. Although Barlow claims this was 'a mistake', a more likely explanation is that she and Clowes were running their own business, separately and in parallel with that of their employer, using Cannon's offices and telephone number. They may have been selling non-competing products such as house and car insurance. Even so this would have been a breach of the contract Clowes had signed pledging himself to work only for Cannon. Had he or Barlow been found out they would have been summarily dismissed and the Barlow Clowes business, in all likelihood, stillborn.

CHAPTER TWO

·

THE PARTNERSHIP

·

The village of Hazel Grove lies on the outskirts of the Greater Manchester area. Formerly known as Bullock Smithy, it excited contrary opinions from those who passed through. The *Short History of Hazel Grove*, published towards the end of the nineteenth century by Robert Fletcher, describes a place full of public houses where 'it is very rare for the police to be required to interfere in consequence of the effects of drink'. A different view was taken by John Wesley when he passed through the village in 1747: 'one of the villages in the country famous for all manner of wickedness'. It was at number 2 London Road that Barlow Clowes and Partners first opened for business in 1973.

Before Peter Clowes and Elizabeth Barlow moved in, 2 London Road had been a dog parlour. It was a simple two-up two-down terraced house, the first house on the A6, which runs all the way to London. Next door was the Cut 'n' Curl hairdresser's shop. It was hardly a grand beginning for the two former IOS employees.

Why had they decided to go set up in business on their own? 'He was good at selling, I was good at selling. We wanted to go into a brokerage offering a range of products rather than only one as we did at Cannon,' says Barlow. 'You are limited if you are with one company – you can only sell their products. It made sense to go into business together.'[1]

The main business of Barlow Clowes in those early days involved providing a service to accountants, solicitors and financial middlemen such as insurance brokers. A financial product known as the 'guaranteed income bond' was gaining popularity at that time. It was an insurance company bond, for which investors paid a single lump-sum premium. In return they received a regular income from the insurance company, which received generous tax treatment.

But the market was flooded by insurance companies offering their own guaranteed income bonds with different rates. Barlow Clowes monitored the market and provided a weekly service to the professionals and financial middlemen telling them which were the best income bonds available. 'The rates were bouncing up and down all the time . . . consequently if you were an accountant and had a client who wanted to put £10,000 into a guaranteed income bond it was quite a job for you to know who was offering the best rate that week,' says Clowes.[2] 'We would analyse all the insurance companies that were in the market and we would categorise them according to whether they were small, up to ten million, ten to fifty million or over fifty million and then set out all the rates for the various companies in those categories. And update that record once a week and send it to everybody once a week. Generally the rates held for about a week and were fairly volatile. It was extremely profitable business for us.'

Much credit for the initial success of the business must go to Barlow. She did most of the promoting of the service, and also sold life assurance and pension policies under the auspices of Barlow Clowes. Clowes was the strategist – and the admin man. Their different roles were reflected in their physical appearance. 'She was very professional in her manner and appearance, always wore a skirt suit with matching bag,' says a neighbour from those days in 1973. 'He was small and chubby and used to walk hunched, with his head down. He would wear trousers and a jacket and a polo-neck. He was not the businessman type.'

The London Road neighbours would also joke about the couple's antics performed in Clowes's Volkswagen Beetle, parked at night in the car park of the local public house on London Road, not far from the Barlow Clowes office. Barlow's height provided a tell-tale sign which the landlady interpreted as meaning that the love-making in the car had commenced, and would convey over the telephone to her friend who owned a house near the Barlow Clowes office. 'The legs are out of the window,' she would say.

Clowes's apparent commercial success with the advisory service whetted his appetite. He had already shown signs of his burning ambition by starting up his own insurance business with Barlow while they were still working at Cannon. Now out on their own without the shelter of a large insurance company, Clowes and his partner had started well.

Some foundations had already been laid for the future development of the Barlow Clowes business. To start with Peter Clowes had seen the seductive power of the word 'guarantee'. Applied to financial products it had the same magnetic attraction to the public as it had on consumer durables or mail order offers: it offered security and absence of risk. When Barlow Clowes later devised its own products, it would make much play of the fact that they were 'guaranteed'.

Another foundation for the future was the cementing of Clowes's links with the financial middlemen whom he had visited, trying to get them to recommend Cannon's products to their clients. One such was Denis Cruse Wilson, a tall, gentle man with an aura of caring and understanding which persuaded thousands of people to entrust their savings to him. His company, D. C. Wilson & Co., operated out of simple shop-fronted premises on Bramhall High Street, very near to Barlow Clowes. Wilson liked Clowes and although he did no business with him in his Cannon days – 'there were lots of better known insurance companies to choose from' – he had taken the Barlow Clowes guaranteed income bond service. He would become vital to the development of Barlow Clowes's business.

Clowes was obsessed with computers. While Barlow was out selling, and often into the small hours of the morning, he fed the different insurance company rates into the office computer or devised different programs to present the information. Even now he remembers his first computer with pride: 'It was a Hewlett Packard desktop computer, quite powerful with a big fixed disk, a twenty-two-Megabyte fixed disk.' He was self-taught and considered himself an expert. Others who met him later said that he used outdated computer language and knew far less than he claimed. But in 1973 and early 1974, computers, as well as middlemen and investment guarantees, had made an impact on Clowes and would play a large part on the future path he took.

First, however, Clowes had to endure a setback. In the 1974 Budget Chancellor Denis Healey outlawed many of the tax benefits of guaranteed income bonds, virtually killing the Barlow Clowes service overnight. It had to change tack in order to survive and change it did. For the first time it became a manager of other people's money.

The vehicle Clowes chose to make the transition from financial adviser to money manager was the British Government. The Government issues bonds, known as gilt-edged securities or gilts, on which it pays a rate of interest that is usually fixed. The Government also guarantees to repay the capital value on the date the bonds mature. Some dates are fixed, for instance 13¾% Treasury Stock 2000–2003, and a few have no fixed date, for example War Loan 3½%, so the Government can redeem them at any time. The gilts market was originally a method of raising money in times of trouble – for instance to finance a war. One of gilts' main attractions, particularly to the private investor, is the security of their issuer – the British Government.

Barlow did not approve of the change in direction. She thought that Barlow Clowes should continue to act as a broker, recommending other companies' products rather than introducing its own. She wanted to stay with insurance-based business, an area in which the partners between them now had over a decade of experience. But Clowes was anxious to move on. 'He had big ideas, delusions of grandeur,' she says. 'We had a big disagreement about premises. I said that we should start small and build up. But he went ahead and rented four thousand square feet of offices.' Clowes had taken a lease on an entire floor of an office block near to the London Road premises. 'We were rolling around like peas in a pod. He was in a big hurry. He used to dream up all these weird and wonderful schemes,' says Barlow. The 'schemes' involved devising ways of making money – out of gilts or even from property investment. Clowes was renovating his own home, hoping to sell it. With Barlow he invested in a shop and a series of flats in the Manchester area.

Before the move the business had taken on some extra staff. These included Harry Stead, a salesman – 'a nice enough person, not particularly bright' according to Barlow – who commuted each day from Blackpool. He appears to have been involved with the business almost from its formation, since old records show him ordering stationery for Barlow Clowes in 1973. Another recruit, and one who would play an important part in future events, was Pamela Haydock. She was the wife of Eric Haydock, who had been the bass guitarist of the Hollies, a pop group from Manchester who had been hugely popular, particularly in the 1960s when at times their records outsold even the Beatles. Pamela Done had married Haydock in 1965, at the age of nineteen, in a register office wedding pictured in national newspapers. The new Pamela Haydock thought she was set for a life of glamour, married to a celebrity: 'I married Eric and thought, now I'm going to be rich.'[3] But she was soon disappointed. Shortly after they married, Haydock was fired from the group after a row about his wages. After giving birth to three children, Pamela had eventually decided to take a job. This brought her to Barlow Clowes, where her job was to generate leads for Stead and Barlow. 'She started out as a telephone girl, ringing up brokers and trying to make appointments for us,' says Barlow. 'She was no good and at one point Peter was going to sack her. But she had family problems at the time.'

Gilts were a shrewd choice by Clowes, given the financial climate at that time: investors were running scared after the stock market and property crashes of 1973; confidence in the banking community was at an all-time low. The collapse of several fringe banks in the early 1970s, most notably London & County Securities, had resulted in many individuals – investors who had bought its shares, listed on the stock market – losing their money. There were rumours that even some of the high street clearing banks might collapse and there was a general nervousness about investment. If the banks were not safe, the stock market had crashed and property was in the doldrums, where could investors who wanted security and a reasonable return on their money entrust their savings? A building society perhaps, or the Post Office? – or they could, as many did, invest in gilts.

Nervousness about investment was justified not just by what had happened in the market but also by the flimsy laws in force at that time to protect investors against financial collapses or, equally important, against rogues. The Stock Exchange had a compensation scheme to protect investors whose stockbroker became insolvent or ran off with their money. But apart from that what protection was there? There were tens of thousands of financial advisers, ranging from one-man bands run by someone with no financial training, to large firms operating in major towns. The position was the same with fund managers – people who actually invested money on behalf of their clients.

The answer is that investors who relied on financial advisers or fund managers were largely left to the perils of the market place. One relevant statute was in force – the Prevention of Fraud (Investments) Act – which was administered by a handful of civil servants working in the Department of Trade and Industry. Its aim was to protect the public against fraud by investment advisers or investment managers. It did this by requiring them to apply for a licence.

The legislation was woefully out of date. It was little more than a rewrite of a 1939 statute of the same name, which had been passed largely in response to a series of frauds in the 1930s. Moreover, in practice the DTI turned a blind eye to any financial adviser or fund manager who was operating without a licence. Worse still, anyone who applied for a licence was granted one – provided they could put up the required returnable £500 deposit and had no previous convictions for fraud. The DTI's own statistics show that before 1980 hardly anyone who applied was refused a licence. Licence-holders could, however, have their licences revoked, for instance, if they misbehaved in any way. The figures also show that there were hardly any revocations.

The DTI was aware of the hopelessness of its system of investor protection. In 1974, as Barlow Clowes was preparing to become an investment manager, the Department began a review of the system which would eventually – three years later – conclude that it was inadequate and recommend modest changes.

It is safe to assume that the vast majority of the investing public were unaware of the deficiencies in the licensing system. This made a DTI licence doubly dangerous: not only was it meaningless but it also gave a semblance of respectability to anyone holding one. For a financial adviser in 1974 it could also be a useful marketing tool: 'Licensed to deal with the public by Her Majesty's Government' or similarly grand and hollow claims regularly appeared on promotional literature from investment advisers and managers.

Clowes had actually asked the DTI in April 1975 whether he needed a licence for his business. He wanted to distribute a circular describing the gilts service he was offering. The desultory contact that ensued between Clowes and the DTI became more active when Barclays Bank, asked by Barlow Clowes to provide a custodian account for clients' money, telephoned the DTI to enquire whether Barlow Clowes needed a licence.

In September 1975 Clowes sent the DTI three leaflets describing the services his business provided which included a gilts service. This specified a minimum investment of £1000. The leaflet described how the gilts would be registered 'in a major bank's nominee company' and, significantly, that 'each client is the beneficial owner of his securities'. In other words, each client had his own stock, specifically allocated to him and kept separate from everyone else's.

The Barlow Clowes circulars triggered some confusion within the DTI. Did Barlow Clowes require a licence? There was a school of thought prevailing at the time in the DTI that investment advisers who charged a flat fee for their services rather than taking a percentage commission or a share in the profits they made for their clients did not require a licence. In contrast, advisers who charged a fee on a percentage basis or who shared in the profits of investments which they made on their clients' behalf, were thought to come under the Act and require a licence.

This view concerned 'advisers' only, people who gave advice on investments. It did not generally extend to 'managers' – those who actually managed investments on behalf of the public. There was no doubt that Barlow Clowes was a manager. Generally speaking, if you were a manager, as opposed to an adviser, you needed a licence, however you charged for your service.

Nevertheless the first reaction of the DTI's Companies Division, which handled licensing applications at that time, was that Barlow Clowes did not need a licence. The question was referred to the DTI's Solicitors Department, which advised categorically that Barlow Clowes needed a licence and was operating illegally. The solicitor concerned made it clear also in a written note that the exemption applying to advisers who did not charge a percentage commission was not relevant to Barlow Clowes.

The solicitor's note was read by a senior executive officer within the Companies Division, who agreed with it and instructed a junior official to write to Barlow Clowes advising the firm that it needed a licence. On 3 December 1985 the official wrote to Clowes telling him that the distribution of the three Barlow Clowes circulars meant that the business required a licence. This was an incorrect interpretation of the legal advice from the DTI Solicitors Department. The nature of Barlow Clowes's business was such that it needed a licence regardless whether it sent out circulars or promotional material.

Clowes's reaction to the letter from the DTI was simple: he told the DTI that he had stopped sending out the circulars. The DTI wrote back saying effectively that he did not need a licence, and there the matter lay. Clowes was a manager of other people's money and, because of an internal misunderstanding at the DTI, he could operate without a licence. This error would play an important part in the events to come.

·

CHAPTER THREE

ROBBING PETER TO PAY PAUL

·

'Gilts are the safest investment. What could be safer than Her Majesty's Government?'

                                                        Peter Clowes

The change in direction to gilts brought modest success to Barlow Clowes. According to Clowes the business took in some £7 million from the public to manage and invest in gilts. This is a lie. The Barlow Clowes records show that it raised only around £1 million. The money came through financial intermediaries whom Barlow and Harry Stead would visit regularly, while Clowes would hold the occasional seminar for intermediaries at the Belgrade, in nearby Stockport.

Wilson was one of the intermediaries who attended a Clowes seminar on the merits of investing in British Government securities. Wilson's firm, like many others, had started as an insurance brokerage, and was moving into general investments. Most of the other intermediaries had worked for large insurance companies or national brokerages and left to set up on their own.

Wilson remembers Clowes diffidently spluttering his way through a talk on gilts. But despite the poor presentation Wilson was impressed by Clowes's apparent command of his subject. 'He used to say that gilts were the safest investment. What could be safer than Her Majesty's Government? he would ask. Large companies like ICI might go bust – but the British Government never would.'[1]

Clowes had a unique selling point which he called 'anomaly switching'. This was a familiar concept in the gilts market and involved switching between similar gilts in order to take advantage of a discrepancy in their respective prices. The market would occasionally throw up these discrepancies, or 'anomalies', whereby one gilt looked cheap in comparison to another based on their previous trading relationship. (Anomaly switching depended largely on history repeating itself.) By switching from one to the other you could take advantage of the discrepancy to move into what appeared to be a bargain-priced gilt.

Clowes claimed that he had devised a computer program which, fed with historical and statistical information about the gilts market, would tell him when a particular gilt was looking cheap and therefore should be bought.

Gilts were always a passion for Peter Clowes. His eyes would often glaze over when talking about them, and he would become so deeply involved in the subject that he could easily leave his audience way behind. One person who came across Clowes in his early days describes him as a 'mad professor type'. A senior civil servant within the DTI would later describe Clowes as 'an addict of doing things with gilts, not a crook'.[2]

As an investment adviser and manager, Barlow Clowes could not buy gilts itself. Only members of the Stock Exchange could do this. So Clowes had to operate through a stockbroker, a member of the Stock Exchange, who would buy the gilts from a market maker, known in those days as a 'jobber'. Although there were several gilts brokers, Clowes placed the vast majority of Barlow Clowes's deals with one stockbroking firm: the London-based Hedderwick Stirling Grunbar. Direct telephone lines were installed to connect Barlow Clowes with Hedderwicks simply by picking up the telephone.

Hedderwicks had a highly rated gilts department which was believed to be very profitable. It had evolved from a team of gilts experts, led by broker Terry Webster, who in 1975 had left the rival firm of Vickers da Costa to join Hedderwicks. Among the team was Agnello de'Souza (known as 'Aggie'), who originated from Goa and was an ardent supporter of Crystal Palace football club. While Webster was the Hedderwicks partner in charge of gilts dealings, de'Souza was responsible for 'settlement', making sure that purchases and sales of gilts were properly paid for. The gilts market was, and still is, a 'cash settlement' market – deals must be paid for the next day in cash. (In contrast, the share market works on an 'account' basis – deals are settled at the end of fortnightly or three-weekly account periods.)

This, on the surface, was Barlow Clowes: a gilts investment manager, specialising in anomaly switching. It was unlicensed but placed all its deals through a reputable firm of London stockbrokers. The reality was very different.

Anomaly switching, as a means of making money out of gilts, was a discredited concept by the time Clowes began to preach it.

The huge volumes of new stock being issued by the Government during the 1970s had more or less put paid to the process since the new stock could quite easily make the historical information on which anomaly switching relied totally irrelevant. It was no good spotting an anomaly and switching into a cheaper stock if the Government issued massive amounts of a similar stock which simply made the cheap stock cheaper. 'In practice what often happened was that the cheaper stocks got cheaper and the dearer ones dearer,' says Peter Clarke, a gilts expert who has worked in the market since 1965. 'For anomaly switching to work you could not have a market which moved around a lot.'

Even when it did work, anomaly switching was thought by the experts to add only as little as 0.5 per cent a year to the average return achieved from managing gilts. So what was Clowes doing with the investors' money?

He was gambling with it. It was not unusual for Clowes to be in and out of the gilts market fifty times in a single day, buying and selling, trying to make a quick turn. He still used the jargon of 'anomaly switching' to his own staff, but what he was doing was quite different. He would buy a long-dated stock, that is, one with a long period remaining before it matured, and sell a short-dated stock, one close to maturity, to pay for it. 'This wasn't anomaly switching,' says Geoffrey Farrington, a quietly spoken actuary who worked for Barlow Clowes at the time. 'To move from long-dated gilts to short-dated ones was not a switch as such, it was a change in investment policy. But that was what he wanted to do and did.'

In fact it was worse. Most of the deals Clowes gave instructions for were known as 'in-house deals'. They were not for Barlow Clowes clients, but for Clowes's own personal account and for those of his staff who chose to join him. Worse still, the decision as to which were in-house deals and which on behalf of clients was often taken only after the deals had been completed. If there was a particularly good deal Clowes might decide to call it his own; one that lost money could always be foisted on the clients. This did not happen in every case – clients' money would have been too heavily depleted – but the allocation of deals after the event was a common practice at Barlow Clowes in the early days of the business. (Clowes was by no means alone in this dubious practice. It was fairly common in the mid-1970s for share or gilts bargains to be recorded as 'client' or 'personal' after the event. 'I'll give you the booking at the end of the day' was a well-known sentence in many stockbrokers' offices.) 'The purpose of the [Barlow Clowes] operation was to trade in gilts for the benefit of the partners,' says Farrington. 'Dealing on behalf of clients was almost secondary.'

It is not altogether clear who joined Clowes in the dealing 'syndicates' – to use the name that Clowes himself gave them. Harry Stead appears to have participated in a syndicate involving Clowes and Barlow. 'The practice [of running syndicates] was started before I went to work in the office,' says Stead, who adds that he knew 'nothing of recording [gilts deals] after the event.' What is clear is that the settlement of gilts bargains between Barlow Clowes and Hedderwicks was not in accordance with normal market practice. Clowes enjoyed special terms with de'Souza at Hedderwicks. Clowes often did not have to pay cash the next day for his gilts deals. In return Clowes allowed de'Souza to borrow stock belonging to Barlow Clowes investors. De'Souza would use this stock to satisfy the gilts deals he had entered into on behalf of Hedderwicks. 'Clowes left his clients' stock on the shelf at Hedderwicks,' says Bob Wilkinson, the former head of surveillance at the Stock Exchange. 'There's no way he should have done so.'

Clowes's lifestyle began to change. He swopped his Volkswagen Beetle for a Range-Rover, later adding a burgundy-coloured Porsche. He also became a kind of general benefactor, a patriarch, doling out largesse to various members of his family. In September 1977 he bought his parents a small house in Stockport for just under £12,000, and paid £14,750 for a home for his wife Patricia when they separated in 1978. (A couple of years later he bought a house for Patricia's mother for £19,850.) He had the marital home, Varykeno, in Marple, Cheshire, extensively renovated so that when eventually he placed it on the market, the estate agents' particulars commended its pink-tiled 'luxurious' bathroom equipped with an avocado-coloured 'low flush syphonic WC', as well as Varykeno's five bedrooms and 'oak beamed landing'.

Clowes had meanwhile moved to a block of flats in Heaton Mersey close to the hardware shop on Shaw Road. Norma Oswald, a neighbour from that time, remembers him as 'an extremely nice friendly man who looked after our money'. Clowes was treasurer of the tenants' management company that owned Southpoint flats, and as such responsible for holding the tenants' management fees and using them to defray expenses such as lighting and insurance. He kept a cat called Churchill for company and would be visited at weekends by Pamela Haydock and her three children as well as his own daughter Sarah.

He was meticulous with his own money. He would go through his bank statements writing against each entry exactly what the payment or receipt represented, down to the £4.47 he paid for cat litter. He appeared to prefer cheques to cash since the statements show him regularly writing cheques for very small items.

It would be more convenient to paint a consistent picture of Clowes, to describe him as either mean or extravagant, ruthless or kind, but the man does not fit any stereotype. It is clear that even early on, in the mid- to late-1970s, there were marked inconsistencies in his character and behaviour. On the one hand, he chose to own two expensive cars; on the other, he itemised his cat litter. He handled his fellow tenants' money with care yet seemed to show a reckless abandon with his own clients' funds.

What he certainly possessed was an enormous belief in his own abilities which, combined with a dogmatic, forthright nature and the complete absence of any superior influence on him, proved lethal. Clowes considered himself an expert in gilts. No doubt he had read a few books on the subject, attended a course perhaps, but that would have been the sum total of his 'expertise'. The phrase 'a little knowledge is a dangerous thing' has a prophetic accuracy in the case of Clowes. He was running a business where his forceful personality made him undisputed boss despite Elizabeth Barlow's 50 per cent share. And he was promoting his gilts expertise among a financial community full of untrained and largely unregulated intermediaries. So neither within his own company nor in the immediate financial community was there anyone able to stand up and contradict him. Moreover, the fact that the financial intermediaries recommended Clowes's business clearly conferred on him a status, at least locally, which would have nourished his own self-belief and other people's high opinion of him. But Clowes's tendency to overrate himself would in years to come cause enormous heartbreak for thousands of other people who believed in him and his gilts expertise.

As well as being forthright and self-believing Clowes had another dominant characteristic: he was secretive. This was reflected in the way he structured his own business. Barlow Clowes was a partnership rather than a limited company, which made it less visible to the outside world. A limited company is by its nature a more public creature: companies must file accounts at Companies House; they have to provide details of the directors and shareholders. All this information is made available to anyone wishing to inspect it. In contrast, a partnership is an essentially private entity: it does not need to file anything publicly; it has to prepare accounts, but these are not available for public inspection.

The advantage of a company structure is that it insulates those who own the business from personal liability for the business's debts should it fail. Partnerships offer no such protection. All legal and accountancy practices are structured as partnerships – their respective professional bodies require this. But there is no stipulation that financial services businesses operate as partnerships. Indeed, because of the risk of personal liability, most would shun the partnership structure. Clowes was prepared to run the risk, in return for the advantage of secrecy.

In 1978 Clowes had formed another partnership, with the identical name (Barlow Clowes & Partners) but based in Jersey. He promoted it on the basis that it was for expatriates who because of their non-resident status would be able to avoid income tax on gilts investments made via his Jersey partnership. That was one explanation he gave. Sometimes he would say that his Jersey partnership was for 'large investors': people with sizable lump sums to invest. Whatever the reason Clowes was very secretive about the operations of his Jersey partnership.

Its records were kept on a separate computer. Clowes was the only one to have access to the computer, which, together with Jersey client records, was kept behind a locked door at Hulton House. Geoffrey Farrington, during his three years at Barlow Clowes, had devised a system for recording gilts dealings and producing valuations for the UK-based clients. When he suggested to Clowes that he do the same for the Jersey clients, Clowes refused. 'He didn't want it done. He said Jersey was confidential,' says Farrington.

Barlow Clowes's bank accounts show that Clowes had been taking money in Jersey since 1976 – two years before formalising the arrangement with a partnership structure. A strict separation should have been maintained between the funds taken in Jersey and those subscribed by UK investors. Otherwise it was quite easy to make up any shortfall in the UK with money from Jersey, or vice versa. This practice is referred to colloquially as 'teaming and lading'. A close relation to teaming and lading is the practice of 'robbing Peter to pay Paul'. In the context of fund management this involves paying out one client with another client's money. Barlow Clowes's records show that from 1977 onwards there was intermingling between the Jersey and UK funds. There was no genuine financial justification for this. With Clowes treating the Jersey money as his own personal fiefdom the scope for abuse – or for covering up deficiencies in clients' money – was tempting and obvious.

Clowes was insulated from direct contact with his investors because money came in only via the financial intermediaries. This probably facilitated the cavalier approach he adopted towards the investors' funds. Another likely element is the fact that before he became a gilts investment manager Clowes had no experience of handling funds of this magnitude. Now, with his own business, and having chosen an appealing formula – investment in gilts – Clowes suddenly found himself in control of a million pounds of other people's money. It must have given him a great feeling of power. But it would not be enough to satisfy him.

CHAPTER FOUR

·

A NARROW ESCAPE

·

*'If the stock is not there by three o'clock I am going to physically
start hitting you.'*

Peter Clowes

The Stock Exchange in the 1990s is very different from the Exchange
of the two previous decades. Although it still occupies the Stock
Exchange Tower, one of the tallest buildings in Britain, and letters
sent to the Exchange need be addressed only 'The Stock Exchange,
London', it lost many of its powers and functions when Big Bang
occurred and the new investor protection regime was introduced in
the second half of the last decade.

The Exchange's trading floor, a vibrant, swarming hive of activity
where stockbrokers bought and sold shares face to face, became a
deserted, redundant monument to times gone by. It was replaced
by the new method of dealing over the telephone using electronic
screens. At the same time the Exchange was split in two by the
Financial Services Act 1986 – many of its regulatory functions
being transferred to a separate body, known as the Securities Association.

Many people regretted the passing of the old Exchange, believing
it served investors better than the new system. They point to the
Exchange's compensation scheme for investors, introduced in 1974
after several broking firms collapsed. This virtually guaranteed to
reimburse investors who lost money when an Exchange member
went down. The new compensation system, introduced under the
Financial Services Act, imposes a £48,000 ceiling on the amount an
investor can recoup. However, one power the Exchange still retains
is that of declaring one of its member firms insolvent – unable to pay
its debts. When this happens a firm is 'hammered', in the jargon of
the Exchange. Hammerings are usually announced during market
hours in order to secure maximum publicity.

On Friday 10 April 1981 the Exchange departed from its normal
rule. At 5.45 p.m., after the market had closed, it announced that

the firm of Hedderwick Stirling Grunbar had been hammered. The news was doubly dramatic because, on the same day, Hedderwicks had been due to be taken over by the firm of Quilter Goodison, another stock exchange firm whose senior partner, Sir Nicholas Goodison, was also chairman of the Exchange.

It very quickly became apparent that the reason for its hammering lay deep within the gilts department of Hedderwicks, the same department which for years had been dealing with Barlow Clowes.

Hedderwicks' gilts department had a chequered history. Terry Webster, who led the department, had been expelled by the Exchange in February 1980 for 'acting in a disgraceful manner'. Webster had secretly been making a profit for himself and other people on gilts orders placed by his clients. Three others in the department has been suspended from trading and the firm's managing director was censured by the Exchange in what amounted to an unprecedented public criticism of one of its member firms. A second scandal and a police investigation had followed, but neither led to further action. Not surprisingly, Goodison, when he had announced the 'merger' terms with Hedderwicks (the merger was really a takeover by Goodison's firm), had specifically excluded the gilts department from the deal.

Peter Clowes had been dealing with Hedderwicks almost right up to when the firm was hammered. In fact Clowes, who had by this time moved his business to an office in Warnford Court behind the Stock Exchange tower, had heard about Hedderwicks' problems a day or so before the hammering was announced. Hedderwicks still held some gilts stock for Clowes which could easily have been caught up in the collapse, particularly given the arrangement Clowes had with de'Souza to leave stock 'on the shelf' at Hedderwicks. In a panic Clowes called de'Souza and told him to get his clients' stock out of Hedderwicks right away: 'I wanted de'Souza to transfer all the stock to Midland Bank,' Clowes says. And he added a threat: 'If the stock is not there by three o'clock I am going to physically start hitting you.'[1] De'Souza obliged.

Barlow Clowes was not the reason for the demise of Hedderwicks – it had no outstanding debts to the firm at the time it was hammered. The true cause was a firm very close to Clowes: Farrington Stead, established in Manchester and run by two of his employees – Geoffrey Farrington and Harry Stead. It owed Hedderwicks £2 million and it could not pay.

Farrington and Stead had left Barlow Clowes in 1978 to set up on their own. Clowes clearly did not want them to leave since he offered Farrington a junior partnership in the business and a 10 per cent stake to stay. Farrington turned the offer down, as did Stead when Clowes made a similar offer to him.

Elizabeth Barlow also left in 1978. Clowes says that Barlow was going through a period of uncertainty in her life, thinking of retiring and living abroad but not quite able to make up her mind. Clowes says that he and Barlow were 'not seeing eye to eye on the way the company should go forward', claiming that he wanted to do more insurance broking work, whereas Barlow did not.[2] This view does not appear to tally with what Barlow did next: she rang up her old boss at Cannon Assurance, asked for a job and was given one. Her departure was more likely to have been due to Clowes having switched his affections to another member of staff, Shelley Avril Goldstone, who replaced Barlow not only in Clowes's heart but also as a partner in Barlow Clowes. Peter Clowes gave her a small stake of around 10 per cent in the partnership.

Elizabeth Barlow kept in touch with Farrington and Stead, who set up their business as a limited company in February 1979. One of the four founding shareholders was none other than de'Souza, the Hedderwicks gilts settlement manager. In June 1979 the firm applied for a licence from the DTI, both Farrington and Stead stating their previous employment with Barlow Clowes on their application forms. Farrington described Barlow Clowes as being involved in 'gilt-edged management' while Stead called the firm 'portfolio managers'. The application was supported by a reference from a partner in Hedderwicks, and was granted.

The significance of the references to Barlow Clowes – that it was a business operating without a licence – failed to register with the DTI official who approved Farrington Stead's licence application.

Farrington Stead proved to be something of a Barlow Clowes clone. The firm claimed to be investment managers in gilts, using computers and aiming to produce a capital gain. Like Barlow Clowes those involved speculated wildly in gilts for their own accounts, almost all the deals going through Hedderwicks' gilts department. As with Barlow Clowes the normal rules for gilts dealing were thrown out the window and clients' stock was 'borrowed' to satisfy Hedderwicks' own capital requirements and to finance gambling in gilts.

The way it worked was simple: clients' stock which had been left on the shelf with Hedderwicks, whether belonging to Farrington clients, Barlow Clowes clients or others, would be sold and the proceeds used to gamble with. If a client asked for his stock back it would be bought again and delivered to him. So it was easy to see why Clowes panicked when he heard that Hedderwicks was about to be hammered. He had allowed his clients' stock to be used in the gambling scheme; there is evidence suggesting that he split the profits, if any, with de'Souza. With Hedderwicks about to go under the gambling money had to be converted back into clients' stock and delivered to Barlow Clowes; otherwise it risked becoming lost in the ensuing liquidation of Hedderwicks. (Clowes claims that his clients lost £500,000 in the collapse of Hedderwicks – but both the firm's partners and the Stock Exchange deny this.)

Special gambling accounts had been set up between Farrington Stead and Hedderwicks. Account number 2 on the contract notes issued by Hedderwicks every time a gilts deal was done indicated that the deals were for de'Souza and Stead. Account number 3 was for Stead, Farrington and de'Souza. And, although the firm took in only slightly more than £1 million from 125 clients, it managed in its brief, eighteen-month existence to buy and sell gilts worth a staggering £400 million.

Barlow was also dealing very heavily in gilts at the same time, using Farrington Stead and, like the other participants, making substantial losses. She had a joint account with de'Souza which owed Hedderwicks around £100,000 at the time of the hammering.

Earlier in 1981 de'Souza had been in the news for launching an audacious £600,000 takeover bid for Crystal Palace football club with the chairman of the club, Ron Noades. The press had described him as 'a wealthy stockbroker'[3] and, although the bid had been dropped, he joined the Crystal Palace board as a director and remains there to this day.

On Tuesday 7 April 1981 a £1.8 million debt was discovered in Hedderwicks' books by Touche Ross, the accountants called in by Quilter Goodison to carry out the standard financial investigations prior to the intended takeover. The debt was owed by Farrington Stead, who could not pay. Not only was the takeover abandoned but Hedderwicks was hammered. Significantly for Barlow Clowes, this meant that Hedderwicks' gilts department would be subjected to detailed investigation by the Exchange to discover how it had been able to act in such a cavalier fashion. Its gilts deals with Barlow Clowes were bound to be examined, as would the special relationship and terms enjoyed by Clowes with de'Souza.

It took only a few days for Martin Fidler, the Stock Exchange official acting as Hedderwicks' liquidator, to come across Barlow

Clowes. He noticed that Barlow Clowes gilts had been used by de'Souza and Farrington Stead to finance their gambling. Was Barlow Clowes a willing participant in this gambling scheme?

Five days after Hedderwicks was hammered Fidler rang the head of the DTI's Licensing Unit to discuss Farrington Stead. As a dealer in securities, licensed by the DTI, Farrington Stead would be of obvious interest to the Unit. However, Fidler suggested that the DTI should take a look at another firm, which he described as 'an associate' of Hedderwicks, which he was surprised to see was trading without a licence.

'Don't you think you ought to take a look at Barlow Clowes?' Fidler said. 'It looks pretty similar [to Farrington Stead] to me.'

In 1981 the Licensing Unit was a tiny, backwater section of the DTI with, at most, four staff none of whom had any relevant skills or training. It was standard practice for them to spend a maximum of three years in the Unit before moving on. Within the DTI itself the Unit was regarded as a dead end and a posting to it something to be endured rather than enjoyed. With several hundred firms and individuals to regulate, the four civil servants had a hopeless task. The Wilson Committee on the Functioning of Financial Institutions had reported the previous year on the inadequacy of the licensing system and recommended that new laws be introduced to tighten it up.

The Committee, chaired by former Labour Prime Minister Harold Wilson, had been disparaging about the existing system: 'Licences are fairly readily granted, provided the application is made in the prescribed manner and the required deposit of £500 is lodged . . . There have been only five refusals or revocations in the last ten years.' The Committee pointed out that the previous government, a Labour one, had already 'proposed to tighten up the system for granting licences' following a review in the mid-1970s. 'So far there has been no announcement of any intention on the part of the present government to amend the Prevention of Fraud Act. The present system is, however, generally recognised to be outdated and inefficient in a number of respects. We recommend therefore that legislation along the lines proposed by the last government should be introduced as soon as possible.'

The Wilson report was by no means the first independent report to criticise the system of investor protection. As early as 1962 the

Jenkins Committee had been highly critical of the Prevention of Fraud (Investments) Act.

Within the DTI the situation was even worse than Lord Wilson realised. The DTI had other sections that were relevant to the function of licensing dealers but which did not always co-operate with one another. It had a Companies Investigation Branch (CIB), which would investigate companies using the powers given to the DTI under the Companies Act 1967. It also had an Insolvency Unit, which collected information about company failures and bankruptcies. Often all three sections, Licensing, Investigations and Insolvency, would regard themselves as entirely separate to the point where they would not pass on information to one another. From a regulatory point of view it was a nightmare. 'There were absurd inhibitions within the Department at that time', says Professor Jim Gower, the man appointed in 1981 to review the whole system of investor protection. From 1981 onward, one man in the DTI, a solicitor called Philip Bovey, set about breaking down these internal barriers. He would later play a vital role in the Barlow Clowes affair.

It was against this background that, in April 1981, the Department's Licensing Unit received Fidler's warning about Barlow Clowes. One of its main functions in those days was to investigate cases of unlicensed dealing. Because of its scant resources the Unit generally did not use its powers to close down unlicensed dealing unless there was evidence of wrongdoing or investors' funds being at risk. It preferred to bring firms within the fold by licensing them.

On this occasion, however, Fidler had pointed not just to Barlow Clowes's unlicensed dealing but also to the fact that there appeared to be similarities between the company and Farrington Stead, which had just collapsed so spectacularly. Moreover, Barlow Clowes had been the training ground for both Farrington and Stead, as the DTI would know from the firm's original licence application. The DTI had to make a decision: as well as investigating Farrington Stead, which it was obliged to do given the firm's collapse, should it launch a separate investigation into Barlow Clowes? The head of the Licensing Unit was worried, as he told the Department's solicitors in a note written the day after Fidler's telephone call. 'I think that we should follow up the possibility that they [Barlow Clowes] have been dealing without a licence, but I am not sure whether a section 109 enquiry would be appropriate.' (A section 109 enquiry allowed the DTI to examine a firm's books and records.) In the end it was decided to make Barlow Clowes into a watching brief when Farrington Stead was investigated rather than launch a separate enquiry into the firm itself. The investigation into Farrington was carried out by the Companies Investigation Branch of the DTI, which collected sufficient information during the course of its enquiries to show that Barlow Clowes was not only operating without a licence but had also started an offshore partnership in Jersey.

Meanwhile, at Barlow Clowes's Warnford offices the staff had noticed that Clowes was taking a great interest in the Hedderwicks affair. 'He was both worried and excited by it at the same time,' says a former employee who worked for Barlow Clowes at the time. 'I remember Aggie de'Souza calling up Peter Clowes a couple of times and arranging meetings with him at the Great Eastern Hotel' – a huge, old-fashioned hotel by the side of London's Liverpool Street station. By this time Fidler was on the trail of Elizabeth Barlow. He had discovered the account in Farrington's records which owed £100,000 or so to Hedderwicks and with which she seemed to be involved. Fidler interviewed her on oath twice and got her to admit that the account was in effect jointly owned by her and de'Souza. When he wanted to see her a third time she fled the country and a warrant was issued for her arrest. It remains outstanding to this day.

The City of London police began to take an interest in the Hedderwicks affair and interviewed Clowes. The police wanted to know about his relationship with de'Souza, and whether Clowes himself had been involved in the gambling scheme. Clowes maintained that he knew nothing about it. Although he had left stock on the shelf with Hedderwicks he claimed that he had not given permission for de'Souza or Farrington Stead or anyone else to use it. His version of events would, if he was prepared to support it in court, be valuable for any prosecution. And when de'Souza, Geoffrey Farrington and Harry Stead were arrested and charged with conspiracy to steal gilt-edged stock, Clowes agreed to act as a witness for the prosecution in the subsequent Old Bailey trial.

But what of the Department of Trade's watching brief on Barlow Clowes? It was here that fortune favoured Clowes for a second time. In 1975 there had been a breakdown in communication between the DTI's Solicitors Department and those responsible for licensing which led to the Department failing to license Barlow Clowes. So it was with the Farrington investigation, this time the breakdown of communication involving the Licensing Unit and the Companies Investigation Branch (CIB). The CIB had enough evidence to prosecute Barlow Clowes for unlicensed dealing, but it failed to pass the information to the Licensing Unit when it completed its enquiries into Farrington Stead. The reason for the failure was that the CIB official had not realised that the watching brief on Barlow Clowes had been at the Licensing Unit's request. Given that he had not, when investigating Farrington Stead, discovered anything about Barlow Clowes which was sufficient to warrant a separate investigation by the CIB, he let the matter drop.

Even then evidence of Barlow Clowes's illegal dealing would probably have come to light but for a fluke. The CIB's report on Farrington was lengthy and included several enclosures. The report itself made no mention of Barlow Clowes but the enclosures did contain the details of the firm. Because of its size the CIB sent only the report to the Licensing Unit, saying that enclosures would be copied to them on request. The Licensing Unit made no such request. This was August 1981, only a few months after Martin Fidler's call to the Licensing Unit pointing out his suspicions that Barlow Clowes was operating without a licence. And yet no one in the Unit thought to ask the CIB whether further evidence of unlicensed dealing – beyond Fidler's hunch – had been discovered. Given the proximity of Fidler's warning and the fact that the CIB watching brief on Barlow Clowes had been triggered by fears of unlicensed dealing among other things, this was an astonishing failure by the Unit to follow through its original concerns. So another opportunity to examine and license – or close down – Barlow Clowes was lost.

Three of the people with whom Clowes had worked most closely over the preceding ten years were under police investigation, and had been arrested; another, Elizabeth Barlow, was wanted for questioning by the police, while Terry Webster, the former head of gilts at Hedderwicks and an associate of Clowes, had been expelled from the Stock Exchange. But Clowes himself, due to a combination of luck and his willingness to lie, had emerged unscathed. And, because the Stock Exchange and DTI investigations were private, the investing public knew nothing about this side of Clowes and his business when, a year after the Hedderwicks hammering, Barlow Clowes was launched nationally.

CHAPTER FIVE

·

THE TURNING POINT

·

'Hello and welcome to Money-Box. *In the programme this week
– how basic rate taxpayers can escape the Revenue's clutches and
get a guaranteed high income on their investments . . . an
investment idea that seems almost too good to be true.'*
Louise Botting, introducing Barlow Clowes to listeners of
BBC Radio Four's *Money-Box* programme, May 1982.

Three weeks before the collapse of Farrington Stead another licensed
dealer went into liquidation. Norton Warburg was a high-profile firm
of investment managers and its liquidation in February 1981 sent
shivers through the investment community and the financial establishment. The firm had been allowed into the Bank of England to
advise staff being made redundant from the soon to be disbanded
Exchange Control Division on how they should invest their redundancy money. About twenty Bank of England officials had taken
Norton Warburg's advice, entrusted their money to the firm, and
risked losing it since it now emerged that the firm had run up debts
of around £5 million.

The Pink Floyd pop group had been clients of Norton Warburg
and cricketer Colin Cowdrey had advertised the firm's services, recommending them to fellow sportsmen: 'Large sums of capital can
bring with them many headaches for the inexperienced. The management of Norton Warburg have certainly been of great help to me,'
Cowdrey said in the advertisements. Four hundred people had
invested with Norton Warburg. Millions of pounds of their money
had been diverted into high-risk business ventures by the firm's co-
founder Andrew Warburg.

Articles started to appear in the press criticising the Department
of Trade's role in licensing the firm. For over a year the DTI had
been in possession of a secret report criticising Norton Warburg's
finances and calling for an investigation. 'There were warning signs
which could have been turned up by anyone who made fairly
elementary checks,' wrote the *Daily Telegraph* in May 1981, pointing

to Norton Warburg's accounts for 1977 which had been qualified by its auditors on the grounds that the company had provided insufficient information for a view to be taken on its affairs. The accounts were publicly available. According to the *Financial Times*, the collapse of Norton Warburg 'demonstrates that once the Department of Trade has certified a company as a licensed security dealer its customers may have remarkably little protection'.

It is characteristic of change that it often takes a disaster to effect it. Norton Warburg's collapse, heavily publicised, finally hammered home the point that the investor protection laws had to be changed. The Government was about to launch a full scale privatisation campaign which would create millions of new investors, naive and easy prey for unscrupulous investment advisers. They needed more than the fig leaf protection of a DTI licence to safeguard their interests.

In July 1981 John Biffen, then Secretary of State for Trade and Industry, chose Professor Jim Gower, an eminent company lawyer, to conduct yet another review of the investor protection laws. Gower was asked to look at the existing system and 'advise on the need for new legislation'. From a public relations point of view the Gower review would at least show that the Government was doing something about investor protection while the privatisation programme was being implemented. There were other reasons behind the review: 'It was hoped that I would make proposals which would reduce the manpower of the DTI,' Gower says. 'Norman Tebbit told me that was the policy. When I asked him why he said policy did not have to have its reasons.'[1]

In January 1982 Gower published a discussion document highlighting the shortcomings in the system. Gower made the point that not only were the DTI's resources for policing the market scant, but the Department was already under instructions to reduce its manpower.

Gower pointed out the mess that the system was in. In some instances, such as unit trusts, the DTI exercised too much control; in others, such as the licensed dealers, not enough control. According to Gower, the DTI was guilty of 'underkill and overkill . . . The most conspicuous example of underkill is the failure effectively to regulate the activities of those who offer their services as investment managers and advisers,' Gower wrote.

He continued in the same vein:

> the lack of effective regulation [of investment managers and advisers] had occurred not so much because there is pres-

41

ently a gap in the statutory controls but because the controls
have not been effectively exercised. The legislation is defec-
tive, however, because the powers conferred on the Department of Trade are not really apt for controlling investment
managers and advisers . . . without new primary legislation
a really satisfactory result cannot be achieved.

Tightening up on investment advisers was merely part of a general process of improving control over financial institutions. The
official enquiry into the collapse of the Vehicle and General Insurance
Company in 1971 had led to an improvement in the controls over
insurance companies and in the resources enjoyed by the Department
of Trade's Insurance Division. The fringe banking crisis from 1973–5
had led to the Banking Act 1979, which introduced tighter controls
over deposit taking and was administered by the Bank of England.
The requirements for a deposit-taker's licence were far more stringent
than those which investment advisers and managers had to satisfy
in order to obtain a dealing licence from the DTI. Gower's discussion
document of January 1982 was the opening shot in an attempt to
bring the laws to protect investors up to date.

In May 1982 Clowes received a telephone call at his London office
from Vincent Duggleby, co-presenter of Radio Four's *Money-Box* programme. *Money-Box* is a respected half-hour programme broadcast
every Saturday at noon and repeated the following Monday morning.
Duggleby presents the programme with Louise Botting, who com-
bines her BBC role with running a financial consultancy.

Duggleby wanted Peter Clowes to appear on the programme. He
wanted to interview him on an apparently new method of converting
taxable income into tax-free capital gains, using gilt-edged securities.
Barlow Clowes was, by this time, specialising in this method. It was
called bondwashing.

In its simplest form bondwashing involved buying gilts just after
they had paid a dividend, at which time their price would be lower
to reflect the dividend payment. The same gilts would then be held
until just before the next dividend was declared, at which point the
price would be higher to take into account the imminent dividend.
But instead of holding them and receiving the dividend they would
be sold at this higher price. By buying 'ex-dividend' and selling 'cum-
dividend' you would benefit from the increase in capital value: you
would have made a capital gain rather than received a dividend

which was subject to income tax. In 1982 the first £5000 of capital gain a year were tax free.

In the case of short-dated gilts, ones with five years or less to run, the income or dividend accrued on a daily basis, making the bondwashing process much easier. If a gilt was sold 100 days after it had last paid a dividend, the seller would receive the price of the gilt plus 100 days' worth of accrued dividend. There was no question of relying on the gilts market makers adjusting the price of gilts to take into account the fact that a dividend had been paid or was about to be paid, as was the case with long-dated gilts. With short-dated ones, there was a simple mathematical calculation.

There were two key developments which had enabled Clowes to specialise in bondwashing instead of being simply a gilts investment manager. First, in 1980 an annual exemption was introduced whereby the first £3000 of any capital gains an individual made were exempt from tax. In 1982 the exemption was increased to £5000. The second was a 1980 legal case which effectively ruled that bondwashing was effective for basic-rate taxpayers – they could convert taxable income into tax-free capital gains – but not for higher-rate taxpayers.

Clowes was quick to take advantage of these developments. He put together a bondwashing product which he called Portfolio 30, offering a fixed income from gilts which was completely tax free, and guaranteeing to return the entire investment after a predetermined period. It offered absolute security, guaranteed income and capital, and no tax to pay. Louise Botting described it as 'an investment idea that seems almost too good to be true' in the opening sequence of *Money-Box* on 8 May 1982. She was right but, along with many others, clearly did not know it at the time. She and Vincent Duggleby were about to publicise bondwashing nationally for the first time, using 'investment adviser Peter Clowes' to explain how it worked and, more important, how *he* could do it best. It would be a turning point for Clowes.

Clowes had not initiated his appearance on *Money-Box*. Duggleby's telephone call to him in early May had been the first contact between the two men. Clowes claims that he was reluctant to appear because he thought that the publicity that would inevitably result would trigger enormous interest and the Inland Revenue would then clamp down on the bondwashing scheme. According to Clowes, Duggleby had been sceptical about bondwashing but had checked with the Inland Revenue and found that it worked. In journalistic terms the bondwashing story was a scoop and ideal for a programme like *Money-Box* whose main purpose was to advise people how and where to invest their money. 'I am broadcasting this item on Saturday whether you appear or not', Duggleby told Clowes.[2]

Barlow Clowes was the first item on the programme, introduced by Louise Botting. 'Hello and welcome to *Money-Box*. In the programme this week . . . an investment idea that seems almost too good to be true. . . . Fourteen per cent on your money, total security of capital, no tax to pay and all courtesy of the British Government.'

Duggleby and Botting proceeded to explain how bondwashing worked and the generous tax-free returns it generated.

'But is it something that you can easily do yourself?'

'In theory yes,' replied Clowes. 'In practice, no. We use a computer to monitor the operation because it is necessary to use more than one stock, to avoid dealing on or around the ex-dividend dates when there would be unfavourable price movements.'

'Is there in fact any risk to the capital because government securities can fall in price?' asked Duggleby.

Clowes, talking purely about his own product, replied: 'No, the yield would still be totally guaranteed and the capital is also guaranteed at maturity. The worst that could happen to a client is that, with hindsight, he would know that six months later he might have been able to buy a higher yield had he waited.'

'But provided the gilt has held the maturity there's no risk to capital?'

'No, there's absolutely no risk to capital.'

There was no mention on the programme of Clowes's unlicensed status, and no other 'expert' was interviewed. Looking back, Duggleby says that he did not question Clowes directly about not having a DTI licence because, so far as he could tell, Barlow Clowes was a wholesale operation which did not deal directly with the public. (Later on, in response to readers' letters, *Money-Box* pointed out that Barlow Clowes was not licensed whereas a rival company offering bondwashing was.)

The last part of the *Money-Box* interview had been exclusively about the Barlow Clowes Portfolio 30 product. Its key characteristic was that it guaranteed both the level of income an investor would receive and the return of his capital – provided that it was held until the gilt matured. And the underlying product was a gilt, issued by the British Government. The security it offered, combined with the fact that it was tax free to basic rate taxpayers, made it an ideal product for pensioners with life savings to invest. People who had retired early or been made redundant and had lump sums to invest would also find Portfolio 30 appealing.

Clowes knew this and structured the product accordingly. Pensioners in particular would like the idea of a fixed income paid to them, so Portfolio 30 offered them the choice of having their income from the gilts paid regularly every six months, allowing them to budget accordingly. Another major attraction for pensioners was that Portfolio 30 would not affect their entitlement to age allowance – the increase in the normal personal allowance given to people aged sixty-five or over. This allowance is reduced for pensioners who earn or receive income above a certain level, but the capital gains generated by Portfolio 30 did not affect the entitlement.

The *Money-Box* interview sparked off interest in bondwashing in general and Barlow Clowes in particular. Investors and financial intermediaries wrote to the BBC asking for transcripts of the interview, and the number of enquiries about Portfolio 30 at Barlow Clowes's London office mushroomed. The interview had turned bondwashing into a nationally known loophole which people would rush to exploit. Later that year, on Saturday 7 August, the *Daily Telegraph* published an article on bondwashing with the headline 'Get in on this Good Thing'. As in the case of *Money-Box*, Barlow Clowes was the only company cited as capable of bondwashing for private investors:

> The idea would seem one that stockbrokers should be promoting to their clients. But they are not. As they frankly admit, small dealings in gilts (by which they mean less than hundreds of thousands of pounds per bargain) are loss-making, and they are not interested.
>
> However, one non-Stock Exchange firm has packaged a scheme for stripping a guaranteed income out of gilts on this basis. Investment manager Barlow Clowes . . . can switch gilts in large chunks thus avoiding the high dealing costs which afflict individual gilt investors.

The media policy generated an enormous inflow of business to Barlow Clowes. In June 1982 it had only £4.3 million under management in gilts, for 1000 clients. One year later funds under management had risen almost eight times to £33.1 million and the number of clients had tripled to 3000. The fees the company earned for managing the gilts increased from £190,000 to almost £800,000, before taking into account commissions paid to intermediaries.[3]

The publicity had other effects, less tangible but important nevertheless. It had put Barlow Clowes into an entirely different league. It had converted a tiny, anonymous investment management company – Barlow Clowes had made a profit of just £27 the previous year – into a nationally known business and, at the same time, strongly endorsed its claim to be 'gilts specialists'. In short, it had given Barlow Clowes and its co-founder Peter Clowes something they had never had before: status.

It is likely that the publicity had more sinister effects, that it gave Clowes greater confidence in his ability to cheat his investors and get away with it. He had taken liberties with their money for years but at the same time had deliberately kept a low profile. He protected himself by keeping his head down, both literally – never looking people in the eye, chin against his chest, blond fringe covering his eyes – and in his business affairs. Even the home he chose, Varykeno, was isolated and reclusive. He never advertised his business directly to the public; the financial middlemen did that for him. Often their advertisements did not even mention Barlow Clowes by name, referring instead to 'monthly income plans' or 'guaranteed income service'. When Clowes opened his London office in 1981 he did not take out any advertisements in the press to announce his arrival; he did not employ a public relations company to introduce him to key journalists. For Clowes, secrecy had counterbalanced his cheating.

His anonymity had also meant that he avoided the Department of Trade's licensing system. The DTI had erroneously advised him that he did not need a licence provided he did not distribute promotional material. But by 1982 he was sending out single-sheet leaflets on Portfolio 30 with his company's name prominently displayed. As he was flouting the rules he was therefore taking a risk by going public about his business on *Money-Box*. But nothing came of it. The radio programme made no impact on the Department's Licensing Unit, money poured in, and Barlow Clowes became better known.

CHAPTER SIX

·

THE ADVERTISING CAMPAIGN

·

'My life began and my luck changed when I married Pamela.'
Peter Clowes, on his second marriage.

Swingate Cottage is what local estate agents would describe as a 'substantial' property. Located in the quiet village of Whitley Green, Macclesfield, it boasts stables, an indoor swimming pool, six bedrooms and a huge sprawling garden. It is separated from the road, Holehouse Lane, by tall hedges, and protected in the rear by fields and a small forest. A plaque on the front maintains that the cottage was built in 1772. The occupants, Mr and Mrs Peter Clowes, like to hold children's parties around the indoor pool, turning the temperature up to 90 degrees so that the pool is like a bath for the children to splash around in. They throw lavish dinner parties with Clowes doing the cooking. Guests report that he is an excellent cook, with a fine sensitive palate. Pamela cannot cook.

Divorced in 1979, Clowes married his former secretary Pamela Haydock in January 1982. 'My life began and my luck changed when I married Pamela,' Clowes would say. This was the third time he had fallen for someone he worked with and made them into his business partner. Pamela followed Elizabeth Barlow and Shelley Goldstone (who left in 1981) into Clowes's affections and was given a 25 per cent stake in Barlow Clowes. This pattern may simply reflect that Clowes felt most at ease with women in a working environment, although this does not explain why all three women also became his business partners. Clowes appeared to connect love with money, perhaps as a result of the hard grafting atmosphere of his childhood home where he had to earn his pocket money rather than be given it. 'Peter Clowes seemed to feel he had to buy his way into women's affections.'[1] He was Pamela's second husband. Her first marriage, to Hollies pop star Eric Haydock, had failed and, after an affair with another Barlow Clowes executive, she had chosen Clowes, bringing three children from her first marriage, a daughter Nikki and twin boys Robert and James, with her. She was materialistic; she liked expensive clothes, jewellery and holidays, and Clowes was happy to indulge her. Later, Eric Haydock would join them. Clowes employed him as a chauffeur to ferry Pamela around, and as a general dogsbody. 'It was a perfectly straightforward arrangement. Eric needed a job and Peter gave him one,' Pamela says.[2]

Clowes bought Swingate in early 1982, shortly before he made his appearance on *Money-Box*. It was on the market for £125,000. But there was a problem: Clowes could not sell his own home, Varykeno, in the unfashionable Marple hillside, because work needed to be done to it. He managed to raise the deposit and arrange a bridging loan of £25,000 for Swingate and drew the balance of the purchase price, £87,500, out of his clients' bank account in Jersey. This was not his money. It was part of the few hundred thousand pounds, which he managed separately in the Jersey business on behalf of investors. The money was not replaced when the sale of Varykeno was completed.

The move to Whitley Green represented quite a change for Clowes. It was a move into a new social milieu, that of the highly paid commuters and *nouveaux riches* who inhabited the nearby village of Prestbury, dubbed the 'Weybridge of the North'. Its high street offers hair design, rather than cutting, properties for sale starting at £100,000 and rising to half a million, and an array of BMWs, Jaguars and Rolls-Royces. It was a far cry from the slums of Moss Side and the drab, working-class streets of Heaton Moor and Heaton Mersey, where Clowes had spent most of his life. The rise in his social status coincided with both his marriage and the massive increase in the funds under his control.

The centre of Barlow Clowes's activities had, by this time, moved to Warnford Court, London, so Clowes would spend the week in a flat in London and his weekends in Swingate. He was not a member of the City establishment. He was, after all, still a little lad from Manchester, with a broad Mancunian accent which would have met with concealed disdain from the upper echelons of the stockbroking and banking communities. Clowes felt his isolation keenly. To this day people who worked for him remember he would often wince whenever the word 'stockbrokers' was mentioned in his hearing; he would sometimes repeat the word aloud, his face contorted with anger. It was almost a trigger, a reminder to him of his lack of acceptance. He felt that the brokers envied him his bondwashing business, and resented him because he had taken private clients away from them. This was not true – bondwashing for small, basic-rate taxpayers was not the sort of business that City stockbroking firms were keen to attract. The returns were not high enough. Blind prejudice, more than anything else, was the most likely explanation for the unreceptive attitude which Clowes came up against. Later there would be more concrete reasons for the City to shun Clowes.

Around the middle of 1983, with almost £40 million under management, Clowes decided to advertise his bondwashing product. He had never approached the public direct before, preferring to rely on recommendations from middlemen. Clowes arranged a meeting with Moorgate Advertising, a small London-based advertising company. His purpose, he explained, was to try out a test advertising campaign for his Portfolio 30 bondwashing product. The advantage would be that Barlow Clowes could keep the 3.5 per cent charge it levied when people invested in Portfolio 30. Until then he had paid 3 per cent to the intermediaries in return for introducing the business. The obvious downside was that Barlow Clowes would have to fund the advertising campaign from its own resources.

'He wanted us to do a test campaign first,' says Brian Feelan, one of the Moorgate staff who attended the first meeting with Clowes.[3] 'We told him it would cost £30,000 for a month's advertising. He said that was far too little – he wanted to spend £120,000. We were gobsmacked. That was a lot of money to spend in those days on a single month.'

The campaign went ahead with quarter-page advertisements placed in the *Daily Telegraph, Sunday Times, Observer* and other papers. The advertisements offered 'a guaranteed monthly income from gilts'. Clowes had further refined Portfolio 30 so that investors could take their income from the underlying gilts monthly, quarterly or every six months:

Now, thanks to Portfolio 30, basic-rate taxpayers can achieve a high guaranteed income without deduction of income tax – with these major advantages:

1. Absolute security of capital.
2. Up to £5300 a year income – free of tax.
3. Prompt payment of income.
4. Easy withdrawal.

5. Full refund of investment guaranteed at your selected maturity date.

Respondents were invited to write for a free quotation and an application form.

The single month's advertising soon became a full-blooded campaign, with Clowes committing £750,000 to the advertising budget and targeting the weekend press. This was a phenomenal amount of money for a small financial services company to spend. Clowes claims that he had seen the writing on the wall for bondwashing and, 'like any sensible financial institution', had wanted to get as much money on the books before the curtains came down.[4] This smacks of the old IOS dictum: 'Write the business first, fix the sweat later.' Clowes may simply have been carried away by his first taste of national advertising, like a child obsessed with a new toy. Certainly the amount of money he threw at the advertisers – often no less than three Barlow Clowes advertisements would appear on the same day in the same Saturday newspaper – bears this out. 'At the time this was remarkable,' says Feelan.

Clowes refused to be drawn on how much money the advertisements were bringing in for the business. 'I called him up to ask about the response figures – there were none,' says Feelan. 'Peter was a very discreet person. In September 1983 all he would say was: "We're doing fine." Despite our asking him several times he would never say how much he had under management.'

Moorgate were impressed with Clowes's professionalism. Every Monday during the campaign, which lasted several months and well into 1984, he would hold advertising meetings at the Warnford Court offices. Feelan describes these meetings as 'focused and to the point – much more professional than many of our other clients'. With Clowes at the meetings would be Dr Peter Naylor, a highly qualified mathematics expert who had joined Barlow Clowes in late 1982. 'The Doc', as he was known, was regarded by the staff as naive and impressionable and easily dominated by Clowes. This was his first paid job. Naylor had spent five years as an academic after graduating from Exeter University and Barlow Clowes was his first job. He had been brought in to work as a programmer on the firm's computerised systems. Like Clowes, he could be very domineering towards the administrative staff working at Warnford Court: 'I want to see you right now – or else,' he would say.

In the meetings Clowes was 'assertive, strong, almost dogmatic', says Feelan. 'If you came out with something he did not agree with that changed the whole course of the meeting, you would have to listen to a ten-minute monologue from Peter. But he was a very focused man. When he started talking he went off into another world, he was so incredibly involved with what he was doing and radiating enthusiasm.'

There was one person who could interrupt Clowes's dogmatic speeches about gilts: his wife Pamela. She would call her husband as many as a dozen times a day, calling him out of meetings, demanding to be put through to him whatever he was doing. 'He changed as a person when Pamela came on the phone', Feelan recalls. 'The assertiveness dropped and it was "Yes dear, no dear" from then on.' But Clowes was shy with women generally. One of the office girls used to put her arm around him and boom out in a loud Mancunian accent, 'Hey, Peter, how are you doing?' Clowes was embarrassed and would shuffle out of the room as quickly as possible.

The advertising campaign prompted Clowes to smarten up the company's image and launch new products. The single sheet of grey A4 paper used to promote Portfolio 30 was replaced with a glossy, smaller brochure. Brochures were also printed for the new products: the Barlow Clowes Gilt Monitor and Portfolio 78. The Gilt Monitor was a 'simple yet certain way to find out when an alternative stock could give you a greater return'. Barlow Clowes offered to review investors' holdings of gilt-edged stock and recommend alternatives that would produce better returns.

'Over the last ten years we have specialised exclusively in gilts and have developed a unique capability in analysing the gilt market and providing meaningful services for our clients', the brochure stated. 'This has been made possible by the installation of two large computer systems in the heart of the City of London, enabling us to provide highly specialised expertise to financial institutions and private clients at a very reasonable price.'

For a flat fee of £12.50 for the first gilt and £6.75 per additional gilt held by the investor, Barlow Clowes would review their holdings and recommend changes. The gilts stayed with the investor. All Barlow Clowes was providing was advice.

The Portfolio 78 product was similar to the bondwashing product in that it offered a tax-free capital gain from gilts. However, Barlow Clowes claimed that it would produce the gain by dealing in the gilts market, switching from one gilt to another whenever profitable opportunities came up, rather than by converting dividends into capital. It offered to produce two rates of return for investors: a guaranteed minimum rate – the minimum return an investor could expect each month – and an expected rate, representing a higher, hoped-for return.

Clowes also instructed Moorgate to act as his public relations advisers, particularly for the launch of the Gilt Monitor service. But the press interest in him and his company centred around Portfolio 30, the bondwashing product. In October 1983 the *Daily Mail* described it in glowing terms: 'timing the buying and selling dates needs skill and knowledge. Barlow Clowes & Partners offer to do it all for you. They can devise a Portfolio 30 plan where the income and overall return are locked in at the outset and as safe as the Bank of England.' Barlow Clowes extracted this quotation from the article and used it on the back of the Portfolio 30 brochures.

Other papers were more discriminating. After a while the *Daily Telegraph* refused to accept any advertisements from Barlow Clowes. Moorgate wanted to book a twenty-six-week series of quarter-page advertisements, costing £5000 each. Richard Northedge, the *Telegraph*'s personal finance editor, was unhappy: 'I had met Peter Clowes and did not like his bondwashing product. It did not add up,' he said, not believing that Barlow Clowes could produce the high returns from gilts which it was promising. 'I had nothing evidential to say they were crooks. So we avoided them. There was no mention of Barlow Clowes in our pages from autumn 1983 until the announcement that bondwashing was going to abolished in March 1985.' Apart from steering clear of Barlow Clowes editorially there remained the question of the advertisements. Northedge took the problem to Andreas Whittam Smith, who at that time was the City Editor of the *Daily Telegraph*. Whittam Smith backed Northedge and refused to accept the advertisements. It was a brave decision to turn away £130,000 of advertising revenue. The *Daily Mail* later refused to take any more Barlow Clowes advertising, on the recommendation of its deputy City Editor Michael Walters.

Other journalists adopted a similar editorial attitude to Barlow Clowes. Diana Wright, now personal finance editor of the *Sunday Times*, lunched with Clowes twice, 'but I consciously did not write anything about him.' Like Northedge she suspected Clowes's ability to produce the returns he was advertising. Lorna Bourke, who edited the 'Family Money' pages of *The Times*, also refused to write about Barlow Clowes. She even went to see Clowes twice, tape-recording interviews with him in which she expressed doubts about his ability to produce the returns. She left unsatisfied with the explanations he gave but, like the others, with no hard evidence against either the man or his firm.

This perspective was not shared with or by the investors who responded to the Barlow Clowes advertising campaign in droves. The number of clients tripled from 3000 to 9000 in the year that the advertising blitz was launched. And Barlow Clowes took in another £19 million.

Inside Barlow Clowes there was a different story to tell. The computer could not cope with the volume of new business and broke down as many as eight times in a day. The printers would not work in any event if the terminals were on. So on a day when journalists were taken around the offices in Warnford Court the terminals all had to be switched off to allow a simple print-out to be produced for their benefit.

The gilts selection and switching was not generated by computer as Barlow Clowes claimed. Instead it was carried out mainly by Margaret Kelly, an executive in the Warnford Court office, who used to pick the gilts out of the *Financial Times*. She had little financial experience; prior to joining Barlow Clowes she had been selling pewter. There was no computerised system for identifying switches. 'The nearest they got to it was a few graphs,' says one of the liquidators who later investigated Barlow Clowes.

Margaret Kelly describes Barlow Clowes as chaotic. The computerised systems for recording the amount each client had invested and how much should be paid out to him or her in regular withdrawals did not work properly. In the end a group of bold, brassy young admin women, nicknamed the 'Barlow Mob' because they used to go out on heavy drinking sprees and play darts matches together, used a combination of manual record keeping and the computer to record client details. Even manual record keeping is too grand a title for what actually happened: one of the secretaries, Lorraine, would pencil in her desk diary how much was to be paid out to each investor. The computer was supposed to do this but the print-outs omitted huge numbers of investors.[5]

As for the advertising campaign, the cost of £750,000 had been funded entirely from money belonging to Barlow Clowes investors.

The advertising campaign represented a landmark for Clowes. It was his most daring move to date. To launch Barlow Clowes nationally, seeking funds from investors while secretly using money belonging to other investors to finance the launch, required particular confidence. The money came from the Jersey side of Barlow Clowes, which had almost £12 million invested in it by the end of 1984. Clowes owned 90 per cent of the Jersey partnership and a local company, Conwyn Services Ltd, the balance. Investors' money could be withdrawn on Clowes's signature alone.

Clowes could not, however, simply write out a cheque from the Jersey clients account and pay it into the office account of his UK business. The amounts – totalling £750,000 – were large and might excite suspicion. And partnerships had to prepare accounts, even though they did not have to be made public. So some form of disguise had to be devised to fool the accountants. Clowes produced a suitable explanation – a company called Hermes Management Services, incorporated in Gibraltar but with a Jersey address. Hermes was in effect a dummy company. It had no staff, sold no goods and at the time of the advertising campaign had no trading function. It existed purely as an excuse for diverting investors' money from Jersey into the UK office account. But if Hermes was the disguise, Clowes still needed an explanation as to why this company was paying him £750,000. 'Software licensing' was the answer. Clowes maintained that he licensed the computer software used for his bond-washing business to Hermes for its own 'clients'. Hermes, so the Clowes explanation went, was a fund management business itself which wanted to use the Barlow Clowes software program. In return it paid a fee, which in 1983–4 was £750,000 and covered the cost of the advertising campaign.

The Hermes sham was a totally private affair, one which provided a bookkeeping explanation for the entry of clients' funds into the Barlow Clowes business. Investors would not have known about it and indeed it would have been impossible for an outsider to detect. It was a technique which Clowes would use again and again to devastating effect in the coming years as his confidence in his ability to deceive grew greater and greater.

CHAPTER SEVEN

·

A LITANY OF WARNINGS

·

The Barlow Clowes advertising campaign, as well as bringing thousands of clients into the business, also unleashed a maelstrom of incredulity and concern about the firm and its products. The common theme, among institutions such as the Stock Exchange, Nasdim – a fledgling organisation established to provide an alternative form of authorisation to obtaining a DTI licence – and several respected fund management groups, was sheer disbelief that Barlow Clowes could generate the high returns it was promising to investors in Portfolio 30. Not only that, the Jersey authorities had realised that Barlow Clowes was running a separate fund management business from the island and were not happy about it.

The concerns about Barlow Clowes ran parallel with the growth in its business generated from the advertising campaign, but neither development overlapped. The fears of the institutions were privately expressed, just as journalists who doubted the firm, but lacked evidence to prove it corrupt, simply wrote nothing abut Barlow Clowes. So despite the consternation behind the scenes, the investing public remained ignorant.

Jersey was the first problem Clowes had to tackle. In December 1983 Clowes had a meeting with Richard Syvret, the Commercial Relations Officer on the island. Barlow Clowes had had a presence on the island since 1977, but for years the partnership had consisted of little more than a small room and a few files in the offices of Anders & Whitehead, a firm of local Jersey solicitors, one of whose partners, Roger Anders, had a separate legal practice in Manchester which advised Peter Clowes.

The Jersey partnership did not raise money in Jersey or indeed manage funds on the island. Clowes or one of his staff would fly to Jersey every two or three weeks to visit the office, which had no permanent staff of its own. It was a step up from being merely a postbox partnership.

The Jersey authorities exercise no control over the *registration* of businesses on the island. However, just as Jersey has strict residence qualifications governing people who want to come to live on the island, it also operates a filtering process to prevent businesses it does not want from actually setting up operations there. Jersey did not and still does not operate a licensing system along the lines of the DTI system for regulating investment advisers and managers. Instead it has two sets of controls. The first requires any business operating a collective investment scheme from the island, such as a Jersey-based unit trust, to obtain a licence. The second applies to all businesses on the island: they must obtain a permit from the Jersey Finance and Economics Committee. The ground rules for obtaining a permit are vague. According to Syvret a business 'must demonstrate that it has a track record established out of the island and is an institution of some stature.' Barlow Clowes had been exempted from this requirement on the grounds that it claimed not to be operating a business on the island.

Syvret called the December 1983 meeting for one simple reason: he wanted Barlow Clowes off the island. He had seen an article in *Financial Weekly* referring to a Barlow Clowes fund 'based in Jersey'. Syvret had also noticed that Barlow Clowes was advertising in the English Sunday newspapers giving two addresses – one in England and also the address of the Jersey partnership. This meant in effect that Barlow Clowes was raising money to be sent to and banked in Jersey and far exceeded the limited presence the Jersey authorities had allowed Clowes to maintain on the island.[1]

What concerned Syvret about Barlow Clowes was the lack of safeguards in place to protect investors. The partnership was under the sole control of Clowes, as were its bank accounts and the clients' money in them. The literature Barlow Clowes sent out to investors made no mention of the fees it was charging. There were probably other reasons which led Syvret to tell Clowes, at the end of the meeting, to take his business off the island. The Jersey partnership, although in existence for six years, had not drawn up a single set of accounts. If Syvret asked Clowes for formal accounts, he would not have been able to produce them. 'We made it clear to them that the island authorities were concerned at what they were doing in the island even though it was not doing much here, and we asked them to wind up their affairs,' says Syvret.

Clowes had resisted at first, claiming that the Jersey authorities should be proud to have a business such as his on the island. But Syvret was adamant. The business must go by the end of the month and with it all the money that it held on the island. The bank accounts holding investors' money in Jersey – with the local branches of Lloyds and Midland – had to be closed down. 'I am anxious that client monies should not be held here in any way,' Syvret later wrote to Clowes's Jersey solicitors, referring to 'the problem of investors believing that their money is in Jersey and looking to the island for recourse should they have any grievance at all'.[2]

What Syvret did not know was that Barlow Clowes's own staff were becoming concerned about the Jersey operations. This was because much of the money that investors sent to Jersey did not seem to be invested in anything. It would be transferred to an account with Midland Bank, known internally as the 'funding' account, and there it seemed to stay. What was going on?

While Clowes was wondering where to move his Jersey business, fears about Barlow Clowes were pouring into the Department of Trade. They started with a letter on 20 January 1984 from Robert Bridges, who ran a firm of investment consultants based in London called John Scott & Partners. Bridges was unhappy about Barlow Clowes and raised five points against the firm. The most telling was the fourth: 'Who are Barlow Clowes and Partners,' he asked, 'and what is *their* guarantee worth?' This was a vital point. On the face of it, as Barlow Clowes was investing only in gilts, its 'guarantee' was that of the British Government, which underwrites all issues of gilts. But on closer examination the guarantee of a fixed income and return of capital was not the Government's, it was Barlow Clowes's.

It was true that investors in Portfolio 30 had their money invested in gilts. But the deal Clowes was promising them meant that he had to achieve a better return than the gilts themselves generated. He was providing a rate of return, fixed from the outset, which was virtually the same as the coupon on the gilts. On top of that, however, he had to pay commissions to intermediaries, his own commission, and the buying and selling expenses. The commissions were sizeable: an initial 3.5 per cent on each investment, of which Clowes took up to 1.5 per cent and paid the balance to the introducing intermediary; and an annual renewal commission of 1.5 per cent – in consideration of Barlow Clowes continuing to manage the money – of which Clowes took 0.5 per cent, the intermediary the remainder. And if interest rates rose, the capital value of the gilts would go down. Clowes was effectively guaranteeing that his technique could beat the market – do better than the Government was offering. The words 'Your Guarantee' were boxed in and highlighted on the Portfolio 30 brochures.

It *was* possible to better the rates of return on gilts, but to do so you had to take risks with the capital – deal in and out of the gilts market. Several financial institutions ran gilt-edged funds which often made higher returns than the average yield on gilts, but they did not guarantee investors the return of their capital. Barlow Clowes did. The implication was that if Barlow Clowes did not achieve the returns, it would provide them from its own resources. That was the 'value' of the guarantee.

The letter from Bridges was read by Noel Dixon, a junior official in the Licensing Unit. He passed it to Roger Louth, the official in charge of licensing, commenting that Bridges had already telephoned a few days previously 'grumbling about Barlow Clowes'. It seems from this response that Bridges's point about the guarantee, which itself raised questions about the financial security of Barlow Clowes and the viability of Portfolio 30, had not struck home. But the Department would soon receive a far more direct exposé of Barlow Clowes and its claims to be a gilts specialist.

Adrian Collins, chief executive of Gartmore, a major City fund management group, hosted a lunch for Louth and John Crease, a DTI official whose responsibilities included unit trusts, on 10 April 1984. Gartmore managed a large number of unit trusts and, as these are regulated by the DTI, it was normal that there should be some contact between Collins and DTI officials. Collins was one of the youngest success stories in the City. He had become head of Gartmore at the very young age of twenty-nine. An extrovert, he was in the habit of walking around the office with a cigarette behind each ear. But on that day in April 1984, Collins was not so sanguine.

Collins was concerned about how Barlow Clowes could spend so much money on advertising and still make the returns which they were 'guaranteeing' to investors. He also told the DTI about his evaluation of the Barlow Clowes bondwashing product. Financial intermediaries who had seen the Barlow Clowes advertisement and its guarantees had asked Collins to provide a similar deal. Collins had made some calculations but found that the product just did not add up.

Collins told the DTI officials that it was 'inconceivable' that Barlow Clowes could guarantee both the income and the capital: the costs of the exercise – commissions to brokers and Barlow Clowes's own fees – rendered it impossible. Merely guaranteeing a fixed income would have been fine because Barlow Clowes could legitimately pay part of that income out of the invested capital. But the return of the entire capital was also guaranteed. 'We simply pointed out that what Barlow Clowes was up to was not deliverable,' says Collins. 'In addition, how were they capable of . . . advertising in an environment which required a licence to deal in securities? And they scratched their heads and said, "Well, we don't really know." '

Unlike the DTI officials, Collins was and is a specialist in the field of devising financial products for private investors. He was a practitioner, they were not. If Collins said that it did not add up, that the Barlow Clowes guarantee was impossible, then it had to be taken seriously. He had evaluated the product and it did not work. All over the City other financial advisers had made the same or similar calculations, had spoken to brokers specialising in gilts and other gilt fund managers selling to the public. They all came to the same conclusion: Portfolio 30 was not viable. 'It wasn't just instinct,' says Collins, 'it was maths.'

Collins's fears were not confined to an analysis of the Barlow Clowes product and the conclusion that it did not work. He took them further and told the DTI officials of a rumour circulating about Barlow Clowes at the time to the effect that the firm was bankrupt to the tune of £4 million. He also passed on suggestions that it had not filed accounts. Like many rumours there were elements of truth. Barlow Clowes Jersey had not prepared accounts, and Clowes was using Jersey funds to top up shortfalls on the Portfolio 30 product.

What Barlow Clowes was doing with its bondwashing product was to offer investors a perfect situation. Investors chose a gilt, they were guaranteed the income which the gilt was offering for a fixed period until the gilt matured, when they would get back all their capital. The gilt would be bought and sold, perhaps switched into a similar gilt, in order to convert the income into a capital gain.

But there were several flaws. The quotations which Clowes provided to investors showing how they would achieve their guaranteed returns completely ignored the dealing costs – the commissions payable to stockbrokers whenever gilts were bought and sold. Bondwashing involved four separate transactions each year – two sales and two purchases – in order to avoid receiving dividends. Moreover, the gilts market makers would take a 'turn' (or profit) each time they dealt in gilts, representing the difference between the two prices – buying and selling – they made whenever anyone wanted to deal in gilts. Added to these were the commissions already described – 3.5 per cent introductory and 1.5 per cent annual – that came out of the investors' money.

The Barlow Clowes literature presented bondwashing as a scientific process, whereas in the case of long-dated gilts – those with five years or more to run – it was not. There was no guarantee that when Barlow Clowes came to sell a long-dated gilt which was close to its dividend date, the market makers would quote a price which reflected the proximity of the dividend. In fact the jobbers, as they were then known, might realise that they were dealing with a seller of gilts and mark the price down accordingly, as they were entitled to do. Many, perhaps most, of the Barlow Clowes investors had their money in long-dated gilts.

There were other factors which explain why Portfolio 30 was a flawed product: the commissions which Barlow Clowes charged were insufficient to cover the firm's overheads; Clowes was drawing money from the bondwashing fund in advance of commissions and sometimes diverting it into his Jersey business. In 1984 £2.8 million was withdrawn from the UK investors' funds. To this date it cannot be traced. If the capital was depleted in these ways the income generated from Portfolio 30 was bound to fall.

It was open to the DTI to regard the concerns voiced by Collins and Bridges as motivated by professional envy. But the Stock Exchange was also worried – as was the Bank of England. The month after the Collins meeting, Bob Wilkinson, head of the Stock Exchange's surveillance department, rang the Bank. Wilkinson, an expert at spotting cheats and fraudsters, told the Bank in no uncertain terms that he did not see how Barlow Clowes could offer the returns that it was. When, a week later, Wilkinson rang the Department direct and spoke to Dixon, he proffered an explanation of the way in which Barlow Clowes was meeting its commitments to clients: it was 'pooling' their money, that is, simply paying one client with another client's money. Provided everyone did not ask for their money at the same time, 'robbing Peter to pay Paul', as it was known, would work.

To an extent Wilkinson was only echoing the views of his own members, the stockbroking firms. Several had complained to him about Barlow Clowes being slow payers and, at least at one point, a black mark had been entered against Barlow Clowes by the Exchange members' Mutual Reference Society, a form of credit-checking agency available only to Stock Exchange members. 'We'd been more or less warned off dealing with Barlow Clowes,' says one gilts stockbroker. 'It was along the lines of perhaps you would not want to do that kind of business.'

The Bank of England's interest in Barlow Clowes was stimulated by Wilkinson's telephone call. Wilkinson told the Bank that he was worried that Barlow Clowes was not subject to any regulatory control. Neither the Bank nor the Exchange exercised control over investment managers or advisers unless they strayed into their jurisdiction. There was a possibility that Barlow Clowes's business constituted deposit taking and therefore came under the Banking Act 1979. At the time that the Bank of England became interested in Barlow Clowes its powers over the financial community stemmed largely from this Act. While the Prevention of Fraud (Investments) Act made it an offence for investment managers such as Barlow Clowes to operate without a dealer's licence, the Banking Act made it an offence to take deposits of money from the public without a deposit taker's licence. On the surface these were two separate procedures – managing clients' money and taking deposits – governed by two separate Acts and regulatory authorities. But there was an overlap: the definition of deposit taking was widely drawn in the Act and in theory many investment managers who invested money on behalf of clients could be said to be taking deposits as well, thus needing a licence. The Bank of England imposed stringent criteria for deposit taking, which many investment managers could not have satisfied. If the strict letter of the law were applied these investment managers would in all likelihood be forced out of business. So the Bank did not usually become involved. With Barlow Clowes it did.

Meanwhile John Grant, the chief executive of Nasdim, rang the DTI to report that he was hearing 'alarming noises on the grapevine' about Barlow Clowes, adding that he had heard gossip that the company was having to cut staff because of cash flow problems. Like many others he wondered how Barlow Clowes could spend so much on advertisements and still make money.

Grant told the DTI that Barlow Clowes had not applied for membership of Nasdim. In fact there had been informal discussions between Clowes and Grant but they had come to nothing. Nasdim and its board did not like Barlow Clowes and they would not allow the firm to join. They also disliked the fact that a number of its own members were promoting Barlow Clowes even though they knew the firm was unlicensed and therefore operating illegally.

'The feeling at the time was that the business was run in a free and easy way with a lot of money sloshing around which was not properly accounted for,' says Robin Hodgson, who was chairman of Nasdim. Nasdim's immediate concern about its own members was to stop them dealing with the firm. But as a fledgling organisation with scant resources it was dominated by the fear that it could be ruined if it took a decision which led to it being sued. Indeed Grant told the DTI that Nasdim feared a defamation action if it went public on its views about Barlow Clowes.

CHAPTER EIGHT

·

JEWELLERY, LIES AND THE DEPARTMENT OF TRADE

·

*'We think there is a serious danger that if the matter is allowed
to drag on the Department will be held to be negligent.'*
DTI solicitor, March 1985.

While warnings about Barlow Clowes were pouring into the Department of Trade, the process of upgrading the system of investor protection was grinding slowly on. In January 1984 Professor Gower, having assessed the responses to his discussion document of two years earlier, published a further report recommending the repeal of the Prevention of Fraud Act, replacing it with a new Investor Protection Act. Gower suggested that the day-to-day responsibility for protecting investors should be removed from the DTI and vested in a network of self-regulating bodies based on existing regulatory agencies such as the Stock Exchange and Nasdim.

Clearly, the review of the system was being afforded low priority by the Government, which was preparing for the sale of a 49 per cent stake in British Telecom – 'the people's share' – later that year. Gower himself pointed out in the foreword to his 1984 report that progress had been hampered because for long periods he had been deprived of the administrative resources normally afforded to him by the DTI.

Temporary measures were, however, introduced to improve the existing system. In April 1983 the Licensing Unit had been enlarged from four to seven and the DTI had introduced new regulations requiring firms seeking a licence to submit more information about the nature of their business. Moreover, once licensed, firms now had to provide the DTI with annual returns – these came to be known as 'monitoring returns' – containing detailed financial information such as the amount of clients' money the firm was holding. The returns had to be endorsed by the firm's auditor, who also had to certify that the business had sufficient resources to continue for another year. Another new requirement was for a statement from a solicitor of not less than five years' standing that he had ensured that the firm understood the legal requirements of being a licence-holder. The DTI did not, however, recruit specialist staff to analyse the huge volume of new financial information it was now requiring from its licensed dealers.

By this time the Licensing Unit came within a section of the Department known as the Financial Services Division, the largest in the DTI. It was headed by Brian Hilton, a high flier with a liking for jazz and French wine. Hilton was an extremely bright man who would later be given responsibility for the overhaul of investor protection and the introduction of new legislation. Below Hilton, and in charge of FS1 – the section responsible for licensing and unit trusts – was Colin Lowry, now retired from the Department. Lowry was slightly effete; people who dealt with him remember his limp handshake and his polite, courteous manner. Hilton could be polite and courteous too – but he was far and away the more driven and ambitious of the two. Licensing was only one string to Hilton's bow while to Lowry it was a large if not the main part of his day-to-day activities.

Beneath Lowry came Roger Louth. He was a 'principal' in the Department, and had worked his way up the ranks, leapfrogging on his way to his current position. Finally, there were the two Senior Executive Officers: Noel Dixon, on licensing, and John Crease on unit trusts.

Also working with the licensing civil servants was Philip Bovey, a solicitor in the Department who also assisted Professor Gower as secretary. Acting on his own initiative, Bovey had contacted Barlow Clowes and been sent details of its Portfolio products. Little could he have imagined the enormous repercussions that this solitary act of initiative would have on the Barlow Clowes affair.

It took the DTI more than a month after the meeting with Adrian Collins of Gartmore to write to Barlow Clowes pointing out that in its opinion the firm was operating without a licence, contrary to the prevailing legislation. When Dixon's letter was met with a wall of silence, he did not press the firm with a reminder since he was under the impression that Barlow Clowes was applying to Nasdim instead. In response to more prompting from the Bank of England, in June 1984 Dixon sent a reminder.

In the same month the Stock Exchange passed on to the Bank of

England the news that Barlow Clowes had been told to move its Jersey operations off the island. This was followed up by a letter from Richard Syvret, the commercial relations officer, who told the Bank that he had been unhappy with the content of Barlow Clowes's advertisements. Syvret also pointed out that the situation had changed and that all correspondence for Barlow Clowes was now being sent to Switzerland. All links between Barlow Clowes and the island had now been terminated.

This was not correct, however. Shortly after the meeting with Syvret, Clowes decided to switch his offshore operation to Geneva, taking an office in rue de Hesse, a tree-lined street in the heart of Geneva's financial district. But investors' money was still arriving in Jersey in response to the original advertisements which had provoked the Jersey authorities to evict Clowes in the first place. And Clowes was still arguing with Syvret over the terms of the letter that he would send out to clients informing them that the business had moved. He certainly did not want to suggest that the move had been anything but voluntary, and wanted to play it down, suggesting that the transfer to Geneva represented an improvement over Jersey. Syvret would not agree and it took a long time before a satisfactory form of words was chosen – one which did not, nevertheless, tell the clients that Barlow Clowes had been moved on.

The most important point concerned the Jersey-based bank accounts, with Midland and Lloyds, which held millions of pounds of investors' money. The authorities had wanted Clowes to remove not merely the administration of his business from the island, but the money as well. He never did.[1]

Meanwhile, the reminder letter from Dixon in the Licensing Unit prompted Clowes to telephone the Department. Clowes said that he found the Prevention of Fraud (Investments) Act unclear and had received conflicting legal advice as to whether he might be able to claim an exemption under the Act from the licensing requirement. A fortnight later, Clowes's solicitors, R. J. Anders & Co., a small firm based near Clowes's Hazel Grove offices, wrote to the Department repeating the claim to be exempt. Roger Anders, a close associate of Clowes, claimed that because the greater part of Barlow Clowes's business was effected through the Stock Exchange, a licence should not be required. Dixon was having none of it. Five days later he replied saying that exempt status could not be claimed and that Barlow Clowes had to have a licence. Anders replied, agreeing, and saying that Barlow Clowes would after all apply.

Clowes's acceptance of the need to bring Barlow Clowes within the regulatory fold was not accompanied by a decision to clean up his business. Even had he wanted to – or thought that he should – he was too far committed for that. He had by this time raised over £60 million from the public on the basis of a false prospectus, namely Portfolio 30. He was consistently hitting new peaks in terms of the amount of money people were sending him to manage on their behalf. The more money that came in, the wider the gulf between what he promised and what he could deliver. He was, in effect, promising to exchange every investor's £10 note for £11. If they sent him tens of millions he would be a few million adrift.

At the same time the money that Clowes was managing offshore was increasing. People who contacted the firm enquiring about bond-washing were often recommended to try the offshore product instead. This was originally called Portfolio 28. Later on, Clowes changed the number, calling it Portfolio 68 and retaining Portfolio 28 for those investors who invested through a few of the financial intermediaries who put huge sums of money – in some cases tens of millions of pounds – with Barlow Clowes. Clowes rewarded these select intermediaries for the volume of business they generated by giving them a higher rate of commission – 2 per cent instead of the normal 1 per cent for the offshore business. They included Wilson, Clowes's acquaintance from his days at IOS. Wilson and Clowes were very close, with Wilson's son Mike working on secondment to Barlow Clowes. The old IOS connection paid off – Wilson put well over £10 million into Barlow Clowes. Clowes also loaned small sums of money to Wilson's business, D. C. Wilson.

The Barlow Clowes offshore portfolios did not claim to make money from bondwashing but still offered returns that were free of income tax since they were ostensibly generated from buying and selling gilts – making a capital gain rather than taking dividends. These returns varied each month, whereas Portfolio 30 was offering a fixed return. And investors could have their money back whenever they wanted. Under the terms of their Portfolio 30 agreements, investors who wanted their money back before the gilt had matured risked receiving less than the entire capital. In practice, however, Clowes always returned their capital intact.

There was one aspect of the offshore portfolios that would be particularly appealing to a business, such as Barlow Clowes, which was not making the returns it was promising. Offshore investors had two options: they could have their money paid out to them monthly, or they could leave it to accumulate within the portfolio thereby generating even greater returns. If investors allowed their money to accumulate this reduced the pressure on Barlow Clowes to make and deliver the returns each month. It gave Clowes more freedom.

Meanwhile, the returns were always very attractive: just as with the small Portfolio 78 product Clowes had launched in the UK, there were two rates of return – a guaranteed minimum rate and a higher expected rate. It was seductive, particularly as Barlow Clowes always seemed able to achieve the higher expected rate each month. By the end of 1984 Clowes would have almost £12 million under his control in the offshore funds compared with only £3 million at the beginning of the year.

In September 1984, two months after agreeing that he needed a DTI licence, Clowes and his wife Pamela became directors of a local jewellery business, J. T. Cottrill and Sons. Clowes had become friendly with one of the co-owners of the business, Robin Cottrill, when, as a customer, he came in to buy presents for Pamela. Originally he had bought small items, costing around £1000, but at Christmas 1982, the year of his marriage, he bought a heart-shaped diamond for Pamela costing £10,500. The relationship blossomed. Cottrill took Clowes to the flat in Malaga which he owned. Clowes liked it very much and bought a penthouse in the same block, with grey marbled floors and a large private swimming pool on its roof.

J. T. Cottrill had been established in 1929 by James Thomas Cottrill, Robin Cottrill's grandfather, and Thomas Cattlow, a business associate. The two men fell out a few years later and James Cottrill continued alone, employing twenty workmen to make jewellery which he sold from a single outlet near the centre of Manchester. The company had to survive a number of downturns and James Cottrill once saved it by persuading his bank to accept a bag of diamonds in return for a loan. It was inherited by Robin's father Jack, who in turn brought Robin into the business. The company provided a living for the family and declared annual profits of around £10,000 for several years, which enabled it to build up its cash reserves until, in 1982, it had over £120,000 in the bank.

When Jack Cottrill fell ill with a duodenal ulcer, Robin Cottrill looked around for a new partner. He considered bringing in his brother-in-law, but then Clowes offered to buy 49 per cent of the business for £100,000. Clowes had grand plans for the business. He wanted to open new shops, develop a manufacturing side and a loose gemstone operation, while advertising Cottrills on the local Granada television station. At the last minute Clowes insisted on having majority control for his £100,000, and Cottrill reluctantly agreed. Pamela involved herself in the advertising side and Clowes promised to commit £5 million of his own money to the business. He considered himself a gilts tycoon. Now he would be a jewellery magnate as well. But Clowes did not have £5 million that was legitimately earned and his own. When he and Pamela joined the board in September 1984 he soon began to transfer funds for the Cottrills expansion plan. The money belonged to the offshore investors.

Barlow Clowes's application for a licence arrived at the Department of Trade on 7 November 1984. By that time Dixon had already done some anticipatory work, asking the DTI's solicitors section to advise what action could be taken to close down Barlow Clowes. The fears about Barlow Clowes's viability had struck home. The Bank of England was also now taking a more active role: it had decided that what Barlow Clowes was doing did indeed constitute deposit taking and was not, as it did with many other firms which strayed into deposit taking, going to turn a blind eye to it. The Bank already knew of the Stock Exchange's scepticism about Barlow Clowes, and would not consider granting the firm a licence. Nor, it seemed, would the Department of Trade. Two weeks after the licence application was submitted, Dixon wrote back to Barlow Clowes's solicitors saying that the Department was considering refusing it.

Dixon cited five reasons, most of them technical, for the proposed refusal. The application form had provided no information about Elizabeth Barlow and was therefore incomplete. The error may have been an innocent omission, although by that stage the warrant for Barlow's arrest in connection with the Hedderwicks affair had already been issued. Clowes must have thought the less said about her the better. The most important ground stated for refusing a licence was the fact that the firm had been operating without one for more than ten years. However, Dixon did hold out an olive branch. The Department was prepared to meet Clowes to discuss his business and the application.

The letter masked several other reasons for the DTI's unease about the firm. These were not relayed to Barlow Clowes but an internal memorandum from Louth in the Licensing Section to the Treasury reveals what these were. The business was a partnership under the control of one man: Clowes. It had employed people who had subsequently triggered the collapse of Hedderwicks, and the Stock Exchange and Nasdim had expressed 'disbelief' that the firm could make the level of returns which it was promising investors.

Clowes's next move was shrewd. He instructed the London firm of solicitors Herbert Smith to act for him. Herbert Smith is well known in the City for its highly reputable and tough litigation department. The appointment of Herbert Smith often strikes fear into the heart of those on the other side of a dispute. The firm acted for Guinness after the Government sent inspectors into the company. Its advice was a key factor in the dismissal of Guinness chairman Ernest Saunders, and the firm led the multimillion-pound legal action against Saunders to retrieve millions of pounds illegally paid out by him. The Al Fayed brothers also called in Herbert Smith to help them with the controversial takeover of the Harrods department store. Richard Fleck is the litigation partner who acted for the Al Fayeds. Fleck is a man who is not afraid of battles. In 1990 he asked a series of sharp critical questions of the directors of property and commodities group S. & W. Berisford at the company's annual meeting. These set the ball rolling for the resignation of several of the directors and the eventual hoisting of a 'For sale' sign over the group. Back in 1984 he took on a new client: Barlow Clowes & Partners.

Meanwhile the Treasury had become involved in the case. Like the Bank of England, the Treasury had a general interest in Barlow Clowes because the firm was ostensibly dealing in gilts, which are issued by the Treasury, while the Bank acts as general supervisor of the gilts market. Louth had asked the assistant Treasury Solicitor for advice because the Department faced a problem if it wanted to launch a formal investigation into Barlow Clowes to ascertain whether the warnings it had received were correct. Barlow Clowes was a partnership and the Department's powers of investigation applied to companies, not partnerships. This was perhaps not as serious a problem as the DTI envisaged since the partnership operated in tandem with several other Barlow Clowes entities, all of which were companies and could be investigated. Nevertheless Louth sought advice on alternative methods of attack if Barlow Clowes refused a request by the DTI to lay open its books.

The assistant Treasury Solicitor suggested that Louth might try to obtain a search warrant to seize the firm's books and records with a view to bringing theft charges against Clowes. Alternatively, the Attorney-General might be brought in to appoint a receiver – a temporary custodian for the firm – to take control of the investors' funds and protect them.

On the same day that the assistant Treasury Solicitor advised on the various options available against Barlow Clowes, the Bank of England also wrote to the Department pointing out the firm's breach of the Banking Act. The senior official at the Bank wanted to write directly to Clowes but Louth called him and asked him to hold back for a while. Louth was frightened that if the Bank added its objections to those the DTI had already voiced to Barlow Clowes, there was a chance that Clowes might decide to leave the country, taking his investors' money with him. The Bank agreed to delay its attack.

On 18 December Clowes, together with Fleck, another Herbert Smith lawyer called Zac Barratt and 'Doc' Naylor met Louth and Dixon at the DTI's London headquarters. Colin Lowry, the man in charge of FSI, also attended the meeting as did Bovey from the solicitors section. The Department had fielded its strongest team. This was Clowes's first face-to-face meeting with the Department. He was still advertising Barlow Clowes prominently in the weekend press at the time. Some people in his position, knowing that the authorities were unhappy, would have thought it wiser to adopt a low profile. The odds were against him. He had advertised a financial product which did not stand up to any informed, detailed scrutiny and had funded those advertisements with investors' money. He had already had one meeting with the Bank of England and, although the Bank had held back from telling him that he was contravening the Banking Act, he would have known that the Bank was unhappy with his business. The Jersey authorities had told him to clear off. Nasdim was showing no signs of admitting the firm into its fold. And the DTI had already told him it was contemplating refusing him a licence. On top of this he was using his investors' money for his own self-aggrandisement – a jewellery shop here, an idyllic family home there. In addition, the Jersey fund had been so depleted that it was £3.75 million short on the amount it owed investors.

But Clowes would never have thought of himself in those terms. Many of us use self-delusion or rationalisation to some extent to cope with the trials of daily life. Clowes was the master of it. It was the key to his success, his ability to carry on, to face meetings with sceptical officials and tell barefaced lies – as he would do at the December meeting with the DTI. Clowes saw himself as an innovator, providing a service for the little men which they could not obtain from the City stockbroking firms who turned their noses up at Clowes and his basic-rate clients. He championed their cause. By this stage he was talking openly about his plans to set up a gilts shop in every high street in the country, perhaps even to have his own gilts market. Who would they serve? The 'thousands of little old ladies holding the wrong gilts', Clowes told one of his advisers. They were his targets, he was their saviour. Another associate remembers Clowes saying that he would never go through the

'nothing-to-declare' customs channel if he was so much as one cigarette over the limit. In his mind, or in a large section of it, he was
doing nothing wrong. He would rationalise away the flaws in his
product, and his misuse of investors' money, claiming that so long as
they received their guaranteed return there was nothing untoward.

There may even have been another part of him that enjoyed
flouting authority – advertising nationally despite knowing he had
no licence. He was, after all, a man in control of tens of millions. A
few weeks earlier the London *Evening Standard* had estimated his
group as having £300 million under management. His effrontery –
his ability to tell barefaced lies even though they were capable of
detection – saw him through the meeting of 18 December.

One of the key questions raised at that meeting was the Barlow
Clowes overseas operations. The Bank of England and the Stock
Exchange already knew that Barlow Clowes had been declared undesirable by the Jersey authorities. For some reason neither had told
the DTI. It may simply have been an oversight but it could also have
been sheer carelessness born out of the negative attitude which both
the Bank and the Exchange shared to the Department of Trade's
abilities as a regulator. 'They viewed us with tolerable contempt,'
says a former DTI official who worked in the Companies Investigation Branch of the DTI. Shortly before the meeting a Bank of
England official had refused a request from Louth to put the Bank's
fears about Barlow Clowes in writing. In fact the Bank had scant
reason for smugness at the time. A few weeks before Clowes met
the DTI, Johnson Matthey Bankers had collapsed and exposed the
shortcomings in the Bank's own licensing system. Whatever the
reason, Louth was hopelessly ill-informed when he asked Clowes
about the overseas business.

Clowes lied to Louth. He told him that his Jersey business – he
did not volunteer the fact that he had been asked to move on – dealt
only for expatriates. It was an important and obvious lie: important
because if Barlow Clowes's overseas business truly dealt only for
expatriates, it would not come under the licensing system or be
subject to any form of regulatory control. Clowes, the man who had
been quick to jump on the bondwashing bandwagon, would almost
certainly have known this. The lie was obvious because a few thousand UK investors had already placed their money with the offshore
operations. Any one of them might have complained to the DTI –
perhaps for some minor reason. Clowes would not have known this,
nor could he have known that news of his departure from Jersey
had not reached the DTI. He took a chance, and he got away with

it. But he should never have been allowed to because all four civil servants sitting across the table from him had seen – and had on file – written material which flatly contradicted what Clowes had just told them about his overseas business: when the DTI had first noticed the Barlow Clowes advertisements, Bovey had responded to them and been sent details not of Portfolio 30 but of Portfolio 28, an offshore portfolio. At the time Bovey had not noticed the Jersey address on the promotional letter he had received. But Dixon, Louth and Lowry, in preparing for the December meeting, had all looked at the Barlow Clowes file and seen the Portfolio 28 material. Dixon had drawn attention to the Jersey address. So Barlow Clowes had itself canvassed the Department of Trade and Industry with an off-shore investment opportunity. Clowes's lie was even more naked than he could have known.

Clowes went on to describe the meticulous records that he main-tained for his clients' investments, keeping every client's money entirely separate, so there was no question of confusing one client's money with another's. This was also a lie.

Other lies emerged. Clowes explained that the firm's clients had lost £6500 in the demise of Hedderwicks, which he had made good himself. Later he would claim the loss was £500,000, which he made up from dealings in the Jersey fund.

From the DTI's point of view Louth came out of the meeting with exactly what he wanted. Clowes agreed to his request to allow two DTI inspectors to investigate the firm's books and records. This meant that Louth would not have to bring into play any of the Treasury's suggested plans to shut down Barlow Clowes, which Louth knew by the time of the meeting were by no means guaranteed of success. Clowes had also agreed to stop advertising. There would be no more flouting of the rules.

But there was to be no announcement of the investigation. The investing public would remain ignorant of the litany of warnings which the DTI had received about Barlow Clowes.

Clowes's performance must have been extremely persuasive and convincing. Whereas previously Louth entertained the possibility that Clowes might skip the country taking investors' money with him, he now took the view that the firm was 'basically honest',[2] as he told the Bank of England shortly after the meeting.

Two top men were assigned the task of investigating Barlow Clowes's records. Gordon Abercrombie was the archetype shrewd Scotsman, regarded by colleagues as an extremely able investigator, and a chief examiner in the Companies Investigation Branch. The other investigator, Brian Killingback, was a much younger man who held the lower rank of senior examiner. He had been promoted to the position after a spell working in Southend for the Official Receiver, the DTI's overseer of bankrupt companies.

It did not take long for Killingback and Abercrombie to discover the mess that Barlow Clowes's records were in. One of their first findings was that the firm had never reconciled its client balances – never in its fourteen-year existence had it checked to ensure that the investments and cash which it held matched what was owed to clients. Clowes's bold assurance about 'meticulous' record keeping had been exposed as a barefaced lie. Louth knew it, but he could not bring himself to accuse Clowes or his firm of lying explicitly. He later wrote complaining to Fleck of Herbert Smith:[3]

> it transpired that contrary to the description of the record-keeping system given at the December meeting, the partnership records were not in a state which could readily show that client assets are being properly held and accounted for . . . This state of affairs is obviously a matter of considerable concern and somewhat surprising in view of the impression given at the December meeting of the accuracy and efficiency of the record system.

The pathetic state of the records was a setback to the DTI. It had been encouraged by the December meeting to think that the Barlow Clowes problem could be sorted out. But the CIB inspectors had been alarmed at the primitive state of affairs which they discovered when they examined the firm's books. 'While it may turn out to have been an accounting muddle, a great deal of clients' money is at stake and a muddle in itself is deplorable,' Abercrombie commented in an official note of his investigation.

Meanwhile, the Bank of England and the Treasury were becoming increasingly worried about Barlow Clowes. The Bank had delivered a written submission of its worries to the Treasury. The Bank had chosen its words carefully but its meaning behind the civil service euphemisms – 'We and the DTI are conscious that we need to tread warily in case BC take any precipitate action which would be to the detriment of investors' interests' – was plain: would Clowes scarper with the money?

Government ministers were becoming involved. The fears about Barlow Clowes were incorporated in a further submission to Ian Stewart, the Economic Secretary at the Treasury. Reading this an official in the Treasury commented: 'I . . . find the Barlow Clowes case very worrying and I think it is a sleeping dog that cannot be allowed to lie.' He added that although immediate action rested with the DTI he thought the Bank of England should be told that the Treasury was 'extremely unhappy' with the situation.

The submission was sent to and read by Nigel Lawson, then Chancellor of the Exchequer. Lawson and Stewart agreed with the conclusion of the Department's submission: that 'extreme pressure' be exerted on Barlow Clowes to regularise its business under the Banking Act, otherwise the Bank and the Director of Public Prosecutions should consider launching their own prosecution.

Abercrombie had pointed out another worrying problem on the horizon. On 27 January the *Sunday Times* had run an article in its business pages headed 'Gilt Scheme Under Threat'. The author, Tony Levene, referred to 'strong rumours' that the forthcoming Budget would outlaw bondwashing. The article said that Barlow Clowes had £400 million under management for 50,000 clients – both Clowes's inspired exaggerations. The abolition of bondwashing could lead to a run on Barlow Clowes. If a shortfall was discovered questions were bound to be asked about how the DTI had allowed the business to operate unlicensed for so long. Philip Bovey summed up his own and the Companies Investigation Branch's fears in an internal note: 'We think there is a serious danger that if the matter is allowed to drag on the Department will be held to be negligent if it turns out that something is wrong, particularly in relation to new business taken on since we became aware of the possible difficulties.'[4]

CHAPTER NINE

·

THE TIME BOMB

·

*'CIB cannot subscribe in a submission to ministers to the
impression that those concerned are not fraudsters.'*
DTI investigator, writing about Barlow Clowes.

If you were to ask which were the most prestigious and successful
merchant banks in the country it is a fair assumption that the names
S. G. Warburg and Lazard Brothers would be at the top of most
people's lists. Both consistently feature at the top of the league table
of merchant banks compiled every month on the basis of the total
value of the takeover bids they are advising on. Warburg has a
reputation for mathematical precision and accuracy in the preparation
of takeover documents. It recruits from Oxbridge, presents a formal,
slightly arrogant face to the outside world and uses a graphologist
to check on the stability of every recruit at or above graduate level.
Lazard Brothers, while not having quite the formality of Warburg, is
nevertheless highly respected, particularly for its corporate finance
department, which advises major corporations such as Guinness and
British Airways. But both these august institutions were unwittingly
used by Clowes to help him siphon off his investors' money.

A month before he met the Department of Trade officials for the
first time, Clowes had purchased an office block in Poynton,
Cheshire. Queensway House is a very ugly, purpose-built office, a
square chunk of grey concrete and brown-coloured window frames
next to a self-service petrol station on London Road. It was bought
in the name of one of Clowes's companies, Megerberry, which was
quite active in buying property in the Manchester area and was
nicknamed 'megabucks' by Barlow Clowes staff. Megerberry owned
the freehold of several flats in Queens Road, Didsbury, a shop in
Davyhulme and a few other minor properties. Its turnover and small
annual profits came almost entirely from rent paid by the tenants of
these properties.

Megerberry was late in filing its accounts at Companies House –
sometimes almost two years out of time – and its accountants, a

firm called Walker & Vaughan, twice stated when signing off the company's accounts that they had been unable to verify the loans of around £100,000 that Megerberry was receiving. Every active company must have its accounts audited – verified by a firm of accountants who state that the accounts represent a true and fair view of the company's state of affairs. In the case of Megerberry, Walker & Vaughan had to qualify their audit certificate by reference to the loan problem: 'We have not been able to confirm the balance of loan creditors as shown in the balance sheet.' For three successive years Megerberry did not have what is termed a 'clean audit'.

In November 1984 Lazard Brothers lent the company £250,000 which it used to buy Queensway House, far and away Megerberry's largest purchase to date. Clearly, Lazard would want security for the loan, and this came partly in the form of £250,000 cash placed on deposit with Lazard's Jersey subsidiary, Lazard Brothers & Co. (Jersey), and held there as security. This is known as a 'back-to-back loan' or sometimes as a 'blocked deposit'. A lends money to B; in return B deposits the same amount of money with A as security. The obvious question is why, if B has the money (which he clearly does since he can deposit it as security), does he not simply use his own money? The answer is that the back-to-back loan is often used as a legitimate device to avoid tax which would otherwise be incurred by bringing money into the country. If he repatriated his own money B might have to pay tax on it, so he borrows from A instead.

In the case of Lazard Brothers and Megerberry, however, no legitimate tax reason lay behind the back-to-back loan. The £250,000 held by Lazard in Jersey had come from Barlow Clowes investors. Unbeknown to them, their money was being used by Clowes to secure finance to enable him to buy his new head office. Of course Clowes could simply have taken the investors' money to pay for the office, but this would have drawbacks. The back-to-back loan gave him secrecy – Megerberry's accounts for the year to the end of November 1984 stated merely that it had a loan from Lazard Brothers. Had the investors' money been loaned directly, the accounts would have had to say that the company had a loan from Barlow Clowes. In this way the back-to-back loan was a crude form of money laundering, converting the illicit and unauthorised loan from Barlow Clowes investors into a loan from a highly reputable merchant bank.

Lazard was not alone in being used by Clowes. He had also been using S. G. Warburg & Co. to finance his partnership. In June 1983 Warburg had lent Barlow Clowes £250,000. This was secured by Hermes Management Services depositing the same amount with

Warburg in Jersey. Hermes, as we know, was a front for Clowes. It was another link in the chain of secrecy which Clowes had set up to disguise what he was doing. As far as Warburg was concerned it was receiving a deposit from a company called Hermes. And as far as Barlow Clowes's auditors were concerned, as we shall see, the business was receiving a loan from Warburg. The use of Hermes, coupled with the back-to-back loan, was an artificial device concealing the unauthorised use of investors' money by Clowes. At the time when the DTI decided to take a closer look at him Clowes was using investors' money to provide his business with both headquarters and working capital. And the two top merchant banks in the country were unwittingly helping him to do it.

Outwardly at least, Clowes was not a worried man. From November 1984 onwards the DTI was anxiously considering whether to close him down. Clowes, however, was working on plans to develop his business.

If the Government abolished bondwashing, Clowes had another investment product up his sleeve, or so he told the *Evening Standard*: 'Depending on exactly what action the Government takes we already have another programme in our computer for providing a capital gain'. He was also effusive about his plans to introduce gilts shops to the nation: 'We have a five-year plan which involves installing a computer system in a 200–strong branch network,' Clowes said. 'That will involve substantial capital expenditure and our auditors are reviewing this. The hardware alone will cost some £30–40,000 per branch and we hope to have fifty opened during 1985.'

Behind the scenes another plan that Clowes had already implemented seemed to be developing teething problems. J. T. Cottrill & Sons, the jewellery business he had bought control of, made a loss of £374,000 in the year to 31 January 1985. Clowes and Pamela had been on board for just fifteen months – and Clowes had in that time lent the company almost £1.5 million of investors' money. The company had never made a loss of this size in its fifty-six-year history. Now it was totally dependent on Clowes for its existence.

The principal reason for the reversal in Cottrill's fortunes was a huge advertising campaign it had launched. Whereas in the pre-Clowes era Cottrill had generally spent less than £10,000 a year on advertising, the Cloweses were largely responsible for running up a bill for a quarter of a million pounds – including advertising Cottrill on Granada Television, the ITV network company covering the

North-West of England. It was too broad a catchment area to advertise a single-unit jewellery shop. People living fifty or more miles away would telephone and ask for the address of a Cottrill shop in their area only to be told there was none. But Clowes had promised £5 million to expand Cottrill, so perhaps this particular extra-curricular investment would come right in the end.

The following month brought more trouble for Clowes. Nasdim, the watchdog for financial intermediaries, was concerned about certain of its members who were recommending Barlow Clowes to their clients even though it was unlicensed. By this time membership of Nasdim had been recognised as an alternative to securing a DTI licence, so it had to demonstrate that it was able to control its members' practices, particularly when, as in this case, it had its own fears about Barlow Clowes's viability. By recommending Barlow Clowes, its members were effectively subverting the DTI's system of investor protection.

Nasdim had been under pressure to take action for some time. Peter Hayes, an investment adviser whose own company Plan Invest was based in Macclesfield, was badgering the organisation to do something about Barlow Clowes. Hayes, like the others who complained, doubted the Portfolio 30 product and had already conveyed his fears to the DTI via his local MP Nicholas Winterton, who had in turn forwarded Hayes's letter to Alex Fletcher, the Minister for Consumer and Corporate Affairs. Department of Trade records show its officials' opinion of Hayes, referring to his warnings about Barlow Clowes as 'naggings'. But Hayes was also making a nuisance of himself with Nasdim. He repeatedly pointed out the inconsistency of Nasdim's position to John Grant, then chief executive. On the one hand, Nasdim was highly critical of Barlow Clowes and Grant had reported 'alarming noises on the grapevine' about the firm to the DTI; yet, on the other, it was standing blithely by and allowing its own members to recommend Barlow Clowes products.

At the time Nasdim was only marginally more developed than the financial intermediaries whom it purported to control. Grant, operating with a skeleton staff from an office in the East End of London, had an unenviable task. As the most senior full-time official he had to front the organisation on a daily basis, dealing with the media and other interested bodies. This often meant defending its supposed position as investor protection watchdog from attack. 'You've got no teeth', one radio journalist screamed at Grant in a programme about a dubious financial intermediary. Grant, a former

ICI manager approaching retirement, would not have relished this kind of attack.

Nevertheless Grant and Nasdim had to do something about Nasdim members who were promoting Barlow Clowes. The organisation's resources were limited and it was terrified of being sued. It did not enjoy the legal immunity that the present-day regulators have, preventing them from being sued if, for instance, they shut down a member firm. The last thing Nasdim wanted was a defamation writ from Barlow Clowes if it issued a notice telling firms to steer clear. (Clowes and his firm were not averse to issuing threats: a local branch of Barclays Bank in Manchester was threatened with libel writs several times for refusing to recommend Barlow Clowes to its customers.) Nasdim sought the advice of Freshfields, the City solicitors whose clients include the Bank of England. Freshfields suggested that Nasdim issue a warning circular on the subject to all its members – but without specifically naming Barlow Clowes.

The circular was sent out on 27 February by Nasdim chairman Robin Hodgson:

> I am writing to you as a member of this Association to let you know of a practice which is causing the Association's Council increasing concern. It has come to the Council's notice that some members of the Association are acting as distributors of investment products which are originated by firms which are neither members of Nasdim nor are regulated by the Department of Trade or any other approved body. This practice has a number of inherent dangers, not the least of which is that a default on the part of the unregulated originator could involve members of Nasdim.
>
> At present only a few members of Nasdim have become involved in practices of this sort. However, the Council has asked me to write to each member pointing out the dangers of this practice and making it clear that it considers that every Nasdim member has a responsibility to consider not only the nature of the investments for which the firm is acting as a distributor but also the demonstrated competence and professional standards of their originator.
>
> [Hodgson ended his circular with a threat, albeit a mild one:] I have to point out that should a member of Nasdim be brought before the Association's Complaints and Disciplinary Committee as a result of an involvement with an 'unregu-

79

lated' firm, the fact that the advice contained in this letter
has been ignored will be taken into account.

The 'unregulated originator' was clearly Barlow Clowes. From
Clowes's point of view the circular threatened to cut off practically
the only remaining lifeblood of his business: the financial intermediaries. He had agreed to a request from Louth to suspend all direct
advertising in the press. If the intermediaries stopped putting business his way then, apart from existing clients who wanted to increase
their investment with the firm, there would be no new business.

The following day, Thursday 28 February 1985, Clowes's position
became far worse. Before the gilts market opened that morning the
Inland Revenue issued a press release stating that the Chancellor,
Nigel Lawson, 'has decided to take action to counter the practice
known as bond washing'. Bondwashing would be abolished, the
release said, except for very small deals – gilts of £5000 or less.
According to the Revenue, bondwashing was costing the Exchequer
£300 million a year. This estimated figure was increasing, the Revenue said, and could well rise more quickly when the Big Bang
changes to the gilts market came through the following year. (One
of the Big Bang changes would allow people to bypass stockbroking
firms and deal direct with gilts market makers. This would reduce
dealing costs and make bondwashing less expensive to effect.) To
Clowes this appeared disastrous. Regardless of his fantastical plans
to open gilts shops throughout the country, his main business was
being almost completely wiped out. There were two glimmers of
hope: small bondwashing deals could continue, and the anti-bondwashing provisions were not due to come into effect for a year.
Clowes had already shown he was a shrewd opportunist. He would
exploit to maximum effect the room for manoeuvre these two caveats
gave him.

There had been no mention of Barlow Clowes in the Inland
Revenue press release. However, the firm's popularisation of bondwashing through national newspaper advertising, coupled with the
concern it had aroused within government departments and the Bank
of England – concern which Nigel Lawson was well aware of – were
almost certainly catalysts behind the anti-bondwashing measures.
Three days after the Revenue's announcement Richard Northedge,
the personal finance editor of the *Daily Telegraph*, recommended his
readers to sell their investments with Barlow Clowes. 'Over the
past five years around £100 million has been invested through this
company by about 12,000 people – even though it is not a licensed

dealer. . . . Investors should always have been wary of such bond-washing schemes,' Northedge wrote. His final paragraph was crystal clear: 'We would . . . advise investors to realise any investments in schemes like Barlow Clowes.' A few days later both *Money-Box* and the *Financial Times* speculated on the future of Barlow Clowes in the light of the Revenue's bondwashing announcement.

Clowes had meanwhile implemented another shrewd move. He had instructed the firm of Spicer & Pegler, one of the largest and most respected in the country, to act as his auditors. Spicers had in fact been giving Clowes some management consultancy advice – probably on his gilts shop plan – since the summer of 1984. Clowes's solicitor, Roger Anders, whose introductions were extremely valuable to Clowes, had introduced him to Christopher Bell, a partner in the Manchester office of Spicer & Pegler. Before taking on Clowes, Spicers had made some discreet enquiries, particularly in view of his involvement with the Hedderwicks affair. Clowes was eventually approved as a client because, as far as Spicers could tell, he had emerged from Hedderwicks with his reputation intact. A partner in Spicers' London office, Julian Pilkington, was to lead the audit team for Barlow Clowes. Spicers' appointment as auditors, like that of solicitors Herbert Smith, was impressive and almost certainly calculated to impress the DTI. It did.

One of the shortcomings unearthed by Killingback and Abercrombie was that Barlow Clowes had never carried out an audit of its clients' accounts. Clowes instructed Spicers to make one. An audit of this type would involve checking that the amount of money held by Barlow Clowes on a particular day matched the amount it owed to investors. Barlow Clowes would produce the figures with Spicers' help. Spicers would check them and then express an opinion on whether Barlow Clowes's figures gave a true and fair view of the clients' affairs. Louth of the DTI wanted to defer any further action against Barlow Clowes until Spicers had reported.

The internal DTI records suggest that some DTI officials were worried that Louth was not putting the case against Barlow Clowes forcefully enough to ministers. Louth was preparing a submission on Barlow Clowes for Alex Fletcher, Minister for Consumer and Corporate Affairs. It was read by the head of the Companies Investigation Branch: 'CIB cannot subscribe in a submission to ministers to the impression that those concerned are not fraudsters', he wrote to Louth.

The decision on what to do rested with Louth – Bovey and the CIB could merely advise. The pressure on Louth was mounting since the Treasury had now written recording Nigel Lawson's and Ian Stewart's desire for 'immediate action [to] be taken to regularise the position at Barlow Clowes'.

Towards the end of March Louth sent Fletcher two submissions about Barlow Clowes. These were vital to the course of action the Department pursued. The spectre of a negligence action against the Department loomed large, pervading both submissions.

'Although advertising has ceased Barlow Clowes are still taking on new business,' Louth wrote. 'Solicitor's advice is that unless this is stopped or *legitimised* whilst the client records are being audited (by the firm's accountants Spicer & Pegler) there is a serious danger of the department being held liable in negligence if funds turn out to be missing.'[1]

Louth was introducing a gloss on Bovey's legal advice: the idea that the DTI could be protected if it legitimised Barlow Clowes – granted the firm a licence. The idea of legitimisation springs from the view among regulators that they can exercise greater control over a business if it is brought within the regulatory fold rather than if it remains without. It is predicated on the belief that the core of an investment firm is solid and respectable and that only its outward manifestations – its client records or its bookkeeping – need bringing up to standard. In the case of Barlow Clowes it was utterly miscon-ceived and inappropriate. The business was an elaborate sham. Its main product, the Portfolio 30 flagship, was full of gaping holes. The firm claimed to be 'gilts specialists' but even when bondwashing was at its peak it never made a legitimate profit from gilts. Barlow Clowes was a 'partnership' but in reality Clowes owned most of it and controlled it. By March 1985 Clowes could not be legitimised. He could not be washed clean like the dividends on his gilts. He had gone much too far for that.

Louth had planted the idea of legitimisation in the Minister's mind, however, and it was regarded as a way of protecting the Department of Trade, the government department whose role was to protect not itself but the investing public. 'A legitimising licence would secure us from liability,' wrote Louth in the same submission to Fletcher.[2] 'So my advice is that legitimisation is a lesser evil than either letting Barlow Clowes continue to take on new business unlaw-fully or attempting to get them to turn it away.'

The seed of self-protecting legitimisation was planted. It immedi-ately developed roots and grew. On 22 March, the very next day after receiving Louth's second submission on Barlow Clowes, Fletcher wrote to Stewart, the Economic Secretary at the Treasury:[3]

> I am now advised that if I allow the firm to continue trading illegally and it is in fact unsound, I may be held to be negligent. I have therefore provisionally decided that the better course is to legitimise them, and thus subject them to monitoring and conduct of business rules provided that adequate reassurances are given.

That was legitimisation. But is clear from the equivocal nature of some passages in Louth's submission to Fletcher that he was not totally confident in this approach. 'For what instincts are worth, mine is that Barlow Clowes are above board,' he wrote. 'I rate Mr Clowes as an addict of doing things with gilts, not a crook: the size of the operation, the time it has existed, and the absence of any investor complaint all point this way,' he added. 'But other – and very worrying – possibilities cannot yet be dismissed.'[4]

Meanwhile, Nasdim's circular on Barlow Clowes was being ignored by one of the two largest producers of business for Barlow Clowes: the Investment and Pensions Advisory Service. IPAS was run from a small shop-fronted office in Addlestone, near Weybridge, Surrey. By March 1985 IPAS, a fully fledged Nasdim member, had already encouraged several thousand investors to put tens of millions of pounds with Barlow Clowes.

IPAS had been founded in 1980 by David Gray, a burly, bearded man who was brilliant at selling. The business took off and in 1983 Gray brought in a junior partner, David Myers, who ran the newsagents' shop across the road from Gray's offices. Myers had only a 10 per cent stake in the business. While Gray was the salesman, Myers's role was primarily to get the IPAS machine running efficiently. Although a tiny office, it received thousands of letters containing millions of pounds' worth of cheques, at least 80 per cent of which were for investment in Barlow Clowes.

Gray developed close links with Clowes. When Barlow Clowes had its literature redesigned by the Moorgate advertising group, the IPAS material was also revamped by the same firm. Some of the promotional material was virtually identical – except that the IPAS name would be used rather than Barlow Clowes.

How did Gray raise so much money for Barlow Clowes? He

decided to target a specific type of investor – the retired person –
and then advertised in publications that specialised in advising them.
These included magazines such as *Choice, Your Taxes and Savings in
Retirement* and *50 Plus*. In some of these publications, such as *50 Plus*,
he also wrote editorials, adding to his status and credibility.

Myers says that a 'major source' of business for IPAS resulted
from prominent advertisements which Gray inserted in an Age Concern booklet for pensioners called 'Your Rights'. At one point a
potential investor contacted Age Concern asking about IPAS and
whether the charity had done any homework on the firm before
accepting the firm's advertisements. Age Concern gave IPAS a glowing testimonial. 'This company has been advertising with us now for
three years and as you may imagine we go to great lengths initially
to ensure that any advertiser has a very high reputation and that
they have the interests of their clients at heart,' Kenneth Bird, head
of marketing at Age Concern wrote. 'I make a point of seeing the
Chief Executive twice a year and I personally know that their loyalty
to their clients is exceptional.'

Gray's selling techniques also involved making presentations to
particular groups of people approaching retirement or redundancy.
These included staff from the Department of Health and Social Security and British Airways. IPAS also issued a brochure aiming to persuade teachers to invest in Barlow Clowes.

Investors invariably posted their money to IPAS. 'There were no
visitors to our offices,' says Myers. IPAS was effectively a mail order
business, with one main product to sell: Barlow Clowes. Apart from
the advertisements and seminars IPAS attracted many of its customers by straightforward mail shots. It had a target list of 75,000
potential customers and used to circularise them with special offers
for Barlow Clowes, which proved to be spectacularly successful. One
particular mail shot, for example, raised £3.6 million.

IPAS's literature was comforting for people anxious to find safe
homes for their investment. The phrase 'safe as the Bank of England'
regularly appeared on IPAS leaflets promoting Barlow Clowes, as
did assurances that 100 per cent of the investors' money would be
put into gilts. Gray was portrayed in the IPAS literature as a solid
family man – exactly the type of person that investors could rely on:

> David, now aged forty-six, is a father of three boys and two
> girls and lives in Sunbury, just a stone's throw from the
> office. His consuming hobby outside working hours is chess,
> but he takes more than a passing interest in sports, particu-

larly tennis and swimming . . . If you were to ask him what constitutes his formula for success, his reply would probably include 'a strong set of principles'.

The IPAS material referred to 'our research team' which 'carefully investigates those few investments which look particularly attractive and will only recommend those which meet our stringent standards of safety or security'. There was no research team. Moreover, statements such as these masked the firm's enormous bias towards Barlow Clowes. Ninety per cent of the money raised by IPAS for investors went into Barlow Clowes in 1984, 1985 and 1986. The IPAS literature also referred to David Gray's 'twenty-five years in the investment world,' which 'has included spells with Legal & General, Sun Life, Guardian Assurance and other financial institutions'. In fact Gray's career as a salesman at Legal & General had been cut short when the insurance giant suspended him after the police accused him and several other people of a mortgage fraud. Gray was subsequently tried at Kingston Crown Court but acquitted. Nevertheless, it is extremely doubtful whether investors would have entrusted their life savings to him had they had a more complete picture of his background.

More important for Clowes, Gray's business accounted for nearly a third of the money that poured into Barlow Clowes. If Gray was in trouble with Nasdim – and in early 1985 Nasdim began disciplinary proceedings against IPAS which threatened its membership of the Association – the consequences for Barlow Clowes could be serious. The adverse publicity that would inevitably follow would remove one of Clowes's most important, and last remaining, sources of business.

The disciplinary proceedings brought by Nasdim against IPAS focused on the extravagant advertising claims which Gray was making, in particular his use of the word 'guaranteed' in conjunction with Barlow Clowes. Nasdim had asked Gray several times to tone down the advertisement but he had not done so to their satisfaction. Moreover, this was not the first occasion that Gray had been in trouble over his heavy promotion of Barlow Clowes. He had difficulties with *Choice* magazine – a very popular magazine which specialises in advising retired people and those approaching retirement. Gray took out full-page advertisements in *Choice* as well as paying to have his leaflets inserted in the magazine. But various members of the editorial staff, including the financial editor Bill Tadd and the editor Roy Johnstone, had their doubts about the IPAS business. Like Nasdim they were concerned that IPAS was promoting Barlow

Clowes when it did not have a licence and was therefore operating illegally. Internal memoranda from Tadd and Johnstone also show that they were unhappy about IPAS using the word 'guaranteed' several times in its advertisements. This too was a breach of the Nasdim rules. 'They [IPAS] were stating that your investment was totally secure, that you couldn't lose any of your capital. These are very strange claims for anyone to make,' says Tadd.

Despite the reservations of the editorial staff, *Choice*'s advertising department continued to accept advertisements for IPAS. In March 1986 Tadd complained bitterly in a letter to the editor: 'In the light of all the misgivings expressed by you and all those responsible for the financial editorial in the magazine, I am surprised that we even contemplate accepting any advertisement from this source.'

Tadd's letter was one of several expressing doubts about IPAS. Tadd had become concerned some months earlier, when Gray was trying to secure from the magazine a favourable editorial mention for the Barlow Clowes products. Tadd had called in a tax expert, Victor Sawle, to examine IPAS and the Barlow Clowes products that it was promoting. They, together with Johnstone, had met Gray and Clowes on 11 December 1984.

Sawle later wrote a letter to Tadd expressing grave doubts about Barlow Clowes and IPAS: 'Mr Gray presently only has a limited understanding of the Nasdim rules and is being pressed by Nasdim to pull his socks up about his advertising matter. He deals only by post, does what his clients want rather than advising them and may be entirely reliant on Barlow Clowes.' Sawle recommended that no advertising should be carried in *Choice* for Barlow Clowes until it obtained a licence and even then he was dubious as to whether advertisements should be accepted.

Following this, the next day Tadd sent a memorandum to Peter Barnes, the advertising manager. Johnstone was also critical of Gray:

> Mr Gray, who presents himself as an investment adviser and as such is a member of Nasdim, is in contravention of the rules of that organisation.
>
> Nasdim rules require that he should examine the financial circumstances of those who approach him – their pension prospects, their tax liability, their current assets and placement – and that he should then advise each individual on the best form of investment or saving to suit their particular situation. He does none of this, when acting for Mr Clowes.

The bottom line was that *Choice* should accept no more advertisements from Gray unless they conformed to Nasdim rules, and until Barlow Clowes had a licence: 'If Mr Clowes or any of his staff took off with £500 million for a far away palm tree there is neither protection nor redress for the investors.' Tadd also said that the word 'guaranteed', which Gray consistently used in his advertisements, should be banned because in the context of financial investment 'there is no such thing as a guarantee'.

Tadd did not get his way. In the February and March 1985 issues Gray was still allowed to advertise. Johnstone sent an angry memo to the advertising department: 'Despite the circulation of the memo, the company in question [IPAS] has been permitted to advertise in the February and March issues. In its copy, the offending word, "guaranteed", appears no fewer than five times.'

Meanwhile, Gray appeared before the Nasdim Complaints and Disciplinary Committee. The Committee was chaired by Geoffrey Pointon, whose long-established business, Pointon York, also ran a rival but legitimate bondwashing fund. Pointon is something of a crusader in the investment community, outspoken and forthright in his views, and – backed by the Committee – he recommended that IPAS be expelled from Nasdim. It was a brave step to take, one which would effectively have closed Gray down, possibly triggering adverse publicity for, and a run on, Barlow Clowes. But Gray appealed and brought in lawyers Herbert Smith to act for him, just as Clowes had done when faced with the DTI's refusal to license his business. A Nasdim official at the appeal hearing recalls how Gray entered the room flanked by an army of heavyweight legal advisers. The full Nasdim Council relented and declined to follow Pointon's recommendation. Gray was let off with a private reprimand. He would go on to raise a total of £56 million for Barlow Clowes. (In the correspondence between Nasdim and IPAS, Gray had insisted that Barlow Clowes was a wholly reputable firm. On one letter, against Gray's assertion that Barlow Clowes was wholly reliable and sound, a Nasdim official had scribbled in the margin: 'Still as naive as ever.')

The private nature of the Nasdim proceedings against Gray, plus the fact that the dispute with *Choice* was never publicised, maintained the vast gulf between the public's knowledge about Barlow Clowes and the behind-the-scenes fears and concerns being expressed. It was as though two films were being shown simultaneously, both on the same subject but completely different. The version the investing public saw was tame and heavily censored. The unexpurgated one contained shocks and surprises which those watching the first film could never have divined. Had they known they would never have watched the film in the first place.

There was another dimension to this dual perception of Barlow Clowes. Gray and other businesses such as D. C. Wilson, the Stockport-based intermediary, put a very high percentage of their clients into Barlow Clowes. (Wilson was for a while the highest producer of business for Barlow Clowes.) From the investors' point of view they could hardly have been more misleading businesses. They were supposed to be independent firms, policing the market and offering the best the market had to offer. In fact in the vast majority of cases they were simply recommending Barlow Clowes. They were almost as good as agents for Barlow Clowes. The nature of their business, with their heavy bias towards Barlow Clowes and their dependence on the company, gave the lie to their 'independence'.

The way Clowes used these intermediaries was masterful. He himself was not a good salesman, so he used others to do his bidding. At the same time it gave Barlow Clowes added status with the investing public if its products were recommended by seemingly independent intermediaries. There were a select few intermediaries like Gray and Wilson whom Clowes used in this way. Their reward was usually a greater slice of the cake – an extra 1 per cent commission.

The Department of Trade's decision to legitimise Barlow Clowes did not proceed smoothly. In late March a meeting was held at the Treasury's Whitehall headquarters between the DTI, Bank of England and Treasury officials working on the Barlow Clowes case. By this stage a joint approach between the officials had been agreed. There would be no more refusals by the Bank of England to supply information to the DTI.

The idea of legitimisation was grudgingly accepted by the Bank and Treasury officials, who made it clear that they still had misgivings. The Bank said that the only reason that it had not already exercised its own powers to prosecute Barlow Clowes under the Banking Act was because it had thought the DTI would arrange for the Attorney-General to close down the firm. The Treasury baulked at the idea that Barlow Clowes might be legitimised before Spicers had carried out its audit. But despite misgivings legitimisation was provisionally accepted by all three as the best way forward. No one wanted to be responsible for a decision to shut down Barlow Clowes.

But action on the legitimisation programme had to begin immediately.

The Bank's misgivings at the meeting spilled over shortly afterwards into a telephone call from a Bank of England official to Louth. The Bank wanted to make sure that Spicer & Pegler was fully briefed for its audit of Barlow Clowes and that it would deliver interim progress reports to the DTI. Louth agreed with the first part but said that he feared interim reports could make Barlow Clowes less co-operative. This seemingly innocuous telephone conversation contained an inkling of the disaster that was about to befall the Government and all the investors who had money with Barlow Clowes. While Spicers would be asked to check that all the money that was supposed to be there was present and correct, no one within the Department would think to ask the accountancy firm or any other specialist to evaluate the actual product Barlow Clowes was selling. Almost all the warnings that had poured into the DTI claimed that the product was not viable; that it would eat into investors' capital and that therefore the guarantee which Barlow Clowes was offering was its own guarantee – not the Government's. What was that guarantee worth? Was Barlow Clowes making sufficient profits to cover it? Did it have enough assets of its own to meet its guarantee commitments? Did Portfolio 30 work? None of these questions was asked. In the face of the specific warnings about Barlow Clowes, the DTI neglected to ask Spicers to examine whether the firm could meet its commitments to clients. The work was therefore never done. Had it been carried out the course of events might have been completely different.

The Department's failure to ask the right questions exasperated the Bank of England. Later, in 1987, when Barlow Clowes had again become an issue, the Bank told the Department that it must get Spicers to examine whether Barlow Clowes had enough resources of its own to meet the commitments under the guarantees. 'We had to tell them how to do their job,' a Bank official says. 'I mean, how much more rude could we have been?'

It is important to be fair to Louth and his colleagues in the Licensing Unit. In March 1985, while Barlow Clowes was simmering within the DTI and threatening to boil over, an internal DTI report had recommended more streamlining of the procedures used to handle licence applications and a reduction in the checks which the Unit's officials were supposed to make on applicants. The priority was speed, to process applications as quickly as possible. This was hardly an inspiring message for a Unit whose function was to regulate and control investment firms.

In the meantime, the concept of legitimising Barlow Clowes had been taken on by the various ministers involved in the case. After being briefed by his own officials, Stewart wrote to Norman Tebbit at the DTI agreeing on a co-ordinated approach between the two departments to legitimising Barlow Clowes. The Treasury's misgivings were plain from the original submission to Stewart and the conclusion of his letter to Tebbit. Martin Hall, the Treasury official who wrote the submission, made the point that Barlow Clowes was probably incompetent rather than fraudulent but that its incompetence 'bordered on the irresponsible'. 'I cannot conceive of a firm handling customers' funds of at least £80 million without having conducted an audit of clients' accounts,' Hall wrote.

Stewart signed off his letter to Tebbit with the view that if Barlow Clowes did not come up with satisfactory responses to the enquiries and questions it was being subjected to, 'the unpleasantness following an enforced cessation of business would be preferable to allowing the present state of affairs to continue with the risk of exposure or default at any time'.

On 2 April 1985 Louth wrote to Fleck at Herbert Smith. The letter, three pages long, informed the solicitors that unless Barlow Clowes complied with a long list of requirements the Secretary of State would be 'minded' to refuse a licence. Despite the mild threat, the message to Herbert Smith was plain: 'The door is still open.'

The process of providing the necessary information to the DTI began at once, with Spicers and Herbert Smith co-ordinating. It was not an easy task. As well as needing to satisfy the DTI, the Bank of England was also involved since in its view Barlow Clowes was breaching the Banking Act. And there was also a question whether the nature of Barlow Clowes's business meant it was operating as an unauthorised unit trust scheme.

A flurry of long, technical letters passed between the parties over the ensuing months, many concerned with the process of bringing Barlow Clowes into line with the Banking Act. What this would involve was making Barlow Clowes put all its investors' money into a special custodian account with a major clearing bank. If what Barlow Clowes was doing constituted taking deposits illegally this could be cured by introducing the bank as a buffer between Barlow Clowes and its clients. All clients wanting to invest with Barlow Clowes would make their cheques payable to the particular bank, not to Barlow Clowes. Barlow Clowes would give instructions to the bank to buy or sell gilts and the gilts would remain in the custody of the bank. In this way Barlow Clowes would hold neither investors' money nor gilts. This was legitimisation Bank of England style, its own alternative to prosecuting Barlow Clowes. The Bank, like the DTI, chose not to prosecute.

Clowes then made a shrewd move, and recruited Derek Tree, a manager with Midland Bank, to be managing director of his business. Tree was a thorough, hardworking type, who had worked for Midland since leaving school twenty-one years earlier. He was one of eight managers at Midland's Threadneedle Street branch in the City of London where Barlow Clowes held money for both its UK and offshore investors. Three months earlier, following an enquiry from the DTI, he had already given a favourable reference about Barlow Clowes: 'I should say that we have no grounds to doubt the integrity of our customers.' Threadneedle Street was at the time the second largest branch in the entire Midland branch network. Here was one of its managers, a man who had been able to see the movement of most of the millions which Barlow Clowes investors had placed with the firm, now teaming up with Clowes.

Tree's appointment provided a considerable measure of reassurance to the Bank of England, Treasury and DTI. Clowes's original licence application, submitted in November 1984, had shown that the entire business, its £80 million and thousands of investors, was under the control of Clowes and Pamela. There were no outsiders, no one removed from the Cloweses who could act as a restraining or checking influence upon them. Tree's appointment, and his status as a Midland Bank manager of some seniority, seemed to cure that problem. From the Bank of England's point of view it would be comforting to have a man with Tree's experience on board to supervise the new custodian arrangements that the Bank was insisting on.

Tree was seduced by Clowes's standard ploy for procuring people to do his bidding: the promise of more money. 'He made me an offer I could not refuse', says Tree.[5] As with the financial intermediaries Clowes knew that money talked. He gave Tree a five-year service contract, with mortgage subsidy, company car, BUPA membership, permanent health insurance and a salary of £40,000 a year.

But Clowes's shrewdness would not of itself suffice to steer him through the licensing system. He would need luck as well.

On 28 April 1985 the *Sunday Times* published an article which sent Philip Bovey, the DTI solicitor advising on Barlow Clowes, straight back to Louth. The tenor of the article indicated that Barlow

Clowes was still taking in money despite its assurances that it would stop. Bovey had throughout adopted a more aggressive stance toward Barlow Clowes than had Louth. The article, written by journalist Tony Levene, was headed 'Gilt Letters that Don't Really Shine'. Levene had found out about Gray's business, IPAS, and the fact that it was promoting two Barlow Clowes portfolios.

Bovey wasted no time. The next day he penned an anxious note to Louth, drawing the article to his attention. He was concerned that IPAS might be acting as a 'front organisation'[6] for Clowes's business, circumventing both the fact that Barlow Clowes was unlicensed and its agreement to stop advertising. Louth called John Grant at Nasdim, who briefed him on the disciplinary proceedings Nasdim was taking against Gray. Louth wrote back to Bovey saying that it was hard to see how the Department could stop referrals of business to Barlow Clowes 'unless of course we wish to pull the plug on this affair. For the moment we do not wish to do so.'[7]

Bovey was not satisfied. He was tenacious and unremitting and practically the only person in the Department involved in the Barlow Clowes affair who showed any great initiative: he had written to Barlow Clowes in 1983, asking for details of the firm's portfolios. This action alone had brought the firm to the DTI's attention and started the whole process of ensuring that the firm was either licensed or closed down, depending on which way the Department chose.

So on 7 May, a few days after his first note to Louth, Bovey penned another, this time concerning an item which had appeared on the BBC's *Money-Box* programme the day before. The *Money-Box* item had also featured Gray's IPAS business and its promotion of Barlow Clowes. In his note to Louth, Bovey voiced his suspicions that the relationship between IPAS and Barlow Clowes was 'a good deal closer than simply that of professional intermediary and producer'.[8] He also suspected that Barlow Clowes was doing rather more than just accepting business from independent intermediaries who referred it to them.

Bovey could not have known it at the time but he was completely accurate. Clowes and Gray were very close – far closer than a fund manager and an independent financial intermediary should have been. Gray used to submit his advertising material to Clowes for approval; Clowes lent Gray's business money and paid him extra commissions secretly through an offshore bank account which Gray did not at the time declare to the Inland Revenue as he should have done.

For the time being, however, all Bovey could do was to voice his 'misgivings' which, he told Louth in no uncertain terms, still remained. Louth himself was not free of doubt. Problems were developing. Midland Bank had withdrawn from the custodian trustee arrangements for Barlow Clowes – the Bank could not cope with the amount of administration that was potentially involved. Louth asked Bovey to draft a notice of intention to refuse a licence. Louth wanted the notice 'on a contingency basis'. Bovey obliged. His draft notice accused the firm of breaching the Prevention of Fraud (Investments) Act in such a way as to put clients' money at risk. It accused the firm of breaching the Banking Act too. And, for good measure, Bovey included allegations that Barlow Clowes had dishonestly concealed the fact that it was continuing to take in new money when it knew that to do so was in breach of the Act.

Lloyds Bank replaced Midland as potential custodian trustee for Barlow Clowes but the Bank of England, the Treasury and the DTI itself were worried that Lloyds might pull out too. On 24 June Colin Lowry, the assistant secretary and Louth's immediate superior, wrote to both the Bank and the Treasury. The letter anticipated that everything was working out and would continue to do so, but also said there needed to be contingency plans if Lloyds withdrew. If everything was not sorted out by 3 July, the Department would refuse Barlow Clowes a licence and close down the business. The Department's previous caution and prevarication about the legal difficulties involved in closing Barlow Clowes appear to have evaporated. It would take steps, via the firm's bankers, Midland, to have a receiver appointed. Everything hinged on the resolution of outstanding problems by 3 July. If they were not resolved, the firm would be closed. The day came and went and matters were still not resolved. The DTI simply allowed its own deadline to pass by. Another chance to close down the business was missed.

At one point the DTI was hours away from refusing a licence. On 31 July Louth was still waiting for the long-promised report on Barlow Clowes's records from Spicer & Pegler. Herbert Smith had told him the previous week that it was being typed but he had still not received a copy. When an official from the Bank of England telephoned him the same day, Louth, who was about to go on leave, told him that he was minded to recommend refusing to license Barlow Clowes. On the very same day Herbert Smith wrote, enclosing Spicers' report. Barlow Clowes was saved.

Spicers had carried out an audit of Barlow Clowes's client accounts as at 28 December 1984. An audit is really a snapshot. In

Barlow Clowes's case it should involve the auditors checking that on that particular day all the money and gilts which were supposed to be there for clients were indeed there. The Spicers report said that £89 million was owed to clients and that there were, correspondingly, £89 million worth of gilt-edged investments held on their behalf. This was accurately recorded in Barlow Clowes's book of accounts.

But this was an oversimplification. When Spicers had first carried out the work the figures had not matched. Barlow Clowes was holding too much money – about £220,000 more than it actually owed to its investors! What was it doing there? It was money belonging to the overseas investors which Clowes had intermingled with the UK investors' money. Julian Pilkington, the Spicers partner responsible for signing off the figures given to the DTI, decided that this was an inadvertent mistake, the result of the chaotic state of Barlow Clowes's record keeping before Spicers became involved. The surplus money was transferred back into the Jersey accounts, the new matching figures were signed off, sent to the DTI and that was that. The DTI saw only what appeared to be a perfect situation.

The incident illustrates some of the shortcomings behind audit work. The books had not balanced, but the audit said that they did. Spicers had acted within the standards laid down by the professional bodies which give firms scope to rectify what they see as inadvertent, rather than fraudulent, practices. Moreover, Spicers had been instructed by Barlow Clowes, which was its client, not the DTI. The audit was required for a specific task – to procure a DTI licence. It is easy to see how a kind construction of the surplus could be taken. And, to be fair to Spicers, it was dealing with a well-practised liar in Clowes. When Pilkington and Clowes discussed Barlow Clowes's move from Jersey, Clowes told him this was due to 'marketing' and 'technical' reasons. Clowes told Pilkington that from a marketing point of view Geneva had a better image than Jersey. And Jersey suffered from lack of support for the Hewlett-Packard computers that the Barlow Clowes offshore business needed. This was the technical reason for the move. It was utter nonsense. But Clowes, a man who often seemed to believe his own lies, was convincing and Pilkington believed him.[9]

Spicers' report arrived when Louth had gone on leave. A junior official in the Licensing Unit therefore referred the report to a DTI accountant. The accountant had never seen an audit of client accounts before and had no idea whether or not it conformed to the normal standards for such a report. His advice to the Licensing Unit was couched in generalities and equivocation which reflected his inexperience: '. . . it does appear to be a comprehensive statement which, while it cannot guarantee that no client money is missing (and no audit will ever provide a guarantee) gives as reasonable an assurance that all is well as one can expect.'

Unforgivably the accountant was given nothing in writing about the background of Barlow Clowes, its history of uncertainty and illegality. He was given the report and asked to comment. So he did not probe deeper, ask further questions about the nature of the problems or examine whether it dealt with the concerns which had been raised to the DTI. Louth may have briefed the accountant verbally, but nothing more took place. So the accountant could not have spotted that the Spicers report did not address the vital question whether the firm had enough money of its own to meet its liabilities to investors under the guarantee commitments.

The DTI thus ended up with a report stating that the assets which Barlow Clowes held matched the amounts due to clients on one day in December 1984. But it said nothing about the offshore funds held by Barlow Clowes – Spicers was not required to look at these. All Clowes needed to do to make sure that there was enough money showing on the books at 28 December was to move some across from the offshore investors. This is exactly what he did. It was his standard 'teaming and lading' trick. No one would spot the hole in the offshore funds because no one was instructed to examine them.

While the Department of Trade, Bank of England and Treasury were agonising over Barlow Clowes, Clowes was again playing around with his investors' money. On 30 September, shortly before Louth returned from leave, Clowes transferred just over £1 million of his overseas investors' money into a newly formed Gibraltar company called Sandover. The money would not stay there for long.

By one of those strange quirks of fate the Old Bailey trial of de'Souza, Farrington and Stead started just as the DTI was going through the final stages of the licensing process with Barlow Clowes. Clowes was called to give evidence. The three had been charged with conspiring to steal gilts worth £4.8 million and Clowes had agreed to give evidence for the prosecution. The case, which threatened to expose some of the unorthodox dealing methods that Clowes had allowed de'Souza to employ with Barlow Clowes investors' stock, could not have come at a worse time for Clowes. He was on the verge of being licensed. A ghost from his distant past had returned to haunt him.

The case against the three men was that they had used stock which clients had left with Hedderwicks to finance their own gilts dealings. All denied the charges. One of the arguments used in their defence was that those who were in the habit of leaving stock with Hedderwicks had given their permission for de'Souza to 'borrow' this stock. As a witness for the prosecution, Clowes was supposed to say that, in the case of his clients' stock, he had not given permission. That, at least, was what he had told the police when they tried to find out how deeply Clowes himself was involved.

Farrington, one of the defendants, recalls that Clowes's evidence from the witness box turned out to be 'more in favour of the defence than the prosecution.'[10] Clowes changed his story: he said that he *had* given permission.

Watching the case with great interest was an official from the Stock Exchange, Brian Rawlins. Rawlins was amazed by Clowes's evidence. He seemed to be saying that it was normal practice in the gilts market to leave stock in bearer form with a stockbroker, a form which would allow the broker to use it for his own purposes. This was blatantly untrue. Rawlins was furious and reported back to Martin Fidler, the Hedderwicks liquidator at the Exchange.

'We were very unhappy with him [Clowes] as a witness', says Fidler. 'He was to have said that he was not aware of his stock being used but in fact said the opposite. Our reaction was "bloody Peter Clowes, he said this is normal practice. He said that he knew about it and it was nothing unusual." ' Clowes had given his evidence on oath. If the Stock Exchange viewed it as highly unsatisfactory this was a serious matter. But possibly because it thought it had already done enough to discourage the DTI from licensing Clowes, the Exchange did not relay its dissatisfaction with his evidence back to the DTI.

On his return from leave Louth, armed with the Spicers report, made a submission to Michael Howard, the new Minister for Consumer and Corporate Affairs, who had not previously been involved with Barlow Clowes. The Banking Act problem had been resolved – Lloyds was in place as custodian trustee – and Louth's views were clear: 'The business has now engaged reputable City firms of solicitors and accountants to advise them on their activities . . . I recommend that the licences should be granted without further delay.'[11]

The date was 17 October 1985. On the same day the Gibraltar Registrar of Companies was putting his seal to the incorporation of a new company: Barlow Clowes International. It was offshore, unlicensed and unregulated. And it would play a central part in the unfolding drama of Barlow Clowes and thousands of investors who would send over £200 million of their life savings to it. Perhaps the DTI had a premonition of this. Certainly it did not license Barlow Clowes with an entirely easy mind. Even as it sent out the licences the DTI was entertaining thoughts that it had been deceived.

On 21 October Howard approved Louth's submission and wrote to Stewart at the Treasury and to Sir Kit McMahon, the Deputy Governor of the Bank of England, informing them of the decision to license. Two days later an official in the Licensing Unit suggested to Lowry that he send the licences with a covering letter to Herbert Smith pointing out that the DTI had relied heavily on Herbert Smith's assurances: 'this may give them [Herbert Smith] an incentive to let us know quickly if they find in the future that they have been hoodwinked', the DTI official wrote.[12] On the same day de'Souza, Farrington and Stead walked free from the Old Bailey, all the charges against them dismissed. The ghosts of the past had been laid to rest. Clowes had been legitimised by the British Government. He had duped three government departments, the Bank of England and some of the best firms of lawyers, accountants and merchant bankers in the country. He was now unstoppable. The Department of Trade had licensed a time bomb.

CHAPTER TEN
·
CORPORATE FORAYS
·

Tucked in the rolling Gironde countryside, twenty-five miles south-east of Bordeaux, is Château d'Auros, a thirteenth-century château with fifty acres of vineyards yielding a full-bodied red and a lighter white wine both bearing the château's name. The vineyard's Merlot, Malbec and Cabernet Sauvignon grapes produce the red wine while the white, a light dry wine, comes from Sémillon and Sauvignon white grapes. The château itself has seen better days. It consists of a horseshoe-shaped complex of farm buildings, some of which are beginning to crumble, although the wine itself is made and stored in a modern addition. The château describes its wines as 'some of the most commendable wines of Bordeaux. And some of the best wine values anywhere. A truly delightful combination.'[1]

While the Department of Trade was in the final throes of the licensing process, committing itself to a legitimised version of Barlow Clowes, Clowes himself, accompanied by 'Doc' Naylor, flew to Switzerland to negotiate the purchase of Château d'Auros for $850,000. The money came entirely from Barlow Clowes overseas investors, who, like their UK brethren, were told their money would be invested in gilts.

The château was owned and managed by an American couple, who wanted to sell. The château was losing money – $15,500 in its last year – and Clowes came forward as a buyer. The deal was concluded quickly and anonymously. Clowes knocked $50,000 off the asking price in return for letting the American couple stay in the château two weeks a year. The Barlow Clowes investors' money was hidden behind two Liechtenstein-registered companies.

The army of government officials, lawyers and accountants which had been summoned to legitimise Clowes could have no idea quite how much he had fooled them. The French château was perhaps the most ostentatious example, but throughout the period when the legitimising task force was struggling to bring Barlow Clowes within the regulatory fold, Clowes was off and away on a huge and diverse spending spree with his investors' money. By this time, with almost £100 million of other people's money under his control,

Clowes liked to describe himself not as a plain investment manager but as a 'financier'.

He had started with jewellery, having bold plans to expand the Cottrill family business. This was followed by a company called Mekom Computer Products. Until Clowes became involved Mekom was a partnership run by Diane Jackson and David McKay from a small unit in Birmingham city centre, supplying daisy wheel and dot matrix printers. They had two staff. One of their customers was Clowes, who at the time was still pursuing his idea of launching nationwide gilts shops. He had the notion that every customer would be issued with a gilts passbook, like a Post Office savings account book, showing how much they had deposited with the gilts shop. Clowes wanted a printer that could produce the passbook and discussed the project with Mekom.[2]

McKay and Jackson wanted to capitalise on the advent of laser printers and were at the time looking for funding. Clowes was very keen to be involved. Once again his plans were on a grand scale: 'He said he would provide the funding the company needed to take the laser market by storm, to be the largest distributor in the country,' says Jackson. Clowes obliged, transferring several hundred thousand pounds to Mekom during the course of 1985 while the licensing process was proceeding. Within a year Mekom had fifty-five staff and offices in three different towns.

Another venture was the Victoria Appointments and Contracts employment agency run by a husband and wife team – Phil and Veronica Waller – who were friendly with Clowes and Pamela. This time the plan was to inject capital so that the company could float as a public company three years later.

These abuses, involving as they did money belonging to overseas investors, were mild compared to Clowes's other manoeuvres while he was going through the licensing process. Starting in August 1985 when Herbert Smith was finalising the custodian trustee documentation with the Bank of England, and the DTI was studying the Spicer & Pegler reconciliation, hundreds of thousands of pounds were transferred out of the Lloyds client account in Jersey. The first payment, £36,500, was on 20 August; the next, for £328,500 came eight days later. There was a brief interval until October, when another £46,350 was transferred out of the Lloyds account – an account which Clowes should have closed after Richard Syvret, the Commercial Relations Officer, told him to leave the island, almost two years earlier. The next payment, £463,500, was made in November 1985, two weeks after the licence had been granted.

All these payments, and a further one of £149,007 at the beginning of December, went directly into the clients' account of Roger Anders, Clowes's solicitor, with Barclays Bank in Rochdale. From here, together with other money from the Jersey account, it was used to buy a magnificent country home in Woking, Surrey, for Naylor and his wife Vicky and a farm, Tudor Barn Farm, a few hundred yards away. The farm was bought for Clowes. The purchase of Send Barns, as Naylor's new home was known, was theft by Clowes of investors' money – but Naylor assumed it came from Clowes's own resources. They were partners in crime now. Naylor had found the home but had nowhere near enough money to buy it. Send Barns cost £365,000. Naylor did not even have to take out a mortgage on it. Peter Clowes may have viewed the property as a way of buying Naylor's loyalty and co-operation and, if necessary, his silence.

Naylor had by this time developed from the naive and impressionable academic to become Clowes's right-hand man. The 'Barlow Mob' had regarded Naylor as something of a wimp. 'His voice would become a high-pitched squeak whenever he got annoyed or upset,' says Margaret Kelly. However, Naylor was now at Clowes's side on his private company ventures. He was very often appointed director of any new company Clowes set up or invested in, along with Clowes himself. He was far closer to Clowes than was Derek Tree, the respectable ex-Midland Bank manager. Clowes had also been active on his own behalf. In August 1985 he had bought himself a smart mews house near London's Hyde Park at a cost of £335,000 – paid for out of investors' funds.

The purchases Clowes made expose the double life he was leading throughout. The story of Barlow Clowes is peppered with duality, with gaps between perception and reality. Clowes and his advisers were promising to comply with the DTI rules, have meticulous records, audit investors' funds. At the same time another Clowes was scattering investors' money into private company ventures and homes for himself and a fellow director. This was but one level of the duality. To behave like this Clowes would also have to fool all the financial intermediaries who put clients' money with him on the basis that he was a gilts specialist and would invest the money in gilts. These were not faceless people whom Clowes could deceive without ever seeing or meeting them. Dennis Wilson, the Stockport intermediary, saw Clowes regularly and, by 1985, had known him for almost fifteen years. Others might not have such a long acquaintance with Clowes but they too had developed close links with the man and his business.

Then there were the investors, mainly retired people. It is important to remember that the money for Clowes's private company forays almost always came from the overseas funds, Portfolios 28 and 68. These were the funds which advertised seductive 'guaranteed minimum' rates and higher 'expected' rates of return that would be earned by Barlow Clowes's trading in the gilts market. The rates changed every month. In reality they were plucked out of the air; they were false. They could not bear any relation to the actual returns made if the investors' money was being diverted into private companies or property for Barlow Clowes. The fears of Barlow Clowes's own staff were confirmed. They had watched money sent to Jersey remain uninvested in a Midland Bank account and wondered how Clowes could calculate and put out rates of return for this money every month. The answer was simple: he made them up.

The Inland Revenue's curtailment of bondwashing did not put the brake on Clowes's activities. Small bondwashing deals were still allowed so Clowes launched a new product, Portfolio 37, to take advantage of the albeit reduced opportunity for bondwashing. It meant that he would still keep many of his clients. Not only that but Clowes started offering more attractive rates of return if investors put their money with him offshore, in his Geneva-based operations. Every month the rates advertised for Geneva were higher than those in London. Clowes made the product more attractive even than bondwashing since offshore clients could have their capital back at any time without penalty. Geneva too was income tax free – ostensibly because it generated capital gains on gilts, rather than dividends. By the end of 1985 Clowes had almost £31 million managed for investors offshore – three times as much as had been invested with him at the beginning of the year. The increase almost completely offset the fall in funds which Clowes held in the UK due to the bondwashing announcement. By abolishing bondwashing the Government had the unhappy effect of driving many Barlow Clowes investors offshore, into a pool of money which Clowes regarded as his own personal fund.

The end of 1985 heralded the beginning of a new era for investor protection. On 19 December Leon Brittan, the Secretary of State for Trade and Industry, published the Financial Services Bill. This followed on from Professor Gower's report and the publication by the

Government of a White Paper on financial services at the beginning of the year. It promised a far tougher regime for investment businesses, which would be policed by a new body – the Securities and Investments Board (S1B) – given wide-ranging powers to crack down on fraudulently run investment firms. The SIB published its own blueprint for investor protection: firms would have to show that they were honest, competent and solvent. Barlow Clowes failed on all three and the SIB would ultimately play a vital role in its destiny.

The Bill also contained important provisions about offshore funds: these would come within the new investor protection laws. They would either have to be based in a country offering equivalent investor protection to the UK or be specially authorised by the SIB. In either case the new watchdogs would require audits and other detailed information of the funds before any UK business, such as Barlow Clowes, could sell them to UK investors. On the face of it the Financial Services Bill represented a serious threat to Clowes – his offshore funds would never stand up to the new kind of scrutiny. It was a threat which Clowes would have to address.

Just before the Financial Services Bill had been published an obscure Liechtenstein entity called Tifa AG began buying shares in a small public company called C. H. Bailey. Commonly referred to as a 'Welsh ship repairer', Bailey's interests were spread much further afield than that. Run by marine engineer Christopher Bailey it owned a Tanzanian game reserve, a 550-bedroom hotel in Malta and the world's largest floating dock, moored off Hawaii. Caribbean cruises were another of its specialities, hiring out huge luxury yachts, at £25,000 a week. They were more like floating palaces than yachts – one of them, the *Welsh Princess*, was once the home of American car magnate Henry T. Ford. Another, the *Welsh Falcon*, built for the King of Sweden, had sixteen bathrooms, three state rooms and open fireplaces. In addition, C. H. Bailey had a controlling interest in an ailing public company which did focus on ship repairs: Bristol Channel Ship Repairers.

Bailey was a controversial company. Although rich in assets it had not paid its shareholders a dividend since 1980 and Christopher Bailey, who owned shares giving him 46 per cent of the voting rights, rarely talked to the press. Even though it had been held on New Year's Eve, some hundred angry shareholders had attended the company's 1984 annual general meeting, demanding more information about the company.

Bailey's assets were the main reason for the stock market valuing it at almost £17 million when the mysterious Liechtenstein shareholder appeared on its register. Certainly its profits could not justify such a rating. Its latest figures showed profits before tax of £204,000, but that included the benefit of a rate rebate without which the company would have made a loss. Meanwhile Christopher Bailey's salary had increased by more than 80 per cent to almost £100,000. So who was stalking the company?

At that time a shareholder had to disclose his stake in a public company if he bought 5 per cent or more of its shares. (New rules introduced in 1990 have reduced the disclosure level to 3 per cent.) Fairly soon, Tifa AG had exceeded the limit and when it disclosed its interest press articles began appearing asking just who was behind Tifa.

Bailey's share capital was divided into two classes of share: A and B shares. The B shares were the more powerful, giving greater voting rights to whoever owned them. By mid-November Tifa was able to disclose that its holding of A and B shares gave it over 11 per cent of the voting rights in Bailey.

The tiny principality of Liechtenstein is famed for the secrecy rules that govern financial dealings there. A Liechtenstein *Anstalt* – a type of company – is regarded by regulators as one of the hardest entities to penetrate. Liechtenstein keeps a central register of directors – and Tifa's directors could be discovered by an examination of the register – but shareholders, the real owners of a company, do not need to be registered. Moreover, Liechtenstein allows companies with bearer shares to be registered. Bearer shares belong to whoever has physical possession of them. Tifa AG was such a company.

A few months earlier a Jersey lawyer named Conrad Whitehead gave instructions for the formation of a company called Sandover Ltd. Whitehead's firm, David Morgan Whitehead, was well established on the island. David Morgan, a partner in the firm, had been the Jersey Commercial Relations Officer before Syvret, and also operated a service providing registered companies to businesses and other law firms.

Sandover Ltd was another company without a business behind it. Whitehead had instructed a lawyer in Gibraltar, John Azopardi, to form the company and register it there. This meant that for legal purposes it was a Gibraltar company. (It is as easy to set up a company in Gibraltar as in Jersey or many other overseas jurisdictions. Essentially it is a form-filling exercise, accompanied by the payment of a fee to the Registrar of Companies.) Whitehead's and Azopardi's law firms had something in common: Clowes as a client.

Sandover was set up with a broad range of directors: a Gibraltar lawyer, Geneva accountant and a company executive based in Guernsey. Sandover had something in common with Tifa: its share capital consisted entirely of bearer shares. Gibraltar, like Liechtenstein, allows the formation of such companies. One of Sandover's first functions was to receive a sum of money slightly in excess of £1 million. The money had come from an account with Midland Bank in Jersey, called the Barlow Clowes & Partners Clients Premium Deposit Account. It was transferred to an account in Sandover's name with Chase Bank. Sandover would receive other funds from Barlow Clowes investors.

Throughout December Tifa continued to increase its stake in C. H. Bailey. What none of the newspapers could have known was where the money to finance the stake in Bailey was coming from. It was, in reality, coming via Sandover, which in turn was funded by unwitting Barlow Clowes investors. A trail of companies, bearer shares and bank accounts, from Jersey to Gibraltar and Liechtenstein, had been used to disguise the true provenance of the money. But very soon a chink would appear in the armour of secrecy.

In the middle of January 1986 there was an announcement that Tifa had bought a 10 per cent stake in Bristol Channel Ship Repairers, Bailey's publicly quoted subsidiary. *Lloyd's List*, the daily paper produced mainly for members of the Lloyd's insurance market, published a short article on this event:

> The purchase has further heightened speculation that Tifa is pursuing the shiprepair company as part of an overall plan to launch a bid for the Bailey group. In the past two weeks Barlow Clowes Nominees, a company beneficially owned by Tifa, has been buying into Bristol Channel and currently holds 8,290,000 ordinary shares (10.38%)

This was the first mention of Barlow Clowes. It was a clue, carelessly dropped by Clowes, to the true source of the funding for these public company stakes. Only three months after being licensed by the DTI he was now engaging in corporate raiding. For Clowes the financier, funding private companies was no longer enough. He had moved into a bigger league, of corporate raiders who took up aggressive stakes in public companies and shook up their management, getting them to agree to a takeover or else to buy them out at a profit. Clowes would say that he was doing it to secure the returns for his investors. He would almost certainly tell himself this, conveniently ignoring the trail of secrecy he had deliberately laid to distance himself and disguise the source of his money.

Now, however, Barlow Clowes Nominees had appeared publicly as a buyer of shares in public companies. A few months earlier the Bank of England had queried the holding of £7 million of gilts in this very same company while it was in the process of sorting out the Banking Act problem. The DTI would have known of Barlow Clowes Nominees as one of the companies in the Barlow Clowes group. What was it doing as a supposed subsidiary of a Liechtenstein company? And why was it buying shares in highly speculative companies such as Bristol Channel Ship Repairers when it was supposed to be merely a holding vehicle for British Government securities, in investment terms the complete antithesis of Bristol Channel?

The DTI, which monitored the national newspapers and various magazines for mentions of investment firms requiring licences, did not pick up the reference. Nor did the Bank of England or anyone else. The clue was allowed to go undetected. Clowes had got away again.

The foray into Bailey and Bristol Channel Ship Repairers had taken Clowes into a different league, a riskier, more ambitious one. He had entered the world of public companies where the rewards could be high. Yet the actions of those taking stakes in public companies were often highly visible and subjected to scrutiny by the financial press, stockbroking analysts and the Stock Exchange itself. It was far more exposed than the private ventures to which Clowes had previously limited himself. Large stakes in public companies would invariably attract comment. People would ask questions about the identity of their owners. When Tifa first appeared as a holder in Bailey, a market rumour went around that the Fiat motor company was the true purchaser, since Tifa was an anagram of Fiat. And there was an added danger in that public companies can issue special notices under the Companies Acts demanding that the true owner of its shares be identified, and can freeze those shares if a satisfactory response is not received.

Clowes was far less likely to be detected in private companies such as Cottrill or Megerberry, the property company which purchased the Barlow Clowes headquarters. Such companies did not offer their shares to the public. There would be no press coverage of them. The only public records relating to them would be the standard information filed at Companies House at Cardiff and London: the accounts, annual report, details of directors, etc. These details are not published in any newspaper – unless someone takes the trouble to search the file at Companies House and, assuming the contents warrant it, to write an article. Public companies have shares which are bought and sold by the public. They have to announce their results to the Stock Exchange twice a year.

To invest in public companies took Clowes further away from the person he was supposed to be – a gilts investment manager – further away from his moral responsibilities to his clients, and closer to danger, detection and the person he now wanted to be: the chairman of his own public company.

CHAPTER ELEVEN

·

THE MAN WITH THE
'VON' IN THE MIDDLE

·

*'Six years ago he [Clowes] was walking the streets of Bramhall
and now he is hiring Lear Jets. . . . Somewhere along the line he
has been terribly sharp.'*
Brian Carlton, aircraft executive.[1]

It is time to meet Guy von Cramer. The 'von' does not connote
aristocratic origins – far from it. Von Cramer was born in Bradford,
on 25 July 1963, the son of an Italian mother, Ioland Violetta, and a
British father, Peter David. People describe von Cramer as a 'whiz
kid' or 'clever' or 'flashy'. He likes to drive Mercedes or Ferraris and
used to own at least one of each – at the same time. His own advisers
privately refer to him as a 'wheeler-dealer type'. He is small, perhaps
only a shade over five feet, given to wearing platform-heeled shoes
and at the time we meet him, in 1986, is sporting a kind of 1970s
hairstyle with the hair at the back of his head shaped at the bottom
like a duck's tail. He looks more likely to be found dancing the night
away at the local discotheque than putting together million-pound
business deals. Clowes was twice as old as von Cramer when the
two men met around the beginning of 1986. But at that stage von
Cramer was being tipped in the national press as a man to watch.
And he would have a marked influence on Clowes.

Simon Preston, a former public relations adviser to von Cramer,
remembers him as 'a man who wanted to be a millionaire in an
afternoon'. This was early on, before the press discovered him.
Preston refers to a 'touching naivety' about him: 'He wrote to the
Reform Club asking to be made a member. No one asks for membership – you are proposed and seconded. His application was rejected.'

But von Cramer was a very determined young man. His passport
to the City, or at least his helping hand, came from N. M. Rothschild,
the prestigious merchant bank born out of the Rothschild dynasty.
He had suggested the occasional deal to Roger Fearnley, a banker in

Rothschild's Manchester office since 1982, although none of them came to anything. Early in 1985 he suggested another; this time it came off. Von Cramer and his associates wanted to buy a complex of buildings, an amusement arcade, theatre, ice-cream shop and others on Scarborough's Golden Mile. A lending facility of £750,000 was agreed of which £600,000 was actually lent to the von Cramer company which was to buy the Futurist Complex.

At the same time von Cramer and his associates were involved in another deal together. They had bought sufficient shares to give them control of James Ferguson Holdings, a virtually bankrupt textiles group which had an undistinguished career as a public company, regularly making losses and failing to declare any dividends for its shareholders. For three years at the beginning of the 1980s the company survived by the skin of its teeth, kept alive by the support of its bankers. It had moved into other areas such as property investment and financial services – at one time owning a pawnbroker – but without much success. Von Cramer joined the board, in July 1985, close to his twenty-second birthday. He was billed as the youngest ever chief executive of a public company.

In stock market parlance Ferguson was a 'shell': a public company whose main asset is the fact that it is quoted on the Stock Exchange. Its business will typically be loss-making or producing small profits. Its appeal is that it provides a vehicle for an entrepreneur to inject his own business interests and expand by issuing more shares. The pre-existing business of the company will typically be sold off and the company as it expands would become completely unrecognisable from its original form. WPP, the international advertising group, began life as Wire and Plastic Products, a shell making supermarket trollies. It was taken over by Martin Sorell and transformed over the years by a series of acquisitions, paid for by issuing new shares, into a leader in the advertising world. This is but one example. In the heady days of the mid-1980s, with rising stock markets, there were many entrepreneurs who made millions for themselves by taking over shell companies. But it was not as easy as it perhaps seems. Taking control of a shell company was only one stage. An entrepreneur needed backers – financial institutions prepared to buy the new shares which would be issued to finance the expansion plans. Reputation was tremendously important. The institutions had to believe in the entrepreneur and his plans for the business. On the surface it looked as if von Cramer had found his own shell in James Ferguson Holdings.

In December 1985 von Cramer and his associates announced the first major deal for Ferguson under his stewardship: they would sell the Futurist Complex in Scarborough, which they owned privately, to James Ferguson. On paper it looked a good deal for Ferguson despite the fact that the Complex sometimes flooded at high tide. Ferguson would issue new shares worth £850,000 to the von Cramer team; the Complex had been professionally valued at £965,000.

A deal of this size would be too small to interest a large merchant banking operation such as Rothschild. But Fearnley, who had agreed the original loan on the Futurist Complex, put von Cramer in touch with a small firm of provincial stockbrokers called Rensburg. There he met two brokers: Tim Jason-Wood and Peter Morrison.

Alongside the Futurist Complex deal von Cramer announced that Ferguson would be raising more money. This was part of the 'shell' strategy. Ferguson would be issuing six million new shares at 10p a share, producing a further £600,000 gross, but only £420,000 once the City advisers had taken their percentage. But the shares had to be placed with people willing to buy them. One or two institutions agreed to take shares, and Rensburg placed three million with its own clients. And, in January 1986, von Cramer and Jason-Wood met another person supposedly very interested in buying Ferguson shares: his name was Peter Clowes.

This was the first time Clowes and von Cramer had met. Clowes was impressed, keen to take up Ferguson shares. He wanted a million shares but in the end, because demand for the shares was great, settled for 500,000.

The January press conference called to launch the new James Ferguson Holdings went well. Von Cramer had been briefed beforehand to expect questions about his age and other potentially sensitive areas such as the lack of time the valuers had been given to examine the Futurist Complex. Press reports that followed talked of von Cramer as 'the stock market's boy wonder'.[2] 'Ferguson looks like one of those uncommon situations where a new team is capable of achieving fast growth,' the *Yorkshire Post* said.[3]

A distillation of the von Cramer stories which appeared in the following morning's papers would resemble this: he sold his bedroom furniture at fifteen to raise money to start a reject china business. This began with a single stall on a Leeds market, which he quickly built up into a chain of stalls in thirty-two different markets throughout the North of England. At seventeen he turned to property, first renovating old mills in the Bradford area but then moving overseas to Spain and the United States. By the age of twenty-two he had a string of properties and investments worth £3 million or more. His resources had been sufficiently strong for him to absorb an £850,000 loss on a deal that turned sour for him.

There were, however, some gaps in the von Cramer story. The first was his age: the papers generally reported him as twenty-four although he was only twenty-two at the time. His age seemed to vary depending on the company he was involved with. He was a director of several private companies. Sometimes he was born in 1960, others 1961 and yet others on his true year of birth, according to his birth certificate, 1963. The von Cramers were known in the Bradford area not only for Guy's china activities but as manufacturers of soft toys. They had a family company – Samantha Toys (Bradford) – which von Cramer became director of at the age of only fifteen. Three years later Samantha Toys was prosecuted and fined £100 for selling dangerous toys.

At the beginning of 1983 an article appeared in the *Bradford Telegraph & Argus* following on from the Harrogate Toy Fair, which had just closed. 'One Bradford soft toy maker with expansion in mind is Samantha Toys, of Britannia Industrial Estate, Portland Street,' the author wrote. 'Sales director Mr Guy Cramer, who for the past six years has run the family business with his father Peter, said he expected 1983 to be a good year for the company.'

A few months later Samantha Toys had collapsed with debts of over £200,000 and a trail of angry trade creditors, none of whom would be paid. There was a fracas at the creditors' meeting, and 'someone got a black eye,' says Richard Stiles, the man who bought the assets of Samantha Toys from the company's liquidators. They were angry at the way Samantha Toys had folded. 'The small suppliers were very badly affected,' says Stiles. 'The directors said that there was no money in the kitty but their lifestyle was pretty good.' The general consensus was that things were unsatisfactory.

Nor was this the first Cramer toy company to collapse. Samantha Toys had a predecessor, Jupeter Toys, a toy manufacturer run by Peter. It failed in 1970, again leaving a trail of unsecured creditors who eventually received 0.085p for every £1 they were owed, when the liquidation was completed in 1976.

The Scarborough deal also had more to it. It was far from being simply an infusion of new assets to revitalise Ferguson. The Complex had been losing money, and the sale to Ferguson had been almost a rescue operation. Clowes claims that at one time prior to the sale to Ferguson there was an attempt to raise money by staging a production of *Snow White* in the theatre in the Complex. There were only six dwarfs and the show flopped.

The reality was even worse. One of Cramer's associates would receive around seven million Ferguson shares in return for his stake in the Scarborough complex. At 10p each they were worth £700,000 on paper but Peter Clowes had already secretly agreed to buy them from the Cramer associate at 14p a share, spending £1 million of his Barlow Clowes investors' money to do so.

Von Cramer would later maintain that he had no idea that Clowes was using investors' money. Clowes had been presented to him as an extremely successful and wealthy man. One merchant banker told von Cramer that Clowes had £40 million of his own money. According to von Cramer, whenever he engaged in any deal with Clowes, he assumed or was told by Clowes that he was using his own money.

Clowes was not content to hide behind dummy companies any more. A fortnight after the Scarborough deal was completed, Clowes and Pamela were announced as owners of 7 per cent of the shares in James Ferguson. 'I thought we could usefully exchange business ideas and that it would be best to be a shareholder in the company,' Clowes told the London *Evening Standard*. This was a massive understatement of his true ambition, which it would take him another year to realise.

The *Daily Mail* was one of the few papers to cast a critical eye over the Ferguson deal. 'Never knowingly would I advise anyone to buy shares in a wooden hut, an ice cream shop, a public house in a state of considerable dilapidation, and an amusement arcade which gets flooded when the tide is high – all in a company headed by a 24–year-old Yorkshire whiz-kid,' wrote Michael Walters, the *Mail*'s Deputy City Editor. 'That, though, is just what I did, unwittingly, when I fastened upon James Ferguson as a highly speculative shell situation at 13p at the end of June. Ferguson soon got suspended, while chairman Guy Cramer sold them a seafront entertainment complex in Scarborough including the above motley collection of assets.' Walters's advice to his readers was clear: 'Take your profits and run fast.'

The *Sunday Times* also took a critical, if lighthearted view, pointing out that units in the Complex destined to be used as a discotheque were currently derelict and that the wooden hut was let to a Mr Spivy.[4]

*

In his new-found role of corporate raider Clowes had set his sights far wider than James Ferguson Holdings. By the turn of the year, 1986, he had taken large stakes in three public companies and was hungry for more. In February 1986 Tifa bought an 11.75 per cent stake in the hotels and property group Belgrave Holdings, paying around £1.4 million. The stake had come on to the market as a result of the Bank of England's rescue for Johnson Mathey Bankers. One of Johnson Mathey's main debtors was Ugandan businessman Abdul Shamji, whose holding in Belgrave was held as security for the £21 million that he owed. Clowes bought half this holding in February and then picked up the other half the following month. In the space of a few months Clowes had spent over £10 million of his investors' money on corporate raiding.

Taking stakes in public companies was not the only visible sign that Clowes now regarded himself as a corporate raider. Another indication, and one which more than any other suggests that he had completely lost touch with reality, was his hiring of executive jets.

In December 1985 Clowes had started modestly enough, paying £200 an hour to hire a Twin Comanche plane for a short business trip. The cost was £600. But then he did something which was highly unusual in the world of private executive jets. He leapt immediately to hiring Lear Jets, far larger and far more expensive, costing £1400 a flying hour. It was an ostentatious move, particularly as Clowes would often hire Lear Jets simply for domestic flights within England, and more often hire them for pleasure trips, rather than business. Then, in March 1986, true madness crept in. Clowes hired a Lear Jet to fly him and his family to Malaga, along with an electrician who was to carry out work on the penthouse flat Clowes had bought in Marbella. A few days later the Lear Jet returned to bring them back to Manchester. These trips cost over £13,500. From then on Clowes would happily pay £13,500 or more to hire Lear Jets for his brief weekend or mid-week breaks in the Marbella flat. A regular pattern was established: a Lear Jet would be booked to fly the Clowes family from Manchester airport to Malaga. Sometimes Clowes's parents Eric and Mary Clowes would join them, arriving at Manchester airport in a rusty, P-registered Austin Maxi. 'They were a very humble couple who used to say things like, "Did you make these sandwiches yourself?" ' says an airline official who came into contact with Clowes.

Clowes had a Range-Rover in Malaga so that he could drive the family to the flat. Meanwhile the Lear, still costing £1400 an hour, would return to Manchester empty. It would return, at the same cost, a few days later to pick up the Clowes family.

Clowes's extravagance did not go unnoticed. Brian Carlton, an aircraft executive working in Manchester, watched with amazement. 'Six years ago he was walking the streets of Bramhall and now he is hiring Lear Jets. This isn't right,' Carlton told himself. 'Somewhere along the line he has been terribly sharp.' Carlton decided that he would keep a close eye on Clowes.

There was no stopping Clowes. In March 1986 he and Naylor became directors of James Ferguson after another share-buying spree which had given Naylor almost 5 per cent of the company. Ferguson's share price had almost tripled, standing at 28p on 13 march, when Christopher Newman, the Barlow Clowes finance director, picked up a quarter of a million Ferguson shares. Later the same month, at a marketing meeting held in the Barlow Clowes head-quarters, Clowes talked of his plans to own a bank – or to apply to the Bank of England for a licence to operate as a bank. Another plan was to recruit a team of door-to-door salesmen in the Iberian penin-sula to sell Barlow Clowes products.

In May Clowes and Naylor were appointed chairman and deputy chairman of James Ferguson, alongside von Cramer. The press release announcing the appointments said they would 'facilitate the Company's planned expansion, in particular into the financial ser-vices sector'. This expansion seemed already well advanced since the press release revealed details of two joint ventures between Ferguson and Barlow Clowes, involving both gilts and computer services. The next month Ferguson announced the formation of a new corporate finance subsidiary, Ferguson & Partners. Von Cramer had brought in some very respectable names to head this new company, including Geoffrey Drain, a former director of the Bank of England and ex-General Secretary of Nalgo. Ferguson's shares soared from 30p to 88p, with the market speculating that Ferguson might actually take over Barlow Clowes or part of it. The shares were now more than eight times the price they had been at the beginning of the year. On the face of it the Ferguson 'shell' seemed to be working like a dream.

If blatancy is an indicator of confidence, then Clowes's confi-dence grew and grew throughout the first half of 1986. A few days after he was announced and installed as Ferguson's chairman, he revealed his stake in the Belgrave hotels group. And he said openly that some of the Belgrave shares which he owned had been bought from 'clients of Barlow Clowes'.[5] The next day he took his wife and children for a quick day out to the Marbella flat, the return flight by Lear Jet costing £7,000.

If Clowes's behaviour suggested that he had forsaken reality, he was nevertheless also capable of recognising it and distorting it to suit his purposes. The results for Barlow Clowes for the year to June 1986 show that, at the time, the company was still being propped up by its own investors. Clowes had rerouted money from investors into the company to pay for the advertising budget, claiming it was 'software licensing' income. He continued to do so. In the year to 30 June 1986 another £750,000 was paid to the Barlow Clowes business, again coming from investors and again disguised as software licensing. This was the 'sham' Hermes arrangement whereby Clowes invented an agreement with a non-existent business to license the Barlow Clowes software to that company. Every element of the plan was fictional. Hermes was a 'brass-plate' company; there was no agreement; no one was paying for the right to use the Barlow Clowes software. Clowes's software was incapable of doing the job properly for his own clients, let alone for anyone else's.

But without this payment Barlow Clowes would have shown heavy losses. To do so could have ruined the elaborate and deceitful plans which, already in June 1986, Clowes had formulated for Barlow Clowes.

CHAPTER TWELVE
·
HELLO GIBRALTAR
·

It is easy to forget that while Clowes was raiding public companies and taking control of James Ferguson, the Barlow Clowes business was still functioning. In February 1986 the anti-bondwashing provisions finally came into effect. While producing a blip in the money that Clowes was able to attract in the UK, the curb served only to increase the apparent attraction of his offshore funds – Portfolio 28 and 68. Five million pounds, more than £1 million a week, was invested in Portfolio 68 alone in the month when bondwashing was abolished.

Nor was this a knee-jerk reaction. Throughout 1986 the offshore funds grew and kept growing until by the end of the year almost £60 million was held overseas, and the overseas funds would, for the first time, be larger than those held in the UK. The balance of the business had shifted in an even more dangerous way. Investors were being pushed by their financial advisers to put their money offshore, into the pool of money which Clowes regarded as his own. Joan Doyle, secretary to Denis Wilson, one of the three most important intermediaries, recalls that after the abolition of bondwashing, D. C. Wilson's clients 'were encouraged to transfer into the offshore fund'. Wilson prepared a standard letter of transfer which his clients could sign, saving them the trouble of coming into the office. Barlow Clowes paid Wilson and the other intermediaries extra commission for transferring clients to the offshore funds even though the intermediaries had already been paid commission for introducing clients to Barlow Clowes in the first place.

By February 1986 the overseas office of Barlow Clowes had been properly established in Geneva. The move from Jersey had been protracted and messy, and it had not been until December 1985 that Naylor, accompanied by his secretary, Shan Swinstead, had flown to the rue de Hesse building to equip the office and recruit staff. An American marketing executive, Robert Posey, was recruited, as was Nicholas Michael, who was taken on as office manager. A local accountant, Donald Macphail, was brought in to do the books.

The Geneva-based Barlow Clowes operated on the fringes of legality. It had no banking licence and no permission from the Swiss authorities to operate as a fund management business. It could not hold investors' money. In March 1986, when the office became fully operational, cheques sent from the UK would be bundled up and sent by post every day to the two Jersey bank accounts which Clowes still maintained. Geneva was the public face of Barlow Clowes's offshore operations, but Jersey was where the money went – and disappeared from.

A familiar and clumsy pattern was established. Clowes or Naylor would give instructions to the Geneva office, usually to Swinstead, who would relay them to one or other of the Jersey banks. In the beginning most of these instructions concerned purchases and sales of gilts, with Swinstead being instructed to transfer money to various stockbroking firms. But there were other instructions too, less obvious ones, for money to be transferred to companies which Swinstead and the other staff at the Geneva office had never heard of.

Initially the amounts involved were small – in early February 1986 £250,000 to Mekom Computer Products' account with Barclays in Birmingham. But the size and frequency of the transfers to unfamiliar companies gathered momentum, and in doing so spread concern among the employees of the Geneva office. One of their functions was to send out monthly notifications to investors in the offshore portfolios, informing them of the rate of return the funds had achieved that month and expected to achieve the next. Naylor usually set the rates and telephoned them through. If the money is not being invested in gilts, reasoned some of the Geneva staff, how on earth are the rates of return being calculated?

In the first fortnight of June instructions were given for £2.2 million to be transferred out of the Lloyds and Midland accounts in Jersey and into a company called Technical Studies. From there, Swinstead and the others would have lost sight of the money. In fact most of it, some £1.4 million, went into Clowes's personal bank account at Barclays Bank in Manchester, and a further £210,000 into his wife's account. On 18 June Clowes drew a cheque for £67,900 on his Barclays account, payable to Strattons of Wilmslow, a car dealer specialising in expensive cars. Clowes had just bought himself a Bentley Turbo. He was not finished: five days later another cheque, this time for £79,500 – Clowes had added a Porsche.

Naylor had also committed a small theft. He entered the name of a fictitious investor on the computer, a Mr Patel, and recorded that this investor had paid in £25,000. Naylor then withdrew £19,000, paying it into his personal account but making entries on the computer stating that Mr Patel had withdrawn that exact same sum.

Naylor's account also received a further £420,000 which came from Lloyds Bank Jersey, via Technical Studies. Naylor used the money for several different purposes, including paying his American Express bill, applying for shares in the TSB share offer and extensively renovating his home, Send Barns, ultimately using over £430,000 of investors' money to do so. Naylor, who later maintained that he was not aware that it was investors' money, bought a Porsche, a cheaper version than Clowes's, costing £36,593. The Geneva staff were right to be worried.

The involvement of N. M. Rothschild is interesting. Like S. G. Warburg and Lazard Brothers, Rothschild is one of the most prestigious and respected merchant banks in the country – and like them it was used by Clowes to help him misuse his investors' money. Rothschild was used to finance Mekom Computer Products, the laser printing company which, by April 1986, had been massively expanded with the help of investors' money. Once again the medium was a back-to-back loan. Instead of lending money directly from investors' funds to Mekom, a loan of £1 million from Rothschild was arranged. This was obtained and secured by depositing £1 million from the Barlow Clowes investors with Rothschild's head office at New Court in the City of London. The £1 million paid to Rothschild as deposit was transferred to the merchant bank's headquarters on 21 March 1986. It came directly from a Barlow Clowes clients account with Lloyds Bank in Jersey. Rothschild has refused to explain how it allowed money coming from a Barlow Clowes clients account to secure a loan to a private computer company.

In the middle of all these transfers, Derek Tree, the ex-Midland Bank bank manager, paid a visit to the Geneva office at the request of Robert Posey. Tree was not happy at Barlow Clowes. Although he was managing director of the UK operations he naturally wanted to know what was happening offshore. Clowes and the others had been evasive. Tree's enquiries had been met with a wall of secrecy.

While Tree was at the rue de Hesse offices, one of the people involved in the Geneva operation handed him two lists of apparently irregular payments and told him that he was worried that the investors' money was not all going into gilts. The lists included instructions to transfer over £211,000 from the investors' bank account with Lloyds Bank in Jersey into the personal account of Guy von Cramer. Tree took copies of the lists and, as soon as he returned, showed them to Clowes. According to Tree, Clowes 'appeared very angry . . . I wasn't exactly sure why'. Tree could get no more than 'bluster' out of Clowes and resolved to take the matter further.[1]

*

The Rock of Gibraltar, two and three-quarter miles of craggy, inhospitable terrain, has no natural industries or produce of its own. It depends heavily on two main sources of revenue: tourism and the provision of financial services. Gibraltar has long promoted itself as an offshore financial centre, even more so since the opening of the border with Spain, which enhanced its status both internationally and with wealthy residents on the Costa del Sol. Every company registering in Gibraltar represents annual fees of at least £200 for its coffers. In 1989 almost 8000 new companies were registered in Gibraltar. As an enticement Gibraltar offers foreign nationals its own brand of tax-exempt company. Unlike most offshore jurisdictions whose tax-exempt companies must be managed elsewhere, the Gibraltar version allows the company to be managed locally and still claim exemption from taxes. It was this feature which appears, at least initially, to have encouraged Clowes to view Gibraltar as a suitable home for his offshore operations.

Clowes had been flirting with Gibraltar since the day his DTI licence was granted. Late in October 1985 he had incorporated a company called Barlow Clowes International. The move to Geneva appears to have been an ill-planned knee-jerk reaction to being evicted from Jersey. Financial institutions based in Switzerland were heavily regulated; there was a strong possibility that Barlow Clowes was contravening Swiss laws even in the limited nature of its Geneva operations and would be closed down. Gibraltar, in contrast, offered a *laissez-faire* system which imposed virtually no controls on investment management businesses such as Barlow Clowes. It had a Banking Ordinance regulating banks, and an Insurance Ordinance, brought on to the statute books following the collapse of the Gibraltar-based Signal Life insurance group in 1982, but on the question of investment managers and advisers it was utterly silent.

Gibraltar also had a psychological attraction for Clowes – he would be welcomed there. He was, at best, tolerated in the UK, he had been evicted from Jersey and he had to operate in a semi-clandestine manner in Switzerland. But Gibraltar, anxious as it was to become a major offshore financial centre, would want this man who flew to the Rock in a private jet and had over £100 million of other people's money under his management.

Clowes instructed the largest law firm in Gibraltar, Hassan & Partners, to act for him. The firm's senior partner, Sir Joshua Hassan, was Chief Minister of Gibraltar at the time. Large advertisements were placed in the local Gibraltar papers seeking staff to join Barlow

Clowes, which was planning to establish 'its international head-quarters' on the Rock.

In June 1986 a standard letter was sent to investors from the Barlow Clowes International offices in Gibraltar, explaining the reason for switching the overseas funds away from Jersey. It was, like other letters covering the same subject, a complete fabrication. The letter was apparently from Peter Clowes, chairman of Barlow Clowes International.

Dear Investor,

Barlow Clowes are pleased to be providing you with an investment service designed to ensure attractive gains and excellent security of funds. Our record of growth and achievement over the past ten years speaks for itself.

As a client of our international portfolios you are well aware of the advantages which such investments can provide and the quality of service.

The expansion of these portfolios has resulted in our outgrowing the Jersey based operations.

We have therefore relocated the base for our international portfolios to GIBRALTAR, a rapidly developing financial centre. At the same time we have established a Servicing & Accounting Centre in GENEVA Switzerland.

Naturally, this new structure remains an integral part of the Barlow Clowes Group and will continue to provide the same service and security to which you are accustomed.

Yours faithfully,

Peter Clowes
Chairman.

PS Why not consider increasing your investment with us now?

Apart from Clowes's sinister invitation at the end, and the mendacious reason given for moving to Gibraltar, the letter also illustrates the confusion in Clowes's thinking. Only a few months earlier Barlow Clowes investors had been sent letters telling them that Geneva would be the international headquarters for the offshore portfolios. In these letters a more subtle disguise was used to conceal the fact that Barlow Clowes had been ordered to leave Jersey:

The client administration of PORTFOLIO 28 has been moved
to our new offices in Geneva. You will be receiving statements and other correspondence from the above address.
Your Portfolio has been redesignated PORTFOLIO 68, for
ease of administration and recognition. In all other respects
the service remains identical.

The redesignation of the portfolio, whether deliberate or not,
was a distraction from the main issue: the move from Jersey to
Switzerland. Being evicted from Jersey was potentially disastrous for
Clowes. If news had got out there would inevitably have been a run
on the offshore funds, eventually bringing down the whole operation. But once again, through a combination of luck, bureaucratic
inefficiency and his downright lies, Clowes avoided disaster.

The advertisements in the Gibraltar papers were noticed by Geoffrey
Burton, Gibraltar's Banking Supervisor. Burton, a former Bank of
England official, was not a full-time supervisor: he commuted to the
Rock from his home in Walton-on-Thames. Seeing the advertise-
ments he spoke first to the Bank of England and then to the DTI to
see if they had 'anything against' Barlow Clowes. 'I was more cau-
tious about their arrival than some,' says Burton. Both the Bank and
Laurence Green, Louth's replacement at the DTI, gave Barlow
Clowes a clean bill of health. Outwardly it had not put a foot wrong.
The DTI had not received any complaints from investors. The pattern
of deceit and diversion of funds had been unnoticed by the UK
authorities. After speaking to Burton, Green made a note on his file:
'I do not think we have cause for alarm. Gibraltar is not perhaps the
location to inspire confidence. But we knew that Barlow Clowes had
some offshore operations when we licensed them.'[2]

Green's attitude was typical of the Department's reactive, unen-
quiring stance. Instead of making some enquiries himself or instructing staff to find out exactly what Clowes was proposing to do in
Gibraltar, he made a note on the file: 'If the opportunity arises we
could ask BC what they are up to and look out for any information
which comes our way.'[3]

The DTI had a chance to question Clowes about Gibraltar in July
1986, when Barlow Clowes came to see the Department with its
lawyers Herbert Smith. This was a key meeting, one which helped
Clowes to continue and increase his massive fraud. Clowes wanted
one thing from the meeting – and he achieved it. He did not want

to have to send clients individual contract notes telling them which gilts he had bought on their behalf. The licensed dealers' rules required him to do this; he wanted a waiver. He also *needed* one. If he was using investors' money to buy stakes in public companies, to invest in other assets such as jewellery, computers and property, there would be no gilts contract notes to send to clients.

Clowes was flanked at the meeting by his right-hand man Naylor and his lawyer, Fleck. Clowes claimed that because of the large number of gilts deals which he was implementing for his clients it would be impractical to send contract notes to clients for every transaction. He wanted to be able to send them only in cases where the client actually requested them. After some discussion the DTI agreed a technical way around the rules which would obviate the need to issue contract notes to clients. By doing so it was making it easier for Clowes to invest his clients' money in assets other than gilts.

The meeting also discussed the move to Gibraltar. Clowes lied to the Department as he had done before. The Jersey operations, he said, had 'run out of space for expansion by 1983' and so moved on to Geneva. A telephone call from the DTI to the Jersey authorities would have exposed this lie. None was made.

Clowes also repeated an earlier lie: that the overseas operations dealt only for expatriates, that is, people who do not live in the UK. Given that there were about 10,000 people living in the UK who had money with the overseas operations it was a rather brazen lie to tell. But Clowes had run rings around the DTI so many times by now that he must have felt he could tell them anything.

He was becoming more extravagant. At the beginning of August Clowes's daughter Nikki fell out with her boyfriend while they were on holiday together in Tenerife. Clowes and his family had already flown to Malaga by Lear Jet. Clowes paid for the jet to fly on to Tenerife to pick up Nikki and bring her back to Malaga. To satisfy Spanish air regulations the plane had first to land in Portugal before bringing Nikki back. The total cost of this jamboree was £12,360.

CHAPTER THIRTEEN

·

A DARK DAY IN AUGUST

·

By July 1986 Clowes had a master plan: he would sell his Barlow Clowes business into James Ferguson Holdings, and receive Ferguson shares in return. It was simple, neat, and would be the springboard for massive expansion. Barlow Clowes was, in theory, far larger than Ferguson so the deal would be what is known as a 'reverse takeover', giving Clowes control over Ferguson. He would in effect be floating the company he had built up over the past twelve years on the stock market. The public, in buying Ferguson shares, would be buying a stake in his Barlow Clowes business. Bernard Cornfeld, Clowes's former employer, had done virtually the same when he floated Investors Overseas Services in late 1969, a few months before Clowes had joined. Clowes was following the master.

Selling Barlow Clowes to Ferguson was just one stage of the plan. The sale would make Peter Clowes the largest shareholder in the company and, with control of Ferguson, he could issue more shares to enable him to take over other companies. Others had done it, why couldn't he? It was, after all, the rationale behind taking control of a shell company such as Ferguson. The shell company's publicly quoted shares would be used to finance acquisitions.

Top on the list of Clowes's desired acquisitions was a bank. James Ferguson Holdings, as a fully fledged financial services company, would either apply for a banking licence or issue new shares to take over an existing one. We shall see later why Clowes wanted to buy a bank and what became of the many attempts he made.

On 29 July, after it announced the deal to buy Barlow Clowes, Ferguson's shares were suspended. This is common practice when a public company announces a reverse takeover. The suspension of dealings in its shares is a form of protection for the public in case the deal does not go through. The announcement of the suspension appeared, from an outsider's perspective, to be a somewhat muddled affair, as the *Birmingham Post* reported the following day.

> At first, the Stock Exchange said this was at the company's request 'pending clarification of the position of the company' – wording that is often a prelude to receivership.

Later the company said the suspension was 'pending finalisation of the timing of the posting of the circular to shareholders relating to certain acquisitions proposed by the company'.

Ferguson's 24-year-old managing director Mr Guy Cramer, said: 'The Stock Exchange got things slightly in a muddle and made the wrong announcement'. The coming announcement concerned four acquisitions and some 'reorganisation' he added.

The SE's spokesman did not confirm there had been a slip up and commented to the *Birmingham Post*: 'It is pretty unusual for us to make a mistake like that.'

The truth was that neither the original nor the corrected announcement disclosed what had actually happened. The company had not requested a share suspension: the Stock Exchange had insisted on it largely because it had become concerned by the astronomical rise in Ferguson's share prices – from 10p at the beginning of the year to 120p in mid-July – and suspected that this rise had been artificially engineered.

The story starts with a section of the Stock Exchange known as its Quotations Division. This is responsible for ensuring that public companies provide sufficient information to their shareholders, about intended acquisitions for example, and that the companies obey the Exchange's rules governing the behaviour of public companies. The rules are laid down in a book entitled *Admission of Securities to Listing*, known – due to its colour – as the Yellow Book.

The Quotations Division had approved Ferguson's acquisition of the Scarborough Complex at the beginning of the year. Had it known the truth about the transaction – the artificial boosting of the Complex's rents – the Quotations Division would never have given its approval. Ferguson's shares had been suspended for almost four months while the Scarborough purchase went through. When they returned from suspension in January they leapt immediately from 10p to 15p and kept rising, hitting 30p the next month. In June the share price had almost tripled, to 88p, fuelled by speculation that the company would be taking over Barlow Clowes. The announcement of the takeover had taken them to 120p – twelve times the level they had been in January.

A hidden factor behind the price rise was the secret buying of Ferguson shares by Clowes through his Gibraltar-registered company Sandover, which he claimed, falsely, was not connected with him.

Sandover's buying should have been publicly disclosed as adding to the stake Peter Clowes held in Ferguson. The Quotations Division was not aware of the link with Clowes but it was sufficiently alarmed by the Ferguson price rise to conduct an investigation after the Barlow Clowes purchase was announced. Conducting the investigation was John Woolland, an accountant on secondment to the Division from one of the largest accountancy firms in the country, then known as Deloitte Haskins & Sells.

Woolland was concerned that there was absolutely nothing to justify the share price rise. Ferguson was still making losses and yet its stock market value had risen from £2 million to £25 million in six months.

One of the reasons was Clowes. Instead of keeping his head down, quietly implementing his plan to reverse Barlow Clowes into Ferguson, he had been bragging. An article in *Accountancy Age* quoted Clowes as saying that Ferguson would be making £2 million profits by 1989. This was typical of Clowes. Although a very secretive man – secrecy was becoming increasingly essential as his diversion of investors' money grew even larger – he was at the same time a reckless braggart. Boasting about Ferguson was equivalent to his extravagant private jet trips: both were underpinned by the secret diversion of investors' money. But Clowes could not do things quietly any more. He was secretive and loud at the same time. This split in his personality mirrored the gap between his public image as an increasingly successful businessman, and his private reality as an ever greater diverter of his investors' funds.

Apart from the *Accountancy Age* article, Woolland noticed that Ferguson had announced a number of acquisitions which, although minor, nevertheless needed prior approval from shareholders. This had not been obtained. Ferguson and its directors were therefore in breach of the Yellow Book rules. Meanwhile the acquisitions themselves had been heralded by a series of announcements designed to boost the share price.

Woolland recommended that Ferguson's shares be suspended immediately and remain so until the company had established a decent track record, one that would justify its high rating. At the same time, because he suspected that Ferguson's shares had been artificially inflated (or 'ramped', to use the stock market jargon), he suggested that the Exchange's Surveillance Division examine dealings in Ferguson's shares. Clowes's master plan threatened to be stillborn.

Both Woolland's recommendations were accepted. But the

announcements of the suspension presented a totally misleading version of events and made no mention of the Exchange's very real concerns. However, it is standard practice, even in cases where public companies are instructed by the Exchange to suspend their shares, to announce that the suspension is at the company's request. To the outside world it looked as if Ferguson, Clowes and the others were correctly following normal procedures. The reality was totally different. The simultaneous versions of events – the heavily censored public showing and the private, unexpurgated one – continued.

The following day, 30 July, a conciliatory von Cramer attended a meeting at the Exchange, accompanied by his stockbroker Peter Morrison of Rensburg. Clowes was not with them; he and his lawyers Herbert Smith were meeting DTI officials, persuading them to relieve him of the obligation to send out contract notes to his clients.

Woolland did not mince his words at the meeting with von Cramer. He told him that Ferguson's behaviour 'showed a total disregard for Stock Exchange requirements'. Von Cramer apologised, wanting to know how the company could make amends. The next day Rensburg wrote to Woolland saying that Ferguson's directors 'deeply regret the Press comment in recent weeks which in our opinion was not accurately reported and represented a fair element of speculative interpretation'. But the shares remained suspended and would do so unless and until the Exchange's Quotations Division approved the takeover of Barlow Clowes. This might provide the acceptable track record the Exchange was looking for. But there were no guarantees. The Exchange would want to ensure that a great deal of information about Barlow Clowes was presented to shareholders before giving its approval.

There remained the Surveillance Division's investigation into dealings in Ferguson shares. The matter was passed to the Insider Dealing Unit within the Division, which examined the dealings, and found nothing wrong. Clowes had hidden his secret share dealings behind front companies, in Gibraltar and Liechtenstein. At that stage, in the absence of an inside source, it would have been difficult to prove that he was the secret buyer behind these companies.

Running parallel with Clowes's master plan was an insanely reckless bid for control of Belgrave Holdings, the hotels group. In March 1986 Clowes had bought a 23.5 per cent holding, concealing his identity, and the fact that he had used investors' funds, behind Tifa, the Liechtenstein company he had previously used to buy shares in C.H.

Bailey. In May his stake was increased to 29.9 per cent and the owner now publicly declared to be International Securities AG.

International Securities was a Liechtenstein *Anstalt*, one of the most secretive entities in the world. Liechtenstein also offers equally private vehicles, known as *Siftungs* (a foundation) or the *Treuunternehmen* – a business trust. An *Anstalt* does not even have shareholders; instead it has a founder whose identity need never be revealed. *Anstalts*, such as International Securities, which merely exist to hold investments, do not even need to file accounts with the Liechtenstein tax authorities.

When the May announcement was made, Clowes and von Cramer declared themselves as directors of International Securities, Clowes claiming they represented wealthy European investors. They wanted to be appointed directors of Belgrave. When the Belgrave board rejected the idea, Clowes and von Cramer used International Securities' 29.9 per cent stake to call for an extraordinary general meeting of Belgrave. The shareholders of Belgrave would decide. This was a hostile and reckless move, highly public and bound to lead to questions being asked about where Clowes and von Cramer were obtaining their finance.

At this juncture it is appropriate to consider the influence that von Cramer had on Clowes, since the two of them were in the Belgrave fight together. Clowes was forty-three, twenty-one years older than von Cramer. What could the younger man offer him?

Von Cramer was a good front man, an articulate and polished public performer in a way that Clowes could never hope to be. While Clowes felt himself to be an outcast, shunned by the City establishment, von Cramer had managed, with the help of City connections, to buy into James Ferguson and sell the Futurist Complex to the company. He had polish and reasonably good connections. Clowes had the money. They also socialised. Von Cramer went on holiday with the Clowes family – at one point staying with them in their Marbella flat. And although Clowes was bright, von Cramer had a quicker, sharper mind. To City professionals and advisers, he was the more impressive of the two men. Clowes could get bogged down in detail, become too technical in his explanations. Von Cramer was far and away the better communicator.

It must also be remembered that Clowes had an ever increasing pile of money to manage offshore. He was committed to achieve a high tax-free return from it by dealing in gilts – and to return investors' money whenever they wanted. Throughout 1986 the rates he offered were far higher than a comparable building society account

– sometimes by as much as 5 per cent. Once again it was a promise he could not hope to deliver. As with his Portfolio 30 bondwashing product, Clowes was raising money on a false prospectus, relying on human greed, ignorance and gullibility to do the rest.

He could not simply invest the money in gilts and pay investors out of the income. He had to deal, to buy and sell, to produce a capital gain. But Clowes had no genuine track record in making gains from gilt dealings. And besides it was somewhat old hat for him: like his gilts shops, a thing of the past. He had moved on, to become a financier and now a corporate raider. He had a continuous positive cash flow abroad – more money was coming in from investors each month than was being paid out. So he could satisfy withdrawals by simply taking from the surplus incoming funds, robbing Peter to pay Paul. Given that he had no hope of making the genuine capital return, and with the comfort of a positive cash flow, the temptation to divert was too great. After the success of his advertising campaign, when people threw tens of millions of pounds at him to manage, he had been bursting with ambition and self-belief. Now he was chairman of a public company. All this had been achieved by deception, was based on little more than his own readiness to lie and cheat, but no matter. Nothing adverse had come of it. On the contrary he had achieved status, recognition and power. There was no reason to stop now. Von Cramer, quick, sharp and ambitious, had fastened on to this phenomenon.

The scale and grandeur of Clowes's plan contrasted markedly with behind-the scenes manoeuvres which threatened to wreck them. As Clowes was proclaiming himself Ferguson's chairman, announcing first the Belgrave demand and then the Ferguson plan for Barlow Clowes, his staff were becoming increasingly edgy and worried. Some of the Geneva staff were worried for their own positions, as they reluctantly but consciously participated in the diversion of investors' money. And Tree, whose appointment as managing director had helped persuade the Department of Trade to license Barlow Clowes, was now a very worried man.

He had shown Clowes the lists of suspect payments an executive had handed him in Geneva, and failed to get a satisfactory reply. On top of this another Barlow Clowes executive claimed that Doc Naylor had been seen putting fictitious entries on to the computer system. He decided to take matters into his own hands.

In the afternoon of Wednesday 13 August Tree rang Derek

Sinstead, the manager in charge of Midland Bank's Threadneedle Street branch where Tree had worked prior to joining Barlow Clowes. Could he come and see him right away? Tree asked, it was important. Sinstead agreed. Later the same day Tree told Sinstead his fear that fraud was taking place in the overseas operations of Barlow Clowes. Tree saw Sinstead twice that week and was clearly a worried man, as Sinstead later noted in an internal memorandum. 'It was obvious that he took the matter very seriously for he talked of resigning his position and specifically said that he thought there might be 'elements of fraud' involved.[1]

Tree's concerns struck home. Midland was banker to Barlow Clowes and together with Lloyds Bank it provided the bank accounts in Jersey which received virtually all of the offshore investors' money. Midland had been aware of the Bank of England's concerns about Barlow Clowes back in 1985, but, according to Sinstead, 'felt able to take a more relaxed view once an audit by Spicer and Pegler had been completed and a Principal's licence . . . had been issued by the DTI'. Now Sinstead was not so sure. Action had to be taken at a senior level within Midland. Sinstead spoke to his superior Neil Blair, regional director at the bank. Blair in turn reported Tree's warning to David Barber, the general manager of the bank. Barber sought an urgent meeting with the Bank of England to discuss the Tree affair. The Bank of England agreed. Sinstead, Blair and Barber could come in that same evening. It was Friday 15 August 1986.

Meanwhile, Tree had decided to take further action. As the top level delegation walked less than a hundred yards from the Threadneedle Street branch to the Bank of England's headquarters, Tree paid a secret visit to Spicer and Pegler. Their offices were also in the City of London, off Fenchurch Street. Tree had, earlier that day, arranged to see Julian Pilkington, the Spicer's partner responsible for the Barlow Clowes business.

Pilkington was an important figure within the accounting profession. He was chairman of a subcommittee of the Audit Practices Committee, the chief UK auditing regulatory body. As such he would have been involved in laying down guidelines for the way in which investment businesses such as Barlow Clowes should be audited.

Tree was going behind Clowes's back in seeing Pilkington and was well aware of it. Had Clowes known about it he would have sacked him. Tree had more or less decided to leave in any event, but in his own time. It was a dangerous step to take, and throughout his meeting with Pilkington he insisted that Clowes should know nothing of his visit. This was Tree's third clandestine meeting that week. During the meeting that evening he was not as forthcoming as he had been when seeing Midland. This was hardly surprising since Tree had previously worked at the bank for twenty-one years, knew Sinstead, and would have felt more comfortable with him. Nevertheless he did tell Pilkington that he was concerned because Naylor had allegedly been seen altering clients' records on the computer. Spicers had been aware of the defects in the Barlow Clowes computer system and had already written to Clowes suggesting improvements. There were several problems with the system, the most serious being that it allowed Clowes or Naylor, the only two people who fully understood it, to delete records without trace. They could wipe the slate completely clean. However, Pilkington had taken some comfort from the fact that two men – Clowes and Naylor – could operate the system because it accorded with the 'Four Eyes' policy laid down by the Bank of England for people who wanted to set up a bank: there had to be at least two people at the top controlling the bank. Naylor and Clowes ran Barlow Clowes. What Pilkington did not appreciate was that both men were actually involved in the diversion of investors' money.

According to his own account of the meeting, Pilkington repeatedly pressed Tree to be more specific about his concerns. Eventually he came away from the meeting with Tree realising that Naylor had possibly done something wrong, but with little more. Tree had not told Pilkington about the lists of suspect payments, possibly because the information about the lists was easily traceable back to him.[2]

Meanwhile, the deputation from Midland Bank had called on the Bank of England where they met with Brian Gent, Deputy Head of Banking Supervision – a very senior post within the bank.

The Midland executives relayed to the Bank Tree's real fears of a possible fraud in the offshore operations. According to Sinstead, Gent's initial reaction was that 'he found it difficult to see a role for the Bank of England'. However, he came away from the meeting under the impression that Gent would speak to the senior partner at Spicer's. In fact, immediately after the meeting an official in the Bank of England called Geoffrey Burton in Gibraltar to relay these concerns. Burton had himself felt uneasy about Barlow Clowes and told the Bank of England. But he had no jurisdiction over the firm – it was not a bank.

That day was a vital one in the life of Barlow Clowes. At the very moment when suspicion of a possible fraud in Barlow Clowes's overseas operations were winging their way around the City and

over to Gibraltar, Sir Montague Prichard, chairman of Belgrave Holdings, sent a letter to his shareholders about Clowes's and von Cramer's attempts to join the Belgrave board. Its contents were dyna-
mite. After deploring the expense and time involved in fighting off
Clowes and von Cramer, Sir Montague went on to question who
was backing them, and where they were getting their money:

> International Securities is a Liechtenstein corporation about
> which very little meaningful information is available. It
> acquired a substantial part of its shareholding in your Com-
> pany from Tifa AG, another Liechtenstein corporation whose
> shareholding had originated from the receiver of Gomba . . .
>
> Following International Securities' purchase of shares in
> your Company we were immediately approached by Mr
> Clowes and Mr von Cramer to consider a request for board
> representation. During the two meetings I had with them,
> attended by our financial advisers, Messrs Clowes and von
> Cramer explained that International Securities had been
> formed by them specifically to acquire a shareholding in
> your Company and that this purchase had been financed by
> expatriate discretionary investment clients of Barlow Clowes
> Limited. We were informed that Barlow Clowes Limited was
> an investment advisory business specialising in small port-
> folios of gilt-edged securities.

This was absolutely correct. Some £4.7 million of Barlow Clowes
investors' money had been invested in Belgrave shares. It should
have been in gilts, and the clients would have had no idea that their
money was being used in this way. Sir Montague's letter, combined
with the simultaneous fears of a fraud in Barlow Clowes's overseas
operations, should have brought Clowes's master plan crashing
down and his new found role as corporate raider to a premature
end. But once again luck, coupled with lack of initiative, played its
part in keeping the fantasy alive.

The Belgrave letter had been reported in the business pages of
the following morning's papers. The *Financial Times* reported that
'the battle for boardroom control of Belgrave Holdings is hotting up'
and that Sir Montague's letter had deplored the 'damaging, time
consuming and expensive action' that Clowes and von Cramer had
taken. The *Guardian* reported on the letter too: 'In a letter to shareholders Sir Montague says both the board and its financial advisers

"consider it is not in the interests of your Company" that the two men [Clowes and von Cramer] should be appointed directors.'

None of the papers, however, picked up the reference to the funding coming from clients of Barlow Clowes. This would have been spoonfeeding the regulators with the information they needed. But the Belgrave bid was reported, the involvement of Clowes and von Cramer and their Liechtenstein vehicle well documented. The regulators passed information about Barlow Clowes to one another, but none of them had sufficient initiative to step outside their immediate regulatory circle and make enquiries about Clowes's activities, his bid for control of Belgrave. They passed the parcel of responsibility among themselves, creating the impression of action and a reality devoid of substance. Warnings were washed through the regulators, from the auditors, to the Bank of England, to Gibraltar and the DTI, just as the investors' money was washed through nominee companies and banks in several countries, both emerging, seemingly anodyne, at the other end.[3]

There is one final, disturbing aspect to the events of 15 August 1986. On that day the Midland Bank had told the Bank of England of the warning received from its former manager of a possible fraud involving the overseas funds of Barlow Clowes. Midland, along with Lloyds, was principal banker to these funds through its branch in St Helier, Jersey. Three weeks after Tree's warning £3 million was transferred out of this Midland branch, secretly and illicitly, into a Gibraltar-registered company. Millions more would follow just as millions had preceded Tree's warning, flowing out of the account to support Clowes's corporate ambitions. But the Midland Bank did not stop this. Despite knowing that Barlow Clowes was supposed to be investing in gilts, and despite a warning of potential fraud it received and implemented instructions to transfer huge amounts of investors' money out of its St Helier branch and into a series of front companies.

How can this be explained? The 'Listening Bank', when served with a writ in July 1990 for its role in the Barlow Clowes affair, protested that it had warned the Government about possible fraud. In doing so it shot itself in the foot. The warning ought to have made the bank more alert to the massive and continuing dissipation of funds from the account in its St Helier branch.

Midland Bank, at the suggestion of the Bank of England, did monitor Barlow Clowes after it had received the Tree warning. Almost every day for several months Derek Sinstead, the manager of the Threadneedle Street branch, aided by two other managers, looked at the cheques drawn on the Barlow Clowes offshore investors' accounts held at his branch. There was one problem with Midland's monitoring. It was only seeing a very small part of the picture. Clowes's massive diversion of investors' funds was mainly coming out of the St Helier bank accounts, not the Threadneedle Street accounts. As if that was not bad enough, no one at Midland relayed the Tree warning to the St Helier branch. The manager there, Derek Denton, never knew a thing about the very real fears that had reached the top echelons of the bank and been relayed to the Bank of England. His branch continued, oblivious, transferring larger and larger chunks of investors' money on Clowes's instructions into dummy companies while Sinstead, back in London, looked at cheques which were largely irrelevant.[4]

Nor were Lloyds Bank blameless in this affair. Tree had relayed his concerns to Derek Piper, manager of Lloyds' branch in London's Mincing Lane where Barlow Clowes banked. 'I certainly said exactly the same to Piper as I said to Sinstead.'[5] Once again Tree's concerns were passed up the hierarchy of the bank. And, as in the case of Midland, Lloyds continued to process Clowes's instructions to transfer funds out of the offshore investors' accounts.

The Midland Bank's response in the face of suggestions of fraud put them in the same category as the other institutions and regulators who played a part in the drama of 15 August 1986. Without their innate caution Clowes could never have gone as far as he did.[6]

CHAPTER FOURTEEN

·

IN THE KINGDOM OF THE BLIND

·

'When the lights go out in Marbella the gilts will still shine in Gibraltar.'

Barlow Clowes advertisement for Gibraltar TV.

The evening of Thursday 18 September 1986 is one which Clowes will never forget. On that evening he was welcomed and praised by government ministers, politicians and civil servants in a way he never had been before or would be again. The occasion was the launch party to celebrate the opening of Barlow Clowes's 'International Head Office' in Gibraltar.

Celebrations for the event had begun the day before when the Gulfstream private jet belonging to millionaire publisher Robert Maxwell had flown a party of financial intermediaries for lunch at the Barlow Clowes Geneva office. The jet, chartered from Maxwell, waited on the tarmac of Geneva airport at a cost of around £4000 an hour while the intermediaries enjoyed a buffet lunch hosted by Robert Posey.

From Geneva the party flew on to Gibraltar where they were housed overnight in two hotels: those generating the highest levels of business for Barlow Clowes went to the Rock Hotel, on the Upper Rock, overlooking the Mediterranean; the others stayed in the Holiday Inn, in the centre of town. (When they left the Holiday Inn the following day several of the hotel's towelling gowns went with them and Barlow Clowes had to send a cheque to cover the expense.)

The launch party was held in the grounds adjacent to the Rock Hotel's swimming pool, where most of the important outdoor functions in Gibraltar are held. It was a sit-down buffet, with Clowes and his wife Pamela sitting with the Governor Sir Peter Terry, the Chief Minister Sir Joshua Hassan and their wives. There were 150 guests altogether, dining under the floral roof which protected them from any unlikely drops of rain. 'It was a very high profile arrival,' recalls

Jo Bossano, the current Chief Minister. 'You know, when a company opens up in Gibraltar, they don't normally throw a party and have a principal guest, the governor of Gibraltar and the Chief Minister and all the leading legal firms and all the leading banks. The entire establishment and even those of us who were on the side of the rebels and not on the side of the establishment turned up. I was a guest at that particular party and frankly, I thought it was a feather in the cap for the government of the day, because here they are, they're bringing a reputable important operation to Gibraltar.'

Sir Joshua gave the first speech. The swimming pool of the Rock Hotel is a favourite haunt on Sundays for Sir Joshua and his wife. That evening he warmly welcomed the tubby little lad from Manchester who had brought his business, and hopefully its £100 million of investors' money (the transfer from Jersey was promised but not effected at the time of the launch), to the Rock. 'It is particularly gratifying that you have chosen us as the location for your international headquarters,' said Hassan.

Sir Peter also gave a short speech of welcome. Then Clowes announced that Barlow Clowes had introduced a new student sponsorship scheme. 'Awards will be granted at the end of the present academic year to the student in each of the local schools who displays the greatest effort and perseverance in the pursuit of excellence,' he said, as a police siren wailed in the background. The announcement of the Barlow Clowes student award drew thanks from the Education Minister, George Mascerenhas.

Six days earlier Clowes had given instructions for the largest diversion of investors' funds so far. Six million pounds had been transferred in two tranches into a nominee company called Lyceum Holdings, registered in Gibraltar. He was bringing to the colony a business that was a complete and utter sham, his private investment pool masquerading as a gilts fund. But that knowledge was locked away in a tiny corner of Clowes's mind as he accepted the plaudits which spilled over from the launch party to that weekend's edition of the *Gibraltar Evening Chronicle*. Large quarter-page advertisements were taken out welcoming Barlow Clowes: 'Norwich Union congratulate Barlow Clowes International Ltd on the launching of their Gibraltar operation and wish them every success', read one. Similar welcomes were advertised by companies such as the Cable & Wireless telecommunications group and the Bland hotels and leisure group.

Somewhere in the Gibraltar system at the time was a warning that Barlow Clowes's offshore operations were possibly fraudulent. Records at the Bank of England show that this warning, which

Peter Clowes's father, Eric, with his paraffin trailer outside the family hardware shop in Moss Side, Manchester, in the 1950s.

Peter Clowes marries the girl next door, Patricia Slann, at the age of twenty-one.

Clowes with his brother John *(left)* who later became a vicar.

Pamela Haydock, after marrying the bass guitarist of the Hollies pop group. Pamela later married Peter Clowes and employed first husband Eric as her chauffeur.

The corporate raiders. Peter Clowes and Guy von Cramer pose for publicity photographs before the James Ferguson purchase of Barlow Clowes is announced.

A proud home owner? Peter Clowes outside his Prestbury home, bought with investors' money.

The *Boukephelas*, named after Alexander the Great's horse. Clowes bought this luxury yacht from Tina Onassis.

Investors' money funded Clowes's private jet trips.

Château d'Auros was purchased by Peter Clowes with investors' money.

Trade and Industry Secretary
Lord Young with the Le Quesne
Report into the government's
licensing of Barlow Clowes.

Peter Clowes outside his offices following the collapse of his empire.
'I have not stolen any money from anyone,' he claimed.

Bailed out: Peter Clowes with his wife Pamela outside Guildhall magistrates' court after being released on bail in June 1988.

Arrested: James Ferguson's finance director, Christopher Newman *(left)*, and Dr Peter Naylor arriving at Guildhall magistrates' court handcuffed together.

Downfall of a whizz-kid: Guy von Cramer outside Bishopsgate police station following his arrest in December 1988.

John Dyer, Chairman of the
Barlow Clowes Investors Group.

Antony Gold, the solicitor who
masterminded the campaign for
compensation.

The first meeting of investors after the collapse of Barlow Clowes. Some hid their faces to
avoid being identified.

originated from Tree, was passed on by the Bank to Burton, Gibraltar's Banking Supervisor. Burton has no recollection of it. His memory may be deficient but, if not, it is not inconceivable that the Bank's note of the conversation is incorrect. A possible explanation is that the call was taken by someone else within the Gibraltar authorities. The Barlow Clowes story is rife with examples of messages that were ignored or did not get through to the right person, or discrete pockets of information held by different regulators and not collated to reveal the whole picture. While the Gibraltar Government was giving Clowes a hero's welcome, someone within the same Government knew that his business might be fraudulent.

But none of this reached the surface on the balmy September evening of the Barlow Clowes launch party. As well as the welcoming advertisements the event received extensive editorial coverage in the Saturday edition of the *Chronicle*. Clowes was pictured for perhaps the first time ever in a newspaper – and praised:

> For the last fifteen years Peter Clowes has specialised in the Financial Services sector and as founder and senior partner of Barlow Clowes & Partners built the practice from inception to its present position where Barlow Clowes are considered market leaders. He has over twenty years' practical experience in data processing and the business applications of computers. He has with Dr Peter Naylor developed systems which are extremely powerful and easy to use by office staff.

The *Chronicle* also introduced a new character in the Barlow Clowes saga: John Perez, managing director of Barlow Clowes International: 'John Perez has a long and wide experience in insurance and more recently in investments. He was sales manager for Norwich Union Gibraltar and was instrumental in the Iberian Peninsula recently. He joined Barlow Clowes in March 1986 and is now spearheading the International Operation.'

Perez had in fact been involved with Clowes in an earlier venture. Clowes and three of his intermediaries had tried to set up a business in Gibraltar. Temple Bar Investments was incorporated in October 1985, its directors being Clowes, Ross Hyett, Denis Wilson and another intermediary named Philip Saunders, of Premier Investment Management. It never got off the ground, and the directors realised that Temple Bar would need a local man in order to be a viable proposition. Perez was recruited. But then Clowes decided that he would set up Barlow Clowes in Gibraltar and so the Temple Bar idea folded.[1]

When appointed managing director of Barlow Clowes International Perez's basic salary was £36,000 a year. In addition, Clowes agreed to pay a further £1250 a month into an Isle of Man bank account in the name of Perez and his wife. Perez would be an important figure in the development of Barlow Clowes International on the Rock.

The Gibraltar launch was a huge success for Clowes. As Maxwell's jet returned the intermediaries to Manchester – the trip cost over £22,000 – Clowes could see what a success he had been. He had found a place whose establishment figures respected him. In Gibraltar he was an important figure, with a very substantial business which the Government was delighted to have. His reception in Gibraltar contrasted with the years of silent disdain and bare tolerance that he had endured. He had been accepted under sufferance in his own country, and he knew it. He knew his reputation and that of his company were, as he himself put it, 'iffy'. He had had to spend tens of thousands of pounds on lawyers and accountants to secure a Department of Trade licence – a procedure which almost every other investment business sailed through, handing over its £500 deposit and receiving the licence in return. He felt, quite rightly, that the Stock Exchange had not liked him ever since the Hedderwicks affair. The Bank of England would not license him; Jersey had evicted him. But in Gibraltar, as he flew in and out by private jet, smoking his Davidoff cigars and opening a small new office in the centre of town, he was respected.

If Clowes steadfastly refuses to fit any stereotype, his behaviour, and the reactions of others to it, does sometimes fall neatly into cliché. 'A little knowledge is a dangerous thing' encapsulates the man's scattergun investments, in jewellery, computers, shipping companies, hotels (Belgrave), property and other assets. It also goes some way towards explaining why he consistently promised more than he could squeeze out of gilts. And Gibraltar, the kingdom of the blind, regarded Clowes as king. Clowes, totally unused to such official approbation, lapped it up, believed in it, and would allow it to catapult him into new levels of personal extravagance and recklessness.

Even at the apparent pinnacle of his achievement, the launch party in Gibraltar, seeds of destruction were taking root and about to sprout. One of the guests at the party was Richard Hooper, an accountant with the Gibraltar branch of Spicer & Pegler. Hooper, a tall, dark-haired man with classical good looks, had been a partner in the branch for five years when he met Clowes. And now, as auditor to the new Gibraltar company, Barlow Clowes International, he was planning a two-day exploratory visit to the Geneva office to see what was there. One of the things Hooper wanted to do was to check the offshore clients' funds – this had never been done. But if Barlow Clowes International was to manage those funds, receiving management fees for doing so, Hooper wanted to check the funds so that he could verify the fees. And if, as was envisaged, the funds were to be transferred to Barlow Clowes International, it would be good practice to check that there were no problems with the funds which would impact adversely on BCI.[2]

A reconciliation would also expose the fact that millions of pounds of investors' money was being diverted into assets other than gilts. The snapshot process described earlier would involve checking not merely whether the clients' records on the Barlow Clowes computer squared with what the clients themselves believed they had invested. It would also involve looking beyond the computerised records to the assets themselves, confirming that they were all there.

There was an important background to Hooper's desire to check the overseas clients' assets: mingling with the guests at the Gibraltar launch party were two men who had secretly gone behind Peter Clowes's back to recommend to Spicers that the checking be done as soon as possible. One was Derek Tree, the managing director of the UK operations who was a reluctant guest at the party. The other was Robert Posey, the marketing executive in the Geneva office who, aware of Tree's concerns, was becoming increasingly nervous himself about how the overseas funds were being managed. Three weeks before the launch party Posey had held a secret rendezvous with both Pilkington and Hooper at Spicers' offices. 'I told them that I did not want them to repeat to Mr Clowes that I was visiting them privately on this occasion but that I wanted them to know that I felt they should take action as soon as possible to audit the assets under management in all the international portfolios based in Gibraltar,' says Posey.[3]

This was not all. Six days later Posey rang Spicers again, this time speaking to another partner, Nic Lewis. Posey told Lewis that he was worried that Barlow Clowes was falsely marketing the return on the offshore funds as tax free. The brochures appeared to claim that the returns were capital gains generated from buying and selling gilts. Capital gains on gilts were exempt from tax. But if, said Posey, the offshore funds were invested in other assets, surely there would be tax to pay? Posey suggested that these other assets might be cash deposits – the interest from them would be subject to income tax.

Posey's concerns hit home. On 3 September 1986, a fortnight before his launch party, Clowes had met Nic Lewis to discuss his overseas funds. Posey was the invisible instigator – 'he was most anxious his name not be mentioned' – a note of the meeting on Spicers' files reveals. Spicers' record of the meeting also shows how, at the very moment when Clowes was launching himself and his products in Gibraltar, he was admitting privately to his accountants that these products did not work. Clowes started by discussing the 'expected' and 'guaranteed' rates of return which the overseas port-folios advertised as a carrot to entice investors.

'He [Clowes] said that in reality the return was completely fixed and the statement in the brochure that there was a guaranteed rate and a higher expected rate was compete hogwash; the expected rate was in fact certain,' the Spicers memo reads. This was in fact only a fraction of the truth – both rates were absolutely bogus. Clowes then launched into a highly complicated explanation of how he managed to produce capital gains and not income for investors in his offshore funds. His explanation, also false, involved offshore companies and lending of gilts. The note of the meeting suggests that Spicers did not accept everything that Clowes said. At one point when Clowes was describing how Barlow Clowes kept separate from the offshore companies involved in his scheme, the note records: 'It emerged this was also an embellishment.'

Spicers were not happy. The firm considered that the offshore portfolios were flawed and did not achieve the tax effects Clowes claimed. Clowes even lied about the amount of money involved, telling Spicers that about £20 million held offshore was owned by UK residents. The figure was actually far higher, and by the end of the year would be £58 million. But the bottom line from Spicers was clear: it was wrong to market the offshore portfolios as 'tax free' to UK investors. They should be given their money back, or it should be transferred to other Barlow Clowes products which worked, as soon as possible.

The fact that Clowes could still go ahead a fortnight later and launch his company and the same misleading offshore products in Gibraltar shows both his bravado and also how little he feared his own advisers. By a stroke of luck Hooper, the Spicers partner, had not been told about the London office's taxation fears for the overseas products. Hooper would not learn about them until several months later, by which time Clowes was promising to withdraw his overseas products and planning to launch new ones – in conjunction with Spicers!

On 12 August 1986, just over a month before the launch party, a Liberia-registered company, Northern Properties SA, using money belonging to Barlow Clowes investors, bought a high-powered speedboat for $88,500. It was named Pam 1, after Clowes's wife, and moored in Marina Marbella, near Clowes's Marbella flat. On the day the boat was purchased a quite different scene was taking place at the offices of the Department of Trade and Industry. Herbert Smith had sent the Department the renewal forms for Clowes's UK business, and these mentioned, in response to a standard question, his appearance as a prosecution witness in the Hedderwicks trial. The forms also declared that another Barlow Clowes executive, Robin Ducret, had appeared as a witness for the defence in the same trial. Both references were noted but it was standard practice in the DTI to disregard disclosures in license application forms by witnesses in the Hedderwicks trial unless they had been found guilty of an offence. As no one was found guilty, all references were disregarded. A telephone call to the Stock Exchange, which had been deeply unhappy with both Clowes's and Ducret's evidence, might have affected the Department's decision to renew the licenses for either the firm or the individuals – Clowes and Ducret. No call was made.

The duality of Clowes's fantastical lifestyle and ambition and, on the other hand, a myriad of warning signs threatening but never managing to expose that reality, was maintained.

CHAPTER FIFTEEN

·

THE FARCE CONTINUES

·

The battle for boardroom representation at Belgrave Holdings reached its peak around the time of the Gibraltar launch party. The day before the party Clowes and von Cramer had sent a letter to Belgrave's shareholders explaining why they wanted seats on the board. The letter was full of generalities and contained no specific ideas for the development of the Belgrave portfolio of hotels and properties. 'International Securities is a substantial Leichtenstein-based investment company with funds provided by its major share-holders, two charitable foundations,' Clowes wrote. 'Guy Cramer and myself are Directors of International Securities and have been authorised by the trustee shareholders to represent them and seek appointment to the Board of Belgrave.'

The notion that Clowes and von Cramer were representing inde-pendently financed shareholders was a complete sham. The money had come from the Barlow Clowes investors. International Securities was set up by Clowes to disguise this. The authorisation Clowes talked about was his own – he had authorised himself to divert investors' money and to use it to buy a stake in Belgrave.

His explanation was greeted with some scepticism in the ensuing press coverage. In an interview with Clowes, the *Birmingham Post* had asked him directly who the individuals behind International Securities were. The article quoted his response: ' "We cannot reveal who they are," said Mr Clowes last night. "It is illegal under Swiss law to disclose the real owners even with their permission." ' It is clear that this explanation did not satisfy the *Post*: 'Odd that Swiss restrictions should govern what a Liechtenstein company can do. It might all be a bit more credible if Mr Clowes could persuade these shadowy folk to reveal their identity themselves.' The *Sunday Tele-graph* was similarly sceptical. It suggested to its readers that they should support the Belgrave board against Clowes and von Cramer 'unless International provides fuller information on its anonymous major shareholder.'

What lay behind the newspaper's scepticism, however, was not the thought that Clowes may have raided his own investors' funds to finance building his Belgrave stake. Rather they suspected that

Clowes might be acting as a front for Abdul Shamji, the African businessman who had forfeited his holding in Belgrave in the wake of the Johnson Mathey collapse. This was a characteristic reaction to Clowes – and one of the reasons for his success. People may have doubted him, thought that he was cutting corners, a shifty character perhaps. But to do what he was actually doing was so outrageous, so brazen, that people with no inside source of information about the man or his business would not suspect it. If they did, lack of proof, coupled with the libel laws, caused them to hold back or rely on innuendo.

In the case of the Belgrave board, all it could do was to point to inconsistencies in Clowes's explanations of International Securities. Responding on 22 September to Clowes's missive, Sir Montague Prichard wrote to his shareholders:

> Your Board, having considered the letter, remain of the view that no information or proposal has been offered which suggests that either Mr Clowes or Mr von Cramer would make a positive contribution to your Company. The major share-holders of International Securities AG are now stated to be two charitable foundations, as yet unnamed. During my two meetings with Messrs Clowes and von Cramer in the presence of our financial advisers, they stated that the investors in International Securities were expatriate discretionary investment clients of Barlow Clowes Limited. Your Board is still not aware of the identity of the shareholders in International Securities.

Four days later the Belgrave shareholders voted overwhelmingly against the motion to accept Clowes and von Cramer on the board of the company. The two pretenders won only 2.2 per cent of the votes cast, apart from their own shares held through International Securities. This would not, however, be the end of the Belgrave story. Clowes issued a press release saying that he was still seeking a place on the board, and there the matter rested for the time being.

The Belgrave defeat was a minor setback for Clowes but was nothing compared to the danger he faced from another quarter. While the Belgrave battle was raging Hooper, the Spicer & Pegler partner, had made his two-day exploratory visit to the Geneva office of Barlow Clowes. In Geneva he had found both administrative chaos and strong indications of fraud. On the plane back to Gibraltar, he wrote out a memorandum to Pilkington in London.

The memorandum contains several indications that investors' funds were being misused. 'It appears that cash required to fund the Geneva office is routinely taken from the clients' funds in round sum transfers,' Hooper wrote. The investors were paying for the expenses of running the Geneva office, Hooper continued, pointing out that the records showed £33 million received from Barlow Clowes investors but only £5 million of this being transferred to the account maintained to pay for gilts purchases. Although he did not say it explicitly, the question following on from this was clear: what had happened to the other £28 million? There was more: 'I trust the reconciliation work will explain what the other apparent payments described as – loan account £221,000, inter-company loans £3.4 million, transfer international system £3.5 million and portfolio transfer £8.7 million – actually relate to. No one in Geneva appears to have the remotest idea.'

This was disturbing. No one in the Geneva office could or would explain what payments recorded in the office of over £10 million represented. Hooper could see that he would have to do more than merely check that clients' records matched the underlying assets held on their behalf. He listed three more tasks:

- how to check the commission fees payable to Barlow Clowes & Partners (Jersey) and against which it appears substantial drawings have been made.
- how we can be sure that there is no switching of assets out of other funds to 'balance the books' for audit purposes at 30 September 1986.
- to what extent we should look at the overall day-to-day procedures and control of client funds since the fund first started.

The 'substantial drawings' Hooper referred to were from clients' funds. A possible explanation for funding the Geneva office from clients' funds was that these were simply payments on account of commissions properly due to Barlow Clowes for managing the investors' money. In reality, Clowes was not earning anything like enough from straightforward commissions to make the offshore operation viable. He therefore used clients' money to fund office expenses. Clowes was not entitled to claim any initial commission out of the clients' money when they first sent it in. The Barlow Clowes brochures told clients that their 'capital is 100% invested because there is no initial fee or bid/offer spread'. And yet he paid his three main intermediaries who generated most of the offshore funds a 2 per cent initial commission. So he was down 2 per cent to start with. He was entitled to an annual management fee equivalent to 1.5 per cent a year, but only out of any profit he made over and above the returns he was declaring to investors. Those returns were simply made up. The fees, the commissions and the returns were all figments of Clowes's imagination. They did not exist in reality. They were part of the multimillion-pound sham that Barlow Clowes's offshore funds represented.

Hooper's second concern – switching between funds to balance the books – was well founded. This was 'teaming and lading', the favourite Clowes trick to make sure he always showed the correct amount of money in a particular fund when it was being checked. He took from one fund that was not being looked at and put it, perhaps only temporarily, in another that was. Hooper wanted to safeguard against it. This was one of the great advantages to Clowes of running a separate fund, over which he had complete control, in Jersey. It could operate, when necessary, as a private top-up fund. Hooper's plan was to prevent this from happening – both the Jersey funds and the UK funds would be audited as at the same date. A simultaneous audit would examine whether on that particular date both the UK and Jersey funds contained the right amount of money. It was tantamount to pinning both Clowes's shoulders to the ground at the same time. So far he had always managed to keep one off the ground.[1]

There was one snag: the computer. The records showing how much money was in the offshore fund and where it had been invested were accessible to only two people: Clowes and Naylor. Only they knew fully how the system worked. They had set up a massive computer system, linking Geneva with London, Manchester and recently Gibraltar, but at the same time devised secret pathways and passwords which they alone knew. Computers had been Clowes's plaything and his obsession and he used them to facilitate the secret diversion of investors' funds.

Hooper asked Clowes for the necessary information from the computer to allow him to conduct the reconciliation. Clowes, who referred to the information as 'the matrix', promised that it would be sent. Meanwhile, Hooper started work, instructing the Geneva staff to circularise a letter to clients in the offshore portfolios, asking them to confirm that the balance showing against their name in the computer records matched with the amount they believed they were owed. Over 2000 letters were sent out to investors in Portfolio 28. This was stage one of the audit – reconciling the client records with clients themselves. Stage two was to check the underlying assets with the records and for that Hooper needed the matrix. It did not arrive so Hooper sent a reminder to Clowes, who again promised to deliver it. But, despite further reminders, the matrix had still not been delivered by the end of 1986, three months after Hooper's memorandum to Pilkington.

Pilkington had also been putting pressure on Clowes. He recalled how when Spicers had audited the UK side of Barlow Clowes to get the licence from the Department of Trade, surplus funds had been found which Clowes said belonged to the offshore side. Spicers had accepted Clowes's explanation that this was an administrative error. Now Pilkington, in his own words, 'wanted to be happy that both UK and offshore were complete in themselves and were not, if you like, still overlapping'.[2] And he had Richard Fleck of Herbert Smith on his side, too. Pilkington wrote to Clowes on 20 November saying that the client reconciliation work had to be done if the Ferguson deal was to go through. 'Both Richard Fleck and I expressed the view that in addition to the audit of the accounts of the companies to be acquired it will also be essential for the client accounts (both in the UK and overseas) to be audited before the acquisition is completed and we sign off on the accounts of the companies and the partnership.' Clowes did not reply. Pilkington sent a reminder just before Christmas, saying that he still did not have the necessary information. A fortnight later, when Clowes and Pilkington met at the Poynton headquarters, Clowes promised to provide the client information before Hooper signed off the accounts for BCI. Clowes was under pressure now from all sides. The Inland Revenue had been probing the overseas side of the Barlow Clowes business, pressing Clowes for the names and addresses of the hundred largest clients of the offshore funds. Exasperated by his lack of response they served a notice on him, demanding details of every investor for whom Clowes had bought gilts exceeding £5000 in the year subsequent to bondwashing being curtailed. The Revenue wanted to know how Clowes was still able to offer a tax-free return from gilts. By a strange coincidence its notice arrived on the day that Clowes had a face-to-face meeting with Spicers in which Nic Lewis confirmed his view that the offshore funds did not work for tax purposes. Clowes could not legitimately offer a tax-free return to UK investors from Portfolios 68 and 28. The answer to the Revenue's notice was simple. Clowes had bought gilts exceeding £5000 for thousands of UK investors, falsely claiming to each one that, despite the demise of bondwashing, their return was tax free. The Revenue's notice was not made public and therefore did not stem the flow of money pouring in: in October 1986, the same month that the Revenue served its notice, a record £6.5 million was invested in Portfolio 28, one of the two main overseas funds. Even taking into account withdrawals by investors and monthly distributions of 'income' this still left £5.8 million in new money for the month: £180,000 a day sent to Peter Clowes to manage.[3]

Meanwhile, it was taking a long time for Clowes to implement his master plan: the takeover of Barlow Clowes by Ferguson. The Stock Exchange, after suspending Ferguson's shares, was insisting on Ferguson shareholders being given a five-year trading record on Barlow Clowes, as a condition of Ferguson regaining its quotation. The circular to Ferguson shareholders would have to show how profitable or otherwise Barlow Clowes had been over the past five years. And it was not simply a question of supplying a figure – a loss or a profit – for each year. The circular also had to show where the money earned by Barlow Clowes had come from. This posed another difficulty for Clowes. Since the days of his advertising campaign in 1983 and 1984 he had rerouted investors' money into his Barlow Clowes business, calling it 'software licensing' income – from Hermes Management Services, the Gibraltar-registered front company which was supposedly paying Clowes for the privilege of using the Barlow Clowes software. Hermes helped Clowes in two ways: first, it paid for large items of expenditure, such as the advertising campaign. In the context of the master plan, however, Hermes had another very important function: to inflate the profits of Barlow Clowes. The more profitable Barlow Clowes appeared to be, the greater the price Clowes could command for it. If Barlow Clowes were to be bought for, say, ten times its annual profits after tax, every £100,000 of bogus Hermes profits would be worth £1 million to Clowes.

The problem was that the Hermes income would fall within the audit of Barlow Clowes and the presentation of the five-year track record on which the accountants were working. Two sets of accountants were involved: Spicer & Pegler was auditing the Barlow Clowes companies; Touche Ross, another of the largest accountancy practices in the country, was Ferguson's accountants, and would have to examine the Barlow Clowes acquisition from Ferguson's point of view. This would entail preparing a written evaluation of the Barlow Clowes businesses, known colloquially as a 'long form report'. A condensed version of this report would have to appear in the circular and it would be Touche Ross, rather than Spicers, who would sign the audit certificate for the Barlow Clowes business as a whole, stating that the figures in its report presented an accurate picture of the company and its finances. Clowes's problem was that Spicers and Touche Ross would both see the Hermes income and require explanations and proof as to how it arose, all the more so because, by the time of his master plan, the bogus Hermes income was the only thing keeping Barlow Clowes afloat. Clowes was losing heavily on his gilts business. The 'gilts specialist' had not, even when bond-washing was at its height, made a genuine profit out of gilts. The master plan entailed Clowes putting his artificially supported Barlow Clowes business under the microscope of two sets of accountants, not to mention the Stock Exchange and a whole range of other advisers involved in putting together the deal. To a rational human being, who fears detection when he has done something wrong, the master plan appeared suicidal. To Clowes it was merely a stepping stone on the road to creating a financial services empire, using the Ferguson shares to buy up other companies.

Investors' money was still being used for his corporate forays. Clowes had not lost interest in C.H. Bailey and its quoted subsidiary, Bristol Channel Ship Repairers. Indeed there had been speculation that chairman Christopher Bailey might be on the verge of selling his subsidiary to Clowes. The speculation had been fuelled by the fact that Bailey had reduced its holding in Bristol Channel to below 50 per cent. Was this the prelude to a sale to Clowes and his interests? On 21 October the *Evening Standard* reported that 'the Barlow Clowes fund management is cagey about its increasing involvement with the world of Christopher Bailey and his two ship-repairing businesses'. The following month Bailey announced that it was negotiating the possible sale of its 46 per cent interest. Clowes – or, rather, his unwitting investors – was obviously the potential buyer.

Meanwhile the farce continued. Three days earlier Brian Gent, the Deputy Head of Banking Supervision at the Bank of England, wrote to Laurence Green, the principal in charge of licensing at the DTI. Gent wanted to know what had come of Tree's warning of a possible fraud which the Bank had conveyed to the DTI in August. Gent explained that the Bank's interest stemmed partly from Midland Bank's involvement (Midland was one of the principal bankers to the offshore funds), and because of Barlow Clowes's large holdings in gilts.

While writing about Tree he also imparted more news about the overseas operations:

> We understand that Barlow Clowes are now very well estab-
> lished and active in Gibraltar and are installing significant
> computer capacity. It occurs to me that they may be conduct-
> ing much of their business over there rather than in the UK,
> even where the clients are resident here; though whether
> this would be to escape your regulatory controls or whether
> it might be associated with tax advantages, I do not know.

This was a good point. If Barlow Clowes International was selling to UK residents it should have been licensed. The Bank of England had got it right. But the Department of Trade, head down and stumbling from one room to another, did not see this.

Green, who had inherited the Barlow Clowes problem at the DTI, replied a few days later:

> I have no concrete reason to worry about Barlow Clowes'
> off-shore expansion, although one naturally tends to look
> askance at businesses controlled from Gibraltar and harbour
> unworthy thoughts about the real motives in moving there.
> If the overseas business is carrying on the business of dealing
> in securities in the UK it will need authorisation under the
> present legislation.

Had Green allowed himself to follow through his unworthy thoughts the course of events might have changed. As for Tree's warning, he had discussed this on the telephone with Pilkington of Spicers. In the absence of hard evidence Pilkington had told Green that he would be extra thorough when auditing Barlow Clowes, and give Tree an opportunity to unburden himself. Nothing would be done for the time being, as Green wrote in his reply to Gent: 'We have received no complaints about Barlow Clowes and have no cause for concern apart from your report of Mr Tree's worries – and these are nowhere near enough to justify regulatory action by the Depart-ment. If you become aware of any other straws in the wind, I would be glad to learn of them.'

Green's reference to a lack of complaints from investors is interesting because it throws further light on Clowes's techniques.

Clowes was very careful to keep his investors happy. He instilled into his staff that they should never become involved in a dispute with a client. If clients of Portfolio 30 wanted their money back early, they were given a complete refund, even though, under the strict terms of their agreement with Barlow Clowes, they were not entitled to one, and Barlow Clowes often lost money in giving it. But it was part and parcel of the business of keeping the clients happy. Happy clients meant no complaints. And the DTI, harbouring unworthy thoughts and regarding the warnings of a Barlow Clowes managing director as straws in the winds, considered investor complaints as a vitally important litmus test of whether a business was operating properly. They were and still are an indicator of wrongdoing, but Clowes was a step ahead, making sure there were no flashing lights to upset the Department. That was one of his most important hall-marks: he kept his customers happy – too happy in fact, offering them more than he could legitimately deliver.

Meanwhile, on 24 November, between the Bank of England's letter and the Department of Trade's reply, a payment of £43,894.97 was transferred directly from a Barlow Clowes offshore clients account with Midland Bank to a firm of builders in Surrey. The builders, P. Howard & Sons, were renovating Naylor's home, Send Barns. It had been Naylor's alleged fabrication of client records which had partly triggered Tree's report of a possible fraud in the first place. Now, as the authorities wrote to one another about Tree's warning, Naylor was taking money directly from a Midland account to renovate his home. The renovation costs would come to over £430,000, much of it coming from Midland client accounts.

CHAPTER SIXTEEN

.

THE HERMES FIDDLE

.

The turn of the year saw no let up in the feverish activity of the professional advisers called in by Clowes and his associates to put the master plan into effect. Audits had to be carried out, the circular to Ferguson shareholders was being drafted and new team members were recruited by Clowes and von Cramer to give Ferguson and its purchase of Barlow Clowes an added layer of respectability.

Stanley Wright, a former high-ranking civil servant in the Treasury, was persuaded to join the Ferguson board as a non-executive director. His appointment was due to von Cramer and his connections; Cramer was friendly with Geoffrey Drain, the ex-Bank of England director, who suggested to Wright that he might like to meet von Cramer and his father Peter. The four men had dinner together, followed later by a meeting with Clowes, who explained his plans for Ferguson. Wright thought Clowes was 'earnest and rather dour' and was struck by Clowes's 'almost evangelical enthusiasm for computers' and how they should be used to support the management of private investors' money.

Von Cramer also introduced merchant bank Singer & Friedlander to the deal. While not top-flight, Singer had a good reputation, particularly for advising smaller companies. Singer had originally been asked by von Cramer to advise on the possible bid for Bristol Channel Ship Repairers. When this fell through in mid-January von Cramer asked David Courtman, the head of Singer's office in Leeds, whether the bank would act for Ferguson in the takeover of Barlow Clowes. After checking on von Cramer and Clowes with the other professional firms involved, Courtman agreed to come on board. With Touche Ross as the reporting accountants, Singer as merchant bank advisers and Wright as a main board director of Ferguson, the master plan would have far greater credibility.

The recruitment of Singer and Wright, however, served only to widen still further the gap between appearance and reality. While they were being brought in, Clowes was implementing his largest diversion of investors' funds to date: the transfer of £12 million into a Gibraltar front company called Lyceum Holdings. The plan was to use the £12 million to provide Ferguson with working capital and money to make acquisitions after the purchase of Barlow Clowes was completed. By January 1987 over £5 million had already been removed from Barlow Clowes's clients account with Midland Bank in Jersey. On 7 January another £1.25 million was removed. For the time being it was placed in bank accounts with Chase Manhattan and Charterhouse Bank in the Channel Islands, awaiting further instructions. On the same day, Clowes met with Spicers and told them that he would shut down the overseas portfolios and launch new projects. He said that he wanted to get out of tax-avoidance schemes altogether. Spicers agreed to explore the idea of working together on new schemes. Nothing would come of it, but Clowes was already working on projects which, if the investors liked them, would avoid the insurmountable alternative of giving them their money back.

Another aspect of the master plan was for Barlow Clowes to become a member of the Stock Exchange, and an application for membership was submitted in January 1987. Clowes had recruited Bernard Osborne, an experienced gilts dealer, to steer Barlow Clowes to corporate membership of the Exchange. In effect Barlow Clowes's UK company, Barlow Clowes Ltd, would be a stockbroking firm, able to buy and sell shares and gilts on behalf of Barlow Clowes clients and members of the general public. Membership of the Stock Exchange would certainly lend more credibility to the master plan since it was a far tougher process, involving more detailed scrutiny than the Department of Trade's licensed dealer requirements. But there were other, more sinister advantages to being a Stock Exchange member. If he owned a stockbroking firm, Clowes could channel all his illicit share purchases through that firm. By keeping the deals in-house the chances of detection would be reduced. There would be an added layer of secrecy since Clowes would not, as he was doing at the moment, need to instruct outside firms of stockbrokers to buy and sell shares on his behalf. The same would apply to his gilts dealings, although here the benefit would not be in terms of added secrecy but in commissions: Clowes could charge his clients commission on the gilts dealings he effected on their behalf, rather than pay that commission to other brokers whom he was currently instructing. As a member of the Stock Exchange, Barlow Clowes could itself float companies on the stock market. For a man such as Clowes, with several 'investments' in private companies, this could be a very advantageous facility.

On 28 January Osborne and Chris Newman, the Barlow Clowes finance director, had a meeting at the Stock Exchange to discuss the application for membership. The Exchange was represented by Barbara Anderson, from its Membership Department, and a medium-sized, slightly dishevelled gentleman with thick, black-rimmed glasses. His name was Julian Varney.

Varney worked in the Surveillance Division of the Stock Exchange and had been keeping a casual eye on Barlow Clowes for over a year, since the Hedderwicks trial. He was an experienced investigator who had come to the Exchange from the Bank of England. While at the Bank he had spent three years tracking down currency fraudsters. He slept most nights with a pencil and notepad by his bed in case he woke up in the middle of the night with a new angle or thought on an investigation he was pursuing.

It was standard practice to involve the Surveillance Division in a membership application since people who sought membership of the Exchange were subjected to a considerable degree of vetting. But Varney was a special case. Bob Wilkinson, head of the Surveillance Division and Varney's boss, had been one of those warning the DTI about Barlow Clowes back in 1984, before it had been licensed. Wilkinson had also been furious at Clowes's evidence at the Hedderwicks trial. He had marked Clowes as a man to watch, and deputed Varney to the job.

The 28 January meeting was merely an exploratory discussion for the Exchange to find out more about Barlow Clowes. Varney thought he noticed a reluctance on Newman's part to discuss other companies within the Barlow Clowes group, such as the Gibraltar-based Barlow Clowes International. He also noticed that Newman and Osborne made no mention of Barlow Clowes's corporate finance activities. This was strange because the latest accounts for Barlow Clowes and Partners Ltd, the company applying for membership, showed that it had received a fee of over £150,000 from an overseas company for giving corporate finance advice. Varney asked to see Barlow Clowes's brochures and the accounts of other companies within the Barlow Clowes group, and there the matter lay for the time being.

On the day of the Stock Exchange meeting, the Hermes 'software licensing' problem reared its head. Clowes was claiming that he had earned a total of £2.1 million over the past three and a half years, by licensing Barlow Clowes's software to Hermes, which, he said, was a fund management group, based in Jersey, with its own separate clients. Clowes assured Spicer & Pegler that the software licensing income was a *bona fide* commercial transaction. But Touche Ross, the Ferguson accountants, learned of the Hermes income only on 28

January when reviewing the Spicer & Pegler papers on Barlow Clowes. Stuart Counsell, the Touche Ross partner in charge of the Ferguson account, was very concerned.

On the face of it the Hermes income looked suspicious. It was the largest single contributor to Barlow Clowes's profits – without it the business would have shown heavy losses. And yet Clowes had never previously mentioned it to Touche Ross and there was no written agreement between Hermes and Barlow Clowes governing payment. Counsell immediately decided to do some checking for himself. He contacted the Touche Ross office in Jersey and asked it to send someone to Hermes's offices on the island to collect Hermes's sales brochures. He also gave instructions for company searches to be made of Hermes Management Services and a related company, Hermes Computer Software, which according to Clowes was to take over the software licensing arrangement with Barlow Clowes.

It did not take Touche Ross very long to discover that the Hermes 'office' in Jersey was merely an accommodation address at which there were no sales brochures. Moreover, the company searches had revealed that one of the Hermes Management Services shareholders was the Jersey lawyer Conrad Winston Whitehead, who had acted for Clowes.

Counsell, an experienced accountant of some twelve years' standing, suspected that the Hermes arrangement was a sham. But his suspicions did not go far enough. He thought that Clowes and von Cramer were using Hermes to repatriate their own capital under the disguise of Barlow Clowes income. If true this would be virtually certain to kill the Ferguson acquisition of Barlow Clowes stone dead: it represented a covert attempt to increase the amount Ferguson would pay by inflating Barlow Clowes's supposed profits.

The truth was far worse: Clowes was not using his own capital to inflate Barlow Clowes's profits, he was using his investors' funds. To do this in such a crude way, with no supporting documents and a couple of front companies – and then have independent accountants examine the flimsy disguise – was recklessness bordering on self-destruction. But Clowes rationalised his behaviour into a legitimate form – perhaps by saying to himself that the Hermes income represented fees due to Barlow Clowes. This would be the springboard. His view of himself as invincible, founded on years of successful deception, would do the rest.

This time, however, he faced a mountain of scepticism from highly respected firms of accountants and merchant bankers who had their own reputations to consider. If the master plan went ahead both Singer and Touche Ross would have their names on the circular sent to shareholders. Touche Ross would have to declare the financial information about Barlow Clowes to be fair and reasonable. Singer would be recommending the acquisition to Ferguson shareholders. How could either firm do this if it had serious doubts, as they both did, about the major source of profits to Barlow Clowes?

Events moved quickly. On Tuesday 3 February Courtman and Counsell met von Cramer to discuss the Hermes income. Von Cramer was chief executive of Ferguson and therefore closely involved in the plan to purchase Barlow Clowes. He told the meeting that none of the Barlow Clowes executives was financially interested in Hermes Management Services. He described it as a fund management group with between twenty and thirty clients. 'At this point,' according to one person present at the meeting, 'Cramer was asked directly by David Courtman whether these funds originated from drugs, racketeering or prostitution and was given a definite no for an answer.'

Cramer may merely have been repeating what Clowes had dishonestly told him. On 4 February, the day after von Cramer's meeting, Clowes flew to Gibraltar and back at a cost of just over £8000. The purpose of his visit was to instruct his Gibraltar lawyers to draw up a software licensing agreement between Hermes Computer Software and Barlow Clowes. The agreement stipulated that Barlow Clowes would be paid an up-front fee of £250,000, and £360,000 a year for licensing its software to Hermes. It was, like everything else connected with Hermes, a sham, but its aim was to persuade the advisers that Hermes was a legitimate company using Barlow Clowes's 'expertise'. Here was a written agreement to prove it. In fact Hermes was a double sham. Not only were there no genuine software licensing arrangements but the Barlow Clowes software, as we have seen, was not worth licensing. It had difficulty servicing Barlow Clowes's own clients let alone those of outside companies who might want it for their own clients.

For Clowes, deception had become a matter of routine. The day after returning from Gibraltar with the bogus licensing agreement he arranged for the transfer of a further £5 million from the investors' accounts into bank accounts in the name of Lyceum Holdings, the Gibraltar front company disguising the intended use of these funds to provide working capital for Ferguson. It would not be a straightforward arrangement. The plan was that the investors' money in Lyceum would be used to secure a loan to Ferguson from the Bank of Credit and Commerce International (BCCI). It was another back-to-back loan of the type Clowes had used in the past. BCCI would

153

lend Ferguson £12 million, on the security of Lyceum's matching deposit of £12 million.

The Lyceum back-to-back arrangement was far and away the largest Clowes had ever attempted. Like the Hermes sham, Lyceum would be questioned by accountants. Assurances would be sought from Clowes about Lyceum and why it was guaranteeing such a large loan. Judging by what he did next these considerations were far from Clowes's mind. On Thursday 5 February he chartered Robert Maxwell's Gulfstream jet to fly him for a three-day break to Saint Martin in the Caribbean Leeward Islands, where he joined his family who were already holidaying there. It was his greatest act of extravagance to date, the round trip costing over £60,000. A telex confirming details of the flight reads: 'PS. Bollinger quite acceptable.'

The Hermes problem still remained when Clowes returned. His advisers wanted to know why the payments from Hermes over the past three years had been so uneven: £750,000 in 1984, only £250,000 the following year and £1.1 million for the fifteen-month period to September 1986. Why the disparity? Clowes threw explanations at his advisers like confetti at a wedding: the introduction of personal equity plans had led to an increase in the servicing Hermes had required from Barlow Clowes. The fall in the stock market had caused a downturn in demand. Hermes was a company with £100 million under management, Clowes explained, and it planned to expand into the United States. It already had offices in Jersey, Geneva and the Isle of Man.

Clowes's master plan was driving him to ever greater heights of deception which, in turn, were bound to make him more vulnerable to detection. Hermes had started as a small, covert operation to reroute investors' funds into Barlow Clowes. The master plan necessitated it being subjected to public scrutiny for the first time. Clowes himself had put it under the microscope. There was an element of naivety as well as brazenness in his behaviour – Clowes probably thought that he would be able to wave the Hermes deal through the accountants and merchant bankers. The master plan was, after all, his first experience of a public takeover bid and all the verification procedures such a bid normally entails. When dealing with the Department of Trade, the advisers had been on his side, instructed by him with a clearly defined goal: to get him a license. The Ferguson deal was a far more public affair and the advisers' responsibilities extended beyond Clowes to the independent shareholders in Ferguson.

The pressures on Clowes to support his Hermes arrangement

eventually led him to produce a file of correspondence between Hermes Management Services and various Barlow Clowes employees. The letters went back as far as 1983 and described the various software licensing arrangements between the two companies. Every letter was fabricated. The letterheading on the Hermes letters had been designed in 1986 – and yet the letters purported to go back to 1983.

Hermes was not his only difficulty. There was the reconciliation of the offshore funds for which Spicer & Pegler was pressing. Any examination of the underlying assets would show that tens of millions of pounds of this money were not in gilts. Clowes himself did not know where all the money he had diverted had gone. He had not prepared any written record of his massive spending spree with the offshore investors' money. Even a cursory scrutiny of the offshore funds would destroy the master plan, and Clowes with it.

Clowes had a simple solution: in late February, he told Spicers that the offshore funds – and the two partnerships which controlled them – would not, after all, be acquired by Ferguson. They were no longer part of the deal. Ferguson would buy only Barlow Clowes's UK operations and the new Gibraltar company, Barlow Clowes International. It was a brazen solution since Clowes was effectively taking out the heart of his business before selling it to Ferguson. He told Pilkington, however, that he would transfer the overseas partnerships and transfer the funds either to his UK company or Barlow Clowes International – after the purchase of Barlow Clowes by Ferguson was complete.[1]

By this stage Touche Ross and Singer & Friedlander were seriously considering whether they could withdraw from the deal. Courtman of Singer knew there were other Singer executives who wanted to pull out. A committee of senior executives at Singer had decided that they would not support the issue of new shares that Ferguson was making alongside its acquisition of Barlow Clowes. Known in stock market terms as a rights issue, it entailed Ferguson issuing 6.9 million new shares at 75p each to raise £4.6 million net of expenses. Singer would not endorse this price for the new Ferguson shares – there was no real basis for it other than the inflated value before the Ferguson shares were suspended by the Stock Exchange. The question then was whether, if Singer would not support the rights issue, it could continue to back the rest of the transaction, in particular the purchase of Barlow Clowes. Some of the senior executives wanted the bank to pull out altogether. The majority had supported staying with the Barlow Clowes purchase on the grounds that, without it, the outside shareholders in Ferguson who had no connection with the board would be left with a company with little or no prospects.

Touche Ross had done some soul searching of its own, examining how it was that the firm had come to act for the 'ex-barrow boy' von Cramer and Ferguson in the first place. Von Cramer had been introduced to Touche Ross's Leeds office by a local firm of accountants. Touche Ross had also refused to support one aspect of the Ferguson deal: Clowes originally wanted to include a profit forecast for Ferguson, stating what its profits were likely to be in the year to 31 March 1987. These would be £608,000, he said, heralding a return to profitability for Ferguson for the first time in years. The master plan would look so much better with this news. But Touche Ross refused to put its name to it. It was rightly suspicious about the genuineness of the forecast profits; most of the profits seemed to be coming from one-off deals rather than a continuing trade, or from projects with people who were or might be linked to Clowes. Clowes had gone too far; the accountants refused to endorse the forecast.

Singer and Touche Ross met secretly on Friday 6 March to discuss whether they could continue. Words such as 'crooks', 'cheating' and 'fiddle' were bandied about during the course of the meeting, which occasionally grew acrimonious. But they were committed to a deal which was due to be announced to the Stock Exchange within the next fortnight. Could they pull out?

If only the advisers could have had a window on parallel events in the Geneva office of Barlow Clowes they would have killed the Ferguson deal stone dead. While Singer and Touche Ross were debating what to do, the Geneva office had been thrown into turmoil by Robert Posey, the marketing executive who had secretly been asking Spicers to audit the offshore funds. Posey now led a revolt which threatened to bring Barlow Clowes crashing down. He was extremely concerned that, acting on instructions from London, staff in the Geneva office had transferred millions of pounds of clients' monies into a series of companies and assets which had nothing to do with gilts. These included payments to computer companies, jewellery companies, property groups and millions of pounds into dummy companies. With the help of the Geneva staff, Posey compiled a list of fifty-six payments from clients' accounts which appeared suspect, totalling more than £20 million. He fired off a series of memos to Clowes, Naylor and staff at the Geneva office. 'It is of particular concern to me as the investment portfolios are based on British Government Securities and the transfer from these client accounts appear to be made to private companies or individuals,' Posey wrote in a memo to the office staff. 'It appears to me that many of the companies to which funds have been transferred have a relationship with Peter Clowes and Dr Peter Naylor.' Posey was more diplomatic with Clowes and Naylor although his underlying fears and suspicions shone through. 'No one would think of questioning your own integrity as managers of the funds under investment in Portfolios 28 and 68 but it is now essential that an audit of all funds under management in these portfolios be carried out . . . in order to assure that our promotion of these investments as being based on British Government Securities is a fair representation.'

According to Posey's version of events later presented at the Barlow Clowes trial, the Geneva office was in turmoil with staff threatening to go to the police. His motive, he said, was to try to contain the situation. But another executive recalled Posey himself saying openly that client funds were being used to pay for 'Bentleys and lavish trips in private jets together with running a bunch of companies on unsecured loans'.

On Thursday 7 March Posey faxed a list of all the suspect transfers to Doc Naylor who immediately called him and said that Clowes would explain everything. Clowes had to act quickly. If news of the revolt in the Geneva office leaked out it would kill the Ferguson deal stone dead and Barlow Clowes with it.

Naylor was immediately dispatched to the Geneva office, arriving the following day. Meanwhile Clowes phoned Posey assuring him that all the transfers made from the client accounts were legitimate. He agreed to provide a written assurance that all the transfers had been made in the best interests of the investors. By the time Naylor arrived Posey had already prepared two lists showing the transfers from clients' accounts with Lloyds and Midland together with a form of wording stating that the transfers were legitimate. He wanted Naylor to take these back to Clowes to sign.

Clowes and Posey spoke several times over the phone during the weekend. Clowes promised to set up a new structure with a bank overseeing investment decisions and an investment committee to review decisions regularly. Posey appeared reassured. Naylor flew back to Geneva on the Sunday with the lists signed by him and Clowes. The two lists, which later became known as 'letters of comfort', stated: 'These transfers represent investments made on behalf of the relevant portfolios in the best interests of the clients.' The staff felt reassured. The crisis in the Geneva office had been averted, at least for the time being.[2]

But Clowes was taking no chances. Within days he had arranged for a convoy of lorries to transfer the Geneva office's equipment, furniture and its records of several thousand investors to Gibraltar.

The letters of comfort were dated Friday 6 March, the same day as the meeting between Singer and Touche Ross. Once again the Barlow Clowes affair had descended to the level of farce. If only the characters in Singer's Leeds office on that Friday could have known what was going on simultaneously in Barlow Clowes's Geneva office, Clowes's master plan would have collapsed. But Clowes's story so far is one of survival and success, facilitated by separate pockets of information, parallel lines of communication which never overlapped – in short by the frailties and inadequacies of human communication. If his story sometimes appears like a farce it also had tragic under-tones, the missed opportunities and unfortunate coincidences of a Thomas Hardy plot.

Singer and Touche Ross discussed a broad range of subjects at the 6 March meeting, ranging from the Hermes software licensing income to the interest-free loans Clowes had ostensibly made to some of the companies in the Barlow Clowes group. These 'loans' were in fact Barlow Clowes investors' money which Clowes had diverted while establishing his network of private companies. Clowes had used this money to buy majority stakes in private companies such as Mekom and to make loans to finance their expansion plans. Now he was selling his stake in Mekom, and a couple of other private companies, to Ferguson. In return he would receive shares in Ferguson. In effect he was converting the investors' money into Ferguson shares for himself. Doubtless Clowes would tell himself that these Ferguson shares were being held by him only as a custodian for the investors. They of course knew nothing of the arrangements and would have been horrified if they had. They thought their money was in gilts – not in a third-rate public company.

The Hermes software licensing income was the main topic of discussion: was it a completely genuine source of income? But it was very late in the day for Singer or Touche Ross to pull out – after several months' work the circular to shareholders announcing the deal was due to be sent out in a fortnight. Could the advisers put their name to it? In the end they decided that they could. The case against Hermes was not proven; there was no hard evidence to show that it was a fiddle.

Singer's decision to continue with the master plan was largely based on the view that it would be in the best interests of the outside shareholders in Ferguson. Touche Ross decided to proceed – but Counsell would make sure that the Hermes income would be very prominently disclosed in the circular to Ferguson shareholders. They could see for themselves that Barlow Clowes was being propped up by software licensing income and that it was losing money on gilts. But both Touche Ross and Spicers needed written assurances from Barlow Clowes about the Hermes income. This is standard practice in the accountancy profession, the assurances being contained in letters known as 'letters of representation'. In a sense they are really letters of comfort, with the directors promising that everything is legitimate. The letter to Spicers, signed by Clowes and Chris Newman, the Barlow Clowes finance director, read: 'There is no connection between the partnership and Hermes Management Services Limited or Hermes Computer Services.' It went on to describe the payments of £2.1 million which Barlow Clowes had received from Hermes as 'arm's length fees for services and facilities provided'.

The 6 March meeting was a turning point for Clowes. But it was not the only obstacle he faced. The master plan also needed clearance from the Stock Exchange and the Takeover Panel to succeed.

The Stock Exchange had taken a tough line on the Barlow Clowes acquisition. It had suspected that the Ferguson share price was being 'ramped' – this had been a factor behind the suspension. It was also highly relevant to the Barlow Clowes deal. The Exchange's rules say that a publicly quoted company whose shares are dealt with on the main stock market must have a minimum of 25 per cent of its shares in public hands. The directors and their families can hold three-quarters and no more. The junior market, called the Unlisted Securities Market (USM), has different rules – only 15 per cent of the shares need to be held by outside shareholders of USM companies.

Ferguson was a fully quoted company, so it was subject to the 25 per cent rule. Clowes and von Cramer had the option of stepping down to the USM but that would have diminished Ferguson's status still further and they preferred to maintain a full listing. The problem was that the purchase of Barlow Clowes involved issuing 12 million new Ferguson shares to Clowes and his associates, which would give them 42 per cent of Ferguson. Added to the stakes of von Cramer and other directors, just over 74 per cent of Ferguson shares would be in non-public hands. It was a tight squeeze. The Stock Exchange wanted to be sure that the limit was not being breached and asked Rensburg for a list of the ten largest outside shareholders. These included several nominee companies which Clowes had assured Rensburg were independent of him and his associates. This was not true. The second company on the list sent to the Exchange was Sandover Limited, which looked like an ordinary UK registered company; in fact it was a Gibraltar-registered nominee company set up by Clowes to buy Ferguson and other shares using Barlow Clowes investors' money. This was not the only company on the list that was fronting for Clowes. Clowes had already spent several million pounds of the Barlow Clowes investors' money secretly buying James Ferguson shares. All in all Clowes would divert £17 million into the Ferguson shares, so that the unwitting investors would eventually own a staggering 92 per cent of the company. It was not a public company in any genuine way. Clowes and his associates held well above 75 per cent. But the Stock Exchange, relying on the advisers who in turn relied on Peter Clowes, was fooled.

Clowes also had to face the Takeover Panel. The Panel administers and enforces the Takeover Code, a non-statutory set of rules governing publicly quoted companies and their takeover deals. Rule 9 of the Code states that if a person acquires 30 per cent or more of a public company he must make a cash takeover bid for the rest of the company. Clowes and his associates had stated that they would own 42 per cent of Ferguson after the Barlow Clowes deal. Strictly speaking, under Rule 9 he would have to make a cash bid. This would scupper his plans since Ferguson would, assuming Clowes could raise the money, become a private company. However, the Panel sometimes allows a waiver of Rule 9, known colloquially as a 'whitewash'. The Panel agreed to whitewash Clowes for a number of mainly technical reasons, and because the Ferguson deal was to be put to shareholders. It could not go through unless the 'independent' shareholders in Ferguson supported it.

What the Panel did not know, however, was that many of the independent shareholders were simply Clowes himself hiding behind nominee companies. Clowes had added the Takeover Panel to the line of venerable institutions which he had fooled in his career of deception.

There was one final act of confusion which helped Clowes on his way. Touche Ross had to review Spicers' files on Barlow Clowes in their capacity as Ferguson's advisers. But the Hooper memorandum, of which there were two copies on file, was not drawn to the attention of Stewart Counsell, the Touche partner in charge of the Ferguson deal. 'Clearly I would have been very concerned indeed,' Counsell later said at the Barlow Clowes trial. 'Because reading the memo there does seem to be a substantial amount of unaccounted-for funds which would clearly have required investigation.' Moreover, Counsell claimed he did not see the Spicers papers warning Clowes that his offshore funds did not work. He claimed that no one at Spicers had pointed out the worrying documents.[3]

The celebrations began even before the formal documentation was posted to shareholders. On 10 March von Cramer took delivery of a red Ferrari Testarossa for £79,668. It was the second car he had purchased in the previous fortnight, having spent over £37,000 on a Mercedes towards the end of February.

Clowes withdrew £1 million cash – funded by Barlow Clowes investors – out of the Barlow Clowes partnership and flew again to the Virgin Islands, for an eleven-day holiday with his family. Once again he went by Gulfstream jet, this time the flight costing £70,000. In a sense the numbers had become irrelevant: Clowes was living a tycoon's life with Pamela, whom he showered with expensive jewellery. They holidayed on luxury yachts in the Caribbean, flown in by fellow tycoon Robert Maxwell's private jet. Clowes met Maxwell afterwards to negotiate buying 150 hours' worth of flying time on his jet at a cost of £2,500 an hour, although the deal never came off. On one private jet trip to Jersey costing thousands of pounds, Pamela wrote one word on the disembarkation card to describe the purpose of her visit: 'lunch'.

The Cloweses had thrown a 'pink' party for Pamela's fortieth birthday, with pink food and pink champagne. Clowes had bought another 'Pam' speedboat for $356,000 and called it *Pam 2*. It was no ordinary speedboat: it was 75 feet long – the size of a yacht – with bathrooms and bedrooms, but faster than a speedboat. *Pam 2* was known as a 'fast launch' – so fast that it needed special permission to be moored in Gibraltar since fast launches were used by drug traffickers to outrun police boats.

Clowes was trapped in a fantasy of his own making. In reality he was not a tycoon: his companies lost money and could be kept alive only by misappropriating other people's life savings. His investors financed his head office, his advertising and ultimately one another as Clowes robbed Peter to pay Paul. The private jet trips, the luxury holidays, the Davidoff cigars and Bollinger champagne were underpinned by a lie.

There were a couple of last-minute hitches. Lyceum Holdings, the Gibraltar front company, proved to be inappropriate for the £12 million back-to-back loan. A new company, Lyceum Holdings (Overseas), was quickly incorporated and used in its place. It was important that the true owners of Lyceum and its sources of funding, the Barlow Clowes investors, were not known. Its shareholders included a Hong Kong company, and two of its directors were residents of the tiny island of Sark, near Jersey. (This is known as the 'Sark Lark' – a method of tax avoidance but also a device to make ownership of a company harder to track down. Directors' fees are a very good source of income for the crofters on Sark.)

The final problem was the underwriting of the Ferguson rights issue. Underwriting is a form of guarantee. When, for example, a merchant bank underwrites a rights issue it guarantees to find takers for the new shares being issued. This guarantee extends to the merchant bank itself: if the bank does not manage to find buyers for all the shares it takes up any remaining ones itself. But in Ferguson's case Singer & Friedlander had declined to underwrite the rights issue – the bank could not endorse the 75p price put on the new shares. In fact, only slightly more than a third of the rights issue needed underwriting because the Clowes and von Cramer camps were taking up the rest themselves.

Rensburg, the broker to Ferguson, agreed to act as underwriters on condition that it was in turn guaranteed. A sub-underwriter needed to be found, someone to whom the underwriter could delegate some or all of the risk of having to take up the Ferguson shares. This is standard practice – a lead underwriter will often minimise his risk by finding sub-underwriters prepared to commit themselves to taking shares. In return the sub-underwriters take a share of the lead underwriter's commission.

Von Cramer produced a sub-underwriter, a company incorporated in the British Virgin Islands called Ryeman. Ryeman was a company which von Cramer effectively controlled. Its shares were held by a Liechtenstein trust of which von Cramer was a director. Who benefited from this trust? Von Cramer's infant son Daniel had 75 per cent of the shares and his brother 10 per cent. The Variety Club of Great Britain had even been allotted 5 per cent, von Cramer's cousins a further 5 per cent, and the 5 per cent balance had not been allocated.

Because Ryeman was a completely unknown entity Rensburg wanted the entire sub-underwriting money deposited with Singer & Friedlander before it would agree. Once again the Barlow Clowes investors unwittingly came to the rescue. On 3 March £1.8 million was transferred through at least four different bank accounts, including two in the Isle of Man, before ending up ten days later on deposit with Singer & Friedlander. It was the final act, guaranteeing that the first and most important phase of Clowes's master plan – the takeover of Barlow Clowes by James Ferguson – would succeed.

CHAPTER SEVENTEEN
·
THE MOLE
·

The Ferguson acquisition of Barlow Clowes was formally announced on Thursday 19 March by Singer & Friedlander, its merchant bankers. 'The acquisition of the Barlow Clowes Group represents an opportunity to acquire a soundly managed group of companies with significant scope for expansion and profitability', Singer's press release stated. The purchase still had to be voted on and approved by the 'independent' shareholders of Ferguson. The vote was of course a formality in this case and went through the following month.

The financial press passed little comment on the purchase of Barlow Clowes. The *Sunday Times*, given advance details of the deal, focused on von Cramer's role, in an optimistic article: 'the management team he [von Cramer] is building up is likely to command a lot of attention', the paper wrote, without a trace of irony. The *Investors Chronicle* analysed the Ferguson deal in depth in its 'Bids and Deals' section. The article carried the headline 'Warning Signs', and said:

> Rarely has a share's unsuitability for widows and orphans been signalled as clearly as in the case of James Ferguson. Despite the acquisition of a Scarborough property for 8.5 million shares, Ferguson managed to incur a pre-tax loss of £379,000 in the six months to September 1986 – a worse figure than the company has produced in any full year this decade. Net borrowings, despite a £600,000 placing early in 1986, have soared from £217,000 in March 1985 to £2.3 million last September.

The author also pointed out the large sums of money earned from 'software licensing'. 'Other little peculiarities include the fees and interest-free loans Barlow has received from others of Mr Clowes' interests and the £1 million cash withdrawal made by Mr Clowes and his wife prior to the acquisition.' The article finished with a warning: 'This is a very speculative investment.'

Once the purchase of Barlow Clowes had been approved, Ferguson's shares could be quoted again on the stock market. On Monday

13 April dealings recommenced for the first time since the suspension the previous July. The shares immediately shot up to 115p, valuing the company at £46 million.

The rise in the share price meant that Clowes had made an instant paper profit of £3.6 million on the shares he received for selling Barlow Clowes. The previous month he and von Cramer had made a profit of £2.2 million when they sold their stake in Belgrave Holdings, the hotels and property group where they had failed to secure seats on the board. Outwardly Clowes looked a winner.

The Belgrave stake had been financed, albeit unwittingly, by the Barlow Clowes investors. They did not, however, share the profits. At the beginning of April the total sale proceeds, some £6.7 million, were paid into a National Westminster bank account in Jersey in the name of International Securities: the Liechtenstein *Anstalt* Clowes had used to disguise the funding for the Belgrave share buying. One million pounds of this money was used, covertly, to fund the purchase of Ferguson shares in the rights issue. Another £145,860 was paid to one of von Cramer's companies as a fee for alleged corporate finance services. Some of the money – over £100,000 – was used to pay bills for Clowes's private jet trips; a further £1 million would later be spent on buying a Lear Jet and on a holiday for Clowes. But the remainder, some £4 million, would be used to fund the most reckless move Clowes would ever make in the field of public company takeovers.

Meanwhile, Julian Varney, the Stock Exchange investigator, had been doing some homework on Barlow Clowes. Varney was closely involved in Barlow Clowes's application for membership of the Stock Exchange. He had checked the latest Ferguson accounts and noticed that the company had been lent £300,000 by Barlow Clowes Nominees. This looked odd; supposedly, Barlow Clowes Nominees existed merely to hold the gilts stock belonging to Barlow Clowes clients. Varney cross-checked, searching the accounts of Barlow Clowes Nominees but finding no mention of the loan. It was beginning to look even more peculiar.

Varney raised the question of the loan at his next meeting with Barlow Clowes and received an evasive reply. 'I felt I had uncovered something which they were anxious not to disclose,' he says.

For the first time Barlow Clowes was being investigated by someone who was prepared to take initiative. Varney had in the past met Derek Tree, who by this time had been pushed out of Barlow Clowes and returned to banking with Lloyds Bank. The two men had met, while Tree was still at Barlow Clowes, on the concourse at Waterloo station. At the time Tree, who had just joined Barlow Clowes, had talked enthusiastically about the group, its intended expansion and plans to join the Stock Exchange. Now Varney wrote to Tree at Lloyds and asked if they could meet.

The two men met on 21 April. 'Tree was clearly a worried man,' says Varney. 'I felt lucky that we were able to meet.' According to Varney, Tree told him he was concerned that some of the UK portfolios managed by Barlow Clowes would be showing losses for clients. Barlow Clowes still held around £50 million for clients in the UK on which it claimed it could produce tax-free gains. Much of these funds was bondwashed – still permitted for small amounts. Alternatively Barlow Clowes claimed to deal in gilts for investors, buying and selling to produce a capital gain. Or it bondwashed in large amounts – with investors having to pay some tax. In all these cases investors were guaranteed the return of the capital. If, as Tree suggested, there was a shortfall, the next question was how good was the Barlow Clowes guarantee? Did it have resources of its own to pay the investors? It was the same question that had been asked many times about Barlow Clowes three years previously when warnings about the firm had poured into the DTI; the same question that the DTI had failed to address when it licensed the firm.

In his version of their conversation, Varney says that Tree told him he had come up against a 'web of secrecy' every time he had tried to find out about the offshore funds. Their whole conversation confirmed Varney's feeling that Barlow Clowes merited further investigation. He felt that Tree knew more than he was at that stage ready to disclose.

Varney's next line of enquiry was an old one: the £300,000 loan to Ferguson from Barlow Clowes Nominees. The explanation that had come back, after Varney had pressed Barlow Clowes about the loan, was that it in fact came from Ryeman: Ryeman was the lender, Barlow Clowes Nominees had merely acted as an agent. Varney started a hunt to discover who was behind Ryeman. He did not know at the time that von Cramer had given instructions for the company to be set up and it contained layers of secrecy which would be virtually impossible to peel away. It was registered in the British Virgin Islands, with bearer shares held by a Liechtenstein trust. The beneficiaries of the trust were members of the von Cramer family including the children of von Cramer's uncle Mario Pacilio, who lived in Venezuela. Five per cent of the shares were held on trust for the Royal Variety Club of Great Britain.

What Varney was able to discover, by looking through Stock Exchange records, was that Ryeman had bought shares in James Ferguson. He looked further and discovered Barlow Clowes Nominees had been buying shares as well, as had other companies connected or seemingly connected to Barlow Clowes.

At this point Varney consulted the Stock Exchange Members Mutual Reference Society (SEMMRS). This is a form of internal credit reference agency which allows stockbrokers to check on any new client that wants to buy or sell shares through them. Every time a stockbroker takes on a new client he must advise SEMMRS, who will make a record of the client, the name of the stockbroking firm he or she is dealing through and the date his or her name was entered in the records. Varney checked with SEMMRS against the names of two Barlow Clowes companies and discovered, to his astonishment, that they had bought shares in public companies through at least twenty-five different stockbroking firms. This was an enormous number of firms to use. Even experienced and active stock market operators do not normally use more than six brokers. 'In my experience this was a danger sign,' says Varney. 'It indicated that member firms had dealt for Barlow Clowes and fought shy of dealing for them again or that Barlow Clowes wanted to conceal their dealings by spreading them among different broking firms.'

Varney examined the prospectus which Ferguson had issued for the acquisition of Barlow Clowes and compared it with another prospectus the company was proposing to issue in conjunction with its purchase of a 10 per cent holding in Bristol Channel Ship Repairers. The information contained in the two documents about who owned Ferguson shares did not tally.

The Stock Exchange has records of every share transaction effected through the stock market. The records are computerised and contain identification codes that reveal the name of the purchaser, or seller, of the shares. Varney decided to monitor all dealings in Ferguson shares. He suspected that the company's share price was being manipulated by systematic buying from companies connected with Clowes.

Varney was also given two audit trails – effectively records of clients' investments – and discovered that in each there was a slight shortfall between the investments Barlow Clowes was holding and the amount it actually owed the clients. If this picture were repeated across the board with every client there could be an enormous deficiency.

There was no way Varney could support Barlow Clowes's application for membership of the Stock Exchange. In fact everything pointed to an urgent need to investigate Barlow Clowes and its parent company James Ferguson Holdings.[1]

CHAPTER EIGHTEEN

·

OUT OF CONTROL

·

'I've only got one motivation and that's money.'
Guy von Cramer.[1]

In 1790 the Reverend James Buckley, an itinerant Methodist preacher, met Maria Child, the daughter of a Welsh entrepreneur, Henry Child. Child owned a number of public houses in West Wales which he supplied with his own locally brewed beer. A devout Methodist himself, he took an instant liking to Buckley and gave his approval for Buckley to marry Maria. When Child died the Reverend Buckley combined looking after a series of different congregations in Wales with running his wife's brewing and public house interests. These became known as Buckley's Brewery and, formed into a company, were handed down through succeeding generations of the Buckley family. The company was floated on the stock market in 1963 by Cazenove & Co., the bluest of blue-blooded stockbrokers. It was Wales's oldest independent brewer, based in Llanelli, and one of the largest employers in the town. It owned around two hundred pubs through which it sold its own, local beers such as Buckley's Best Bitter, Buckley Gold and Buckley's Mild.

Buckley's was one of several regional brewers which came under what was known as the 'Whitbread umbrella': companies in which Whitbread, the brewing giant, held shares, acting as a form of protection against hostile takeover bids. Whitbread interests owned 27 per cent of Buckley's shares and, in turn, supplied most of the lager drunk in Buckley's pubs. It was a cosy arrangement.

Nevertheless Buckley's came under siege from a couple of hostile shareholders. In March 1987 one of them, Tony Cole, a wheeler-dealer who had built up a stake of almost 28 per cent in Buckley's, tried unsuccessfully to secure a seat on the board. He was rebuffed, but pledged to fight on. 'This is only round one,' Cole declared.[2]

*

By the spring of 1987, Shan Swinstead, Naylor's personal assistant, was increasingly worried. Having returned from Geneva to work in the Barlow Clowes Warnford Court office, she was still being instructed to take large sums of money out of the investors' bank accounts. Swinstead herself was planning to leave. 'I was getting unhappy about being asked to . . . make these types of transfers.'[3] In the middle of June she received another order – the largest she had handled. Clowes needed £7 million for what he described to Swinstead as 'a unique underwriting opportunity'. The money was to be transferred to a numbered account with the Union Bank of Switzerland in Geneva.

Swinstead was very reluctant to transfer such a large sum. The most cash she thought she could raise was £3.5 million but it would leave the bank accounts she handled with very little to meet with-drawals that investors might make. Unable to reach Naylor, she typed a letter which she insisted Chris Newman, the Barlow Clowes finance director, should authorise. 'With regard to the three million pounds withdrawn from Midland Bank St Helier, Jersey, and £500,000 withdrawn from the Midland Bank 5 Threadneedle Street, London EC2, I hereby notify that I am acting on instructions and take no responsibility for my action in signing for any transfer, with-drawals or otherwise.'[4] She then sent the money. The balance, another £3.5 million, Clowes took from client accounts in Gibraltar with Barclays Bank. The money was to be used to support a takeover bid, by Clowes and von Cramer, for Buckley's Brewery.

The two men had purchased Cole's stake in Buckley's at the beginning of June for £5.7 million. Most of the money, some £4 million, came from the sale proceeds of their Belgrave Holdings shares. Using a nominee company called Brodian, the bid was launched on Friday 10 July; Brodian was offering 175p a share in cash, which put a price tag of £27 million on Buckley's Brewery. Brodian's funds came from the Barlow Clowes investors. The announcement came an hour before Buckley's annual general meet-ing, held at its traditional venue – the Thomas Arms Hotel, Llanelli, where shareholders could sup pints of Buckley's Best once the for-malities were out of the way. Von Cramer flew down by helicopter; he had been given permission to attend – but not address – the meeting. He would claim, much later, that he thought Clowes was using his own money to make the bid.

The bid for Buckley's was a diversion for Clowes from his master plan. In May 1987 Clowes had presented the board of Ferguson with several proposed acquisitions all of which were to be financed by issuing Ferguson shares. Top of his list was a bank: Clowes wanted to buy the Douglas Bank in the Isle of Man and had agreed to pay £1.9 million for it in Ferguson shares. At the same time Clowes told the board that he would stop taking in any new money in his UK Barlow Clowes portfolios; this he said was part of a phased strategy to move away from tax avoidance schemes altogether.

There were several good reasons for Peter Clowes wanting a bank. He would be able to launder his investors' money far more easily. He was having to use front companies and bank accounts in several different countries; it was messy and, more important, more liable to detection than if he could keep the whole process of converting clients' money into shares or other assets in-house. If he owned a bank investors in his offshore portfolios might be persuaded to convert their 'portfolio' investment into a deposit with his bank. This would be an ideal solution for Clowes, legitimising the portfolios overnight.

Clowes needed a solution because of the Financial Services Act, which was scheduled to come into effect the following year and which heralded a far more detailed and thorough system of investor protection, one which would require Clowes to produce detailed audits of all his funds, including the Gibraltar one. The Act stipulated that offshore funds which were being marketed to UK investors had to be based in a country offering equivalent investor protection to the UK or, alternatively, had to be individually approved by the new investor protection watchdog the Securities and Investments Board. Gibraltar was not recognised as providing equivalent investor protection; and the offshore funds would never stand up to SIB scrutiny. There was every chance that Clowes would have to shut down the offshore funds and return all the money in them to the investors. His accountants had already told him to close the offshore funds for tax reasons. He needed an escape route, which would be provided by converting the investments in the portfolio into a form of deposit with a bank. He could legitimise himself virtually overnight; all he would have to do was to maintain a certain level of cash to pay investors who wanted to take their money out. The jewellery companies, properties, farms, château, shares in Ferguson and other companies could all be quite legitimate investments by the bank. No longer would there be any need for the clumsy back-to-back loans, the washing of funds through dozens of different bank accounts to disguise their provenance.

The £1.9 million which Clowes was offering for the Douglas Bank was considerably in excess of the Bank's net assets of £1.1 million.

This meant that Clowes would be paying £800,000 for the bank's licence. Under normal circumstances this would be a very high price to pay – but circumstances were not normal. His hunt for a bank was by no means confined to the Douglas Bank. Clowes approached the Celtic Bank, another Isle of Man bank, but was shown the door by its owner Albert Gubay when he had suggested that the £10 million payment for the bank would be in James Ferguson shares.[5] He had tried in Gibraltar too, telling James Levy, his lawyer at Hassan & Partners, that he wanted to buy a bank on the Rock. 'I told him quite categorically that there was no way the Gibraltar authorities would allow him to own a bank unless he obtained a banking licence in the UK first', Levy says. Clowes tried in the UK too, picking on an obscure Scottish company called Combined Capital Ltd.

Based in Glasgow, Combined was a licensed deposit taker, a form of junior bank, owned by the Alexander Stone Foundation and managed by Stone himself, an octogenarian, with just one other executive. By July 1987 it looked as if Clowes had done a deal: he would buy 50 per cent of Combined Capital for £500,000 – and possibly the remaining half in three years' time. All Clowes needed was for the Bank of England to give its approval for the intended change in ownership.

Other acquisitions that Clowes was planning at the time also have elements of escape underlying them. Clowes wanted to buy International Trust Corporation (ITC). ITC was an Isle of Man-based organisation unwittingly supplying front companies and nominee shareholders used by Clowes to disguise the diversion of his investors' money. By acquiring ITC Clowes would have greater control over the diversion process – both past and future. This control was very important to his plan. Control of Ferguson meant that he could manipulate the company's share price to ever higher levels – the shares reached £2 at one point. If he also bought a controlling interest in a bank and in ITC he would control the whole process: receipt of funds from the public, the formation of dummy companies, the transfer of funds into those companies, and so on.

On 2 July, a fortnight after Swinstead had reluctantly transferred the funds for the Buckley's Brewery bid, Varney sent the DTI the preliminary results of his investigation into Barlow Clowes. It was in the form of a draft paper on the suitability of Barlow Clowes for membership of the Exchange, and its conclusion was plain to see: 'there must be substantial doubts as to whether the Barlow Clowes and James Ferguson companies and their directors can be considered to be fit and proper for membership of the Stock Exchange'. Varney recommended that the application be rejected and a full enquiry be instigated into James Ferguson and Barlow Clowes.

The report was a summary of the discoveries Varney had made: Barlow Clowes claimed to deal only in gilts, but in reality was a heavy buyer of shares. This fact alone would cast doubt on its published accounts, which mentioned only its gilts dealing activities. Many of the concerns were familiar to the DTI, such as the fear that investors' capital was being eroded and connections with Hedderwick Stirling Grunbar. The conflicting information Ferguson had supplied on its shareholding led the Exchange to doubt that it had given it the full picture when buying Barlow Clowes. Tree's resignation and the wall of secrecy he had come up against were other factors. 'I have no doubt that there is much more to be unearthed on these people by anyone who cares to delve', Varney said in his covering letter.

The Buckley's bid came eight days after Varney's report was sent to the DTI. Buckley's 'has lost its way', Clowes told reporters covering the bid. 'It has no financial director. It has no real property expertise. We want to see the business expand.'[6] Clowes's effrontery was matched by the naivety of some of his statements to the press, none more so than his remarks, in the following morning's *Guardian*, to the effect that he and von Cramer were 'not really interested in owning a brewery'. It was a huge public relations blunder; von Cramer later rectified this, giving assurances to the Buckley's board that if successful they would keep the brewery going for at least another two years. The Buckley's board rejected the bid anyway, describing it, in the timeworn language of takeover battles, as 'unwelcome and unrealistic'.

The view in the industry, however, was that the bid was 'astonishingly generous'.[7] The Clowes offer valued Buckley's at thirty-two times its profits – almost twice the average for the drinks sector at the time. At 175p a share it was pitched at more than a third higher than the price of the shares before the bid.

The Buckley's bid had been von Cramer's idea, but he had nothing like the financial muscle to make it. So he suggested it to Clowes. It appealed to Clowes the tycoon, the chairman of one public company, to go after another. By this stage Clowes was out of control, firing off in several directions at the same time: he was escaping, he was expanding, he wanted to buy the Douglas Bank, he formed a new company to import Lear Jets, he had jewellery, property, fund management, stakes in public companies, and so on. He was scattering investors' money as though he had an inexhaustible supply and an inalienable right to do so.

Clowes had backed von Cramer's plan financially, despite the risks; the younger man was able to step back from the tornado that Clowes had whipped up around himself. Von Cramer skirted it, choosing when to enter – and sometimes when to leave. In July 1987, a fortnight after announcing the Buckley's bid, von Cramer and the company he ran, Cramer Holdings, sold almost 2.25 million Ferguson shares for £1 each, making a profit of well over £1 million. The original announcement said that the shares had been placed with a number of investment institutions, giving the impression that Ferguson shares would appeal to institutional shareholders. The reality was that Ryeman, the British Virgin Islands company, had bought the shares using Barlow Clowes investors' money. Ferguson later corrected its original announcement, admitting that Ryeman had bought all the shares.

The £26.6 million bid for Buckley's coincided with, and provided fresh ammunition for, the renewed anxiety that was being felt about Barlow Clowes within official circles. The Bank of England started pressing the Department of Trade to take action on the Stock Exchange report. In a sense the report disclosed little that was not either known back in 1985 or could have been gathered from public sources. But Clowes was no longer a nuisance that could be confined. His Ferguson master plan and now his bid for Buckley's had brought him into new territories. He was claiming to be a serious stock market player, which meant that the Bank of England, the Takeover Panel and the Stock Exchange were all directly concerned with his behaviour. Clowes's case could no longer be shunted the DTI's way. The Bank of England has an unofficial role as supervisor of the markets, the Panel regulates takeovers and had already been duped once, possibly more often, by Clowes. So too had the Stock Exchange. The DTI might be the body which had licensed him, and it was certainly the one with powers to investigate him, but Clowes was now a problem for everyone. His behaviour was a challenge, and an affront, to four of the most important regulators in the UK.

Throughout July and August there was a flurry of phone calls from the Bank of England to the Department of Trade asking what action the Department intended taking. If it is possible to reduce the Bank's suggestions and requests for progress reports into clear unequivocal language, then its message could be encapsulated in the words: 'Stop Peter Clowes.'

In August Clowes and von Cramer published their formal offer document for Buckley's Brewery. The document attacked Buckley's profit record and, quoting the *Daily Telegraph*, described the company as 'the worst performing regional brewer in the country over the past five years'. Buckley's and its advisers, Kleinwort Benson, immediately hit back, describing the offer document as 'lightweight' and pointing to its lack of information on Clowes's and von Cramer's management record. 'All we can trace for Mr Cramer is at one time he sold crockery in a Leeds market', Buckley's managing director Colin Thomas told Nicholas Witchell on the BBC's *Nine o'Clock News*.

Buckley's defence document asked a series of searching questions, highlighted in red ink, about where Clowes and von Cramer were getting their money:

We believe the offerors should answer the following questions:

– How is the offer being financed?
– Who would be the beneficial owners of Buckley's shares if the offer did succeed?
– Is it intended that Buckley's shares should be used as security for borrowings related to other interests?

Clowes and von Cramer responded three days later in bold capital letters: 'Buckley's Board have accused us of not explaining how the offer is being financed,' they wrote in a circular to Buckley's shareholders. Beneath this they added: 'To divert your attention away from the real issues, the Board of Buckley's seem to be suggesting that there is something unsatisfactory about the financing arrangements.' Within a week, Clowes and von Cramer had actually increased their offer for Buckley's by another 10p a share, now valuing the company at £28 million. 'The bid would not be made unless we were satisfied they had the resources to meet it in full,' said David Courtman of Singer & Friedlander. 'All the funding arrangements have been made on the back of the private means of Mr Cramer and Mr Clowes.'

In fact Kleinwort Benson, merchant bank advisers to Buckley's, had privately raised the issue of the funding of the bid with the Takeover Panel. Kleinwort was sceptical about Clowes's and von Cramer's ability to finance the Buckley bid themselves: were they acting as a front for someone else who had the money but did not want to be identified? The Takeover Panel raised the question with Singer & Friedlander, who said they were satisfied that the two men had the resources and were not hiding an unseen bidder. Clowes had duped his advisers. The Takeover Panel inquiry came to nothing.

The Buckley's board rejected the improved offer from the 'financiers', as Clowes and von Cramer were regularly dubbed by the press covering the bid. More important, Whitbread also rejected it, unfurling its umbrella once more to protect another regional brewer. But when Clowes and von Cramer offered yet another increase – to 192p a share – there was nothing the board could do but accept. This was an astronomical price: it valued Buckley's at £29.2 million, thirty-six times its profits after tax. The Buckley's board could no longer claim with any justification that it was unreasonable or inadequate. Somewhat reluctantly the board capitulated and recommended the bid to its shareholders. Clowes and von Cramer had given further assurances about keeping the brewery open which Buckley's chairman, Griffith Phillips, said had also been a factor in the board's recommendation.

Whitbread also accepted but for part only of its shareholding. It retained sufficient shares to give it 10 per cent of Buckley's. Under Companies Act provisions, takeover bidders needed over 90 per cent of the shares of a company before they could mop up any reluctant shareholders by legally compelling them to sell. Whitbread had not fully closed its umbrella.

Three days after declaring victory in the battle for Buckley's, Clowes announced another corporate foray: he and von Cramer had taken a stake of almost 30 per cent in another public company. J. England, the new Clowes target, made quiches and crisps. It was effectively another shell company, another public vehicle for Clowes to control. Some £2.2 million of investors' money was used to buy the J. England stake. Clowes appointed himself chairman of the company.

There was no logic in buying J. England or Buckley's; these deals appear like the actions of a man buying for the sake of buying. Clowes was doing deals to feed his ego and nourish his vision of himself as a major force in the stock market, just as he once believed he would have a gilts market to himself with a gilts shop in every high street.

Meanwhile Clowes was negotiating to take over two of the financial intermediaries who put large amounts of money into Barlow

Clowes. IPAS, the Surrey-based financial intermediary and the largest single supplier of money to Barlow Clowes, was one target. The
other was Analysis Holdings, the Harrogate intermediary that was
also a major contributor to Barlow Clowes. They and D. C. Wilson
were the three intermediaries who received an extra 1 per cent commission for recommending clients to invest in Barlow Clowes's offshore portfolios.

The purchases were to be in Ferguson shares. David Gray, the
IPAS boss, wanted to sell out and move to Australia. Analysis, led
by Ross Hyett and Nigel Burrows, a director of Manchester United
football club, simply wanted to cash in by selling to a public company.

The proposed purchase of financial intermediaries was another
facet of the control Clowes wanted. If he owned the intermediaries
he could have control over the money coming in through the front
door, over the flow of funds into his business. So long as he kept
money coming through the front door he could take it secretly out
the back, using it to fund his lifestyle and his corporate ambitions.
He thought that he would be in a position to exert greater influence
on the impartial recommendations that the intermediaries such as
IPAS were supposed to make to their clients. For a man who needed
to persuade thousands of clients to switch their investments, it made
sense to try to gain control over the persuaders, the financial intermediaries. And, although it was hard to see how Clowes would
avoid the impact of the Financial Services Act, he was working on a
new investment product which might solve all his problems.

As he spun wildly out of control, looking for solutions and scattering money into new areas, Clowes bought himself a tycoon's
yacht. He paid $2.5 million for the *Boukephelas*, a 101-foot monster
owned by Tina Onassis. Named after Alexander the Great's horse, it
was a sleek, silver, streamlined extravagance, equipped with satellite
navigation equipment, a cinema, huge open lounge, four-poster
beds, telephones and bars. The money to pay for the boat travelled
from the Barlow Clowes investors through twelve different bank
accounts and six different countries. The Cloweses threw parties
on the boat, entertained financial intermediaries in the lounge and
holidayed on it. Business deals were negotiated there and a full-time
crew was engaged at a cost of over £1000 a week. Sometimes the
boat was moored in Gibraltar, at others in Marbella. It was Clowes's
plaything, his status symbol – and, importantly, his wife Pamela's
as well: she was the mistress of the boat. Later Clowes would transfer
a further $1 million of investors' money to buy the *Yara*, another

massive yacht, whose hull had been damaged in transporting it from the Middle East. The tycoon had his yachts. All he needed now were his private aeroplanes. These would not be long in coming.

CHAPTER NINETEEN

·

THE SECRET
INVESTIGATION

·

*'Just as in 1985 our concern remains that the size of the Barlow
Clowes operation could lead to a major "City scandal".'*
Sir George Blunden,
Deputy Governor of the Bank of England.

The day after Clowes and von Cramer announced their successful
192p a share final offer for Buckley's Brewery, officials from the
Department of Trade met to consider what to do about Barlow
Clowes. Although it would be the most important meeting, one
which would change the course of events, no one took any notes.
Until the meeting, which took place on Friday 18 September, the
Department had been prevaricating; it was torn between requesting
Barlow Clowes's new auditors, Touche Ross, to carry out a new audit
of the UK funds and launching a full-scale investigation into Barlow
Clowes.

The Bank of England had been pressing for action. It preferred
an investigation. At the beginning of the month Brian Gent, the
Deputy Head of Banking Supervision, had called the Department for
a progress report and to pass on the view that Ferguson shares were
being 'ramped'. He was 'concerned that no action had been taken
by the Department'. When the DTI official pointed out that there
had been no complaints about Barlow Clowes and that the firm
had had a satisfactory audit two years earlier, Gent challenged both
arguments: 'one could not expect complaints until a crash had
occurred', Gent said, adding that 'since the 1985 audit report the
Inland Revenue's action on bondwashing seemed to have removed
the basis on which Barlow Clowes's gilt plans operated'.[1]

The DTI had also received a call from the Greater Manchester
Police. The police had been tipped off by Brian Carlton, the aircraft
executive in Manchester who had long harboured suspicions about
how Clowes was managing to finance his private jet trips. He thought

that Barlow Clowes was shipping cash out of the country, and that drug money was somehow involved. 'The jets had been making trips to Switzerland and the West Indies', an officer from the Drugs Intelligence Branch told the DTI official.[2]

As a result of Carlton's tip-off Detective Inspector Joe Langlands had followed Clowes briefly – on one occasion sitting outside a Chinese restaurant for hours while Clowes and Pamela ate a meal inside. The customs office at Manchester airport was also alerted. From then on Clowes and Pamela were regularly searched when they flew into the airport. On one occasion customs officials wanted to examine Pamela's fur coat. Clowes was furious: 'You can't do this to me,' he screamed, protesting so much he was eventually led away by customs officials for questioning. Clowes had around £5000 cash on him which he told the officials was 'spending money'. Pamela's fur coat was found to have an English label, so the officials gave it back to her.

It was against this background that the 18 September meeting was held. A new official was in charge of the Licensing Unit. He had received the Stock Exchange report on 2 July. It was now 18 September and no action had been taken. He would later make the point that he had come to the Unit from 'totally different work, without training in or experience of enforcement' and 'that his assistant secretary had joined the unit only a week before he had'.

The meeting ruled that Barlow Clowes should be investigated.

Meanwhile, plans were progressing for the purchase of Analysis Holdings, the Harrogate broker. Analysis was making profits of around £1 million a year; its purchase would bring a much needed flow of profit into Ferguson. Clowes, with a war chest full of heavily inflated Ferguson shares, was willing to pay £10 million – in shares – for Analysis.

Other plans were not proceeding so well. The Bank of England had told Clowes that it would not approve the transfer of the Douglas Bank's banking licence to him. The necessity for Bank of England approval of taking over a bank was an impossible obstacle for Clowes. His chances of obtaining it were nil. On 28 September, Sir George Blunden, Deputy Governor of the Bank of England, wrote of his concern about Barlow Clowes in a letter to the DTI's Permanent Secretary, Sir Brian Hayes. Sir George referred to the Stock Exchange draft paper and the unease felt in the stock market about Ferguson and Barlow Clowes:

We find all this rather worrying. Just as in 1985 our concern remains that the size of the Barlow Clowes operation could lead to a major 'City scandal'. It is clear that at this stage the Bank can play only a limited role but I thought we should make you aware of our general unease, and the need for the situation to be looked at as closely as possible.

The unease in the market that Sir George referred to was reflected in the actions of two major city institutions: Barclays de Zoete Wedd and Phillips & Drew. Both had sold all the shares they held in Ferguson in July. Meanwhile Clowes continued to buy Ferguson shares covertly, keeping the price up. Pouring millions of pounds of investors' money into the exercise, Clowes set up offshore trusts in Gibraltar to buy up many of the spare Ferguson shares that came on the market.

Clowes actually called on the Bank of England in October 1987, to seek approval for his purchase of a 50 per cent stake in Combined Capital, the Glasgow-based licensed depositor run by Alexander Stone. Sir George's letter had only just been sent to the DTI. The Bank of England officials pointed out as politely as possible that there was no question of anyone buying their way into banking by taking over Combined Capital. It was a unique situation, the licence was effectively personal to Alexander Stone. Clowes could not have it.

Clowes also asked the Bank for a banking licence for his own operations; rather than take over a banking institution could he not simply have a licence of his own? The Bank was evasive, telling Clowes that he would have to get his Stock Exchange application through first.

The Bank of England's attitude to Barlow Clowes had changed. Sir George Blunden's letter reveals the bank as insistent, pressing for something to be done. But earlier in the year its attitude had been quite different. When Varney, the Stock Exchange investigator, had begun his enquiries into Barlow Clowes, he had called on an official at the Bank of England, to see if the Bank's files had anything to help him.

Varney recalls several coloured Barlow Clowes files, pink and blue, piled high on the Bank official's desk. He was surprised when help was refused. Later, in two separate telephone calls, the official told Varney and another Stock Exchange official, Martin Powell, that the Bank thought it would be 'in the wider interests of the City' if Barlow Clowes were admitted to membership of the Exchange.[3] This was reverting to its old idea that it was easier to regulate a firm when it was within the system. The Bank changed its tune, however, when it received the draft Stock Exchange report in July, from then on pressing the DTI for action.

On 14 October Frances Maude, the Minister for Consumer and Corporate Affairs, gave his approval for an investigation to begin into Barlow Clowes. The investigation was limited to Barlow Clowes's UK funds: the submission to the Minister had not even mentioned that Barlow Clowes managed money overseas.

It took some time for appropriate investigators to be found. This was to be an external investigation, carried out by a lawyer and an accountant rather than by DTI officials themselves. The problem was finding an accountant – a spate of insider dealing investigations had exhausted the list of accountants recommended by the Institute of Chartered Accountants. Eventually, on 13 November, Walter Max Hoffman, an accountant with the firm of Baker Tilley, and Laurence Ziman, a partner in the West End law firm of Nabarro Nathanson, were appointed. Their brief: to investigate the affairs of Barlow Clowes Gilt Managers, the UK arm of Barlow Clowes.

On the evening of 24 November 1987 Clowes signed the acquisition document to buy Analysis Holdings. It had been a tough day: Naylor, the deputy chairman of Ferguson, had resigned. For several months Naylor and Clowes had not been getting on. The friction between the two men was so great that in July that year Naylor and Shan Swinstead had moved out of the Barlow Clowes offices to an office in Naylor's Surrey home, Send Barns. The reason for Naylor's and Clowes's estrangement is not clear: Clowes accuses the Naylors of being over-ambitious and envious of his success. 'He had a very very ambitious wife behind him and became far too big for his boots', says Clowes. The Naylors for their part may have turned their noses up at the northern origins of Clowes and Pamela, an attitude which Naylor sometimes let slip privately to Barlow Clowes staff. Naylor may also have felt that his role as Clowes's right-hand man had been usurped by von Cramer, who, rather than Naylor, had partnered Clowes in his most recent corporate forays – Buckley's and J. England.

Things had come to a head with the Analysis deal. As a main board director, Naylor's approval was necessary. Shortly before the deal was due to be announced Clowes gave him an ultimatum over the telephone: resign or sign the document. 'If you don't do one or the other I will kill you,' Clowes said.[4] Naylor resigned.

The Analysis deal was due to be announced the following day, Wednesday 25 November. A press release was drafted and sent to the Stock Exchange to be held, ready to go out on the Exchange's Company News service. It never made it. At 10 a.m. the two Department of Trade inspectors arrived unannounced at Barlow Clowes's Warnford Court offices. Ziman and Hoffman asked to see either Clowes or Keith Allsop, the newly appointed managing director of Barlow Clowes Gilt Managers. Neither man was there. Instead they were met by an open-mouthed and incredulous Bernard Osborne, who showed them into the boardroom at Warnford Court. The inspectors handed Osborne a piece of paper formally declaring their appointment. Osborne had his own concerns about Barlow Clowes which he had voiced in a letter of resignation sent to Clowes but not acted upon. Looking at the document from the inspectors he remarked simply that it was a copy.

Once again there was an element of farce. Hoffman and Ziman were at pains to point out that their investigation was completely confidential – there would be no formal announcement. While doing so, Osborne took a call from a fellow stockbroking friend in the city. 'Have you seen today's issue of *Private Eye*?' the friend asked. Osborne had not. 'It says that there is an investigation going on at Barlow Clowes.'

Osborne was flabbergasted and sent someone out to buy the magazine. Sure enough, in the 'City Slicker' column of the magazine Barlow Clowes was mentioned. 'There appears to be considerable interest all at once in the state of financial health at investment brokers Barlow Clowes & Partners,' the article said. It went on to state that 'a number of official sources were "eager" ' to examine Barlow Clowes. Osborne angrily showed it to the two inspectors. 'The Stock Exchange must have leaked it,' he said. Hoffman and Ziman were surprised but made no comment.

With the appointment of the inspectors the Analysis deal was off the table – at least for the time being. Hyett and Burrows of Analysis were not prepared to go ahead until they knew what was going on. Clowes, informed of the investigation, called up the company's lawyers Simpson Curtis to try to find out more about what lay behind it. The DTI refused to say.

Meanwhile, Clowes had a domestic problem. He and Pamela had decided to renovate their home, Swingate Cottage in Macclesfield. The work would be extensive, rendering Swingate uninhabitable for several months. Clowes and his family needed a temporary home. On 27 November – two days after the inspectors had moved into his company – Clowes put down a £27,000 deposit on a house on the outskirts of Prestbury. The deposit came from Clowes's own bank account with Midland Bank in London; but the balance, £243,000, came from the Barlow Clowes investors. It was 4 December, just eleven days after the inspectors had moved in, and Clowes was still misappropriating his investors' money.

Three days earlier Clowes had met Hoffman and Ziman at his Poynton offices. Hoffman had questioned Clowes closely about the Barlow Clowes products, in particular the guarantee that they offered investors to return their capital and income. What if there were a shortfall, Hoffman asked. 'Let's put this into context,' Clowes replied. 'I have personal assets in excess of £20 million.'

There was a discussion about the monitoring of clients' investments, which must have seemed quite innocuous to Hoffman and Ziman at the time. How often was the monitoring done, Ziman asked. Normally it was done every month, Clowes replied. 'You have regular print-outs?' Hoffman asked. 'I will be able to produce calculations,' Clowes replied. It sounded harmless enough, but Clowes's mind had been working quickly when he had replied to Hoffman. When he avoided saying that he kept print-outs of the computer information he was laying the ground for the months to come. The cover-up operation had begun.

CHAPTER TWENTY
·
THE COVER-UP OPERATION
·

There had been no formal announcement of the Government's investigation into Barlow Clowes. The leak to *Private Eye* was not followed up by any newspaper, and so virtually all investors remained ignorant, once again, of the Government's concern. The extent of their ignorance was reflected by the huge sums of money which continued to pour in, every week, to Barlow Clowes's offshore operations. When the inspectors were appointed the money came in at the rate of over £1 million a week and this rate was maintained throughout the following months. Later it would increase.

But Clowes would not be able to keep the investigation completely under wraps. Analysis Holdings, one of the financial intermediaries, knew of it because the appointment of the inspectors had put the Ferguson deal to buy Analysis on ice. Moreover, the government inspectors now had a team of accountants working in the Poynton headquarters of Barlow Clowes. It would be impossible to conceal their presence from some of the local intermediaries, such as Denis Wilson, who had offices nearby and who were closely involved with Barlow Clowes.

The explanation Clowes gave was that the DTI investigation was 'a routine enquiry'. The inspectors would be working in Poynton for a few weeks and that would be that. Clowes also suggested that there might have been a few minor breaches of the licensed dealer rules, but that these were purely technical.

Ironically, Clowes's dismissal of the investigation was given credence by the Department of Trade itself. The Department had instigated the investigation into Barlow Clowes at a time when it knew the firm's licence was due for renewal. Should it refuse to renew? A refusal could bring Barlow Clowes crashing down, pre-empting the purpose of the investigation. It would also lead to lengthy legal proceedings since Barlow Clowes would be virtually certain to challenge the refusal. In the end the DTI decided to renew the licence, subject to receiving 'satisfactory monitoring returns within a reasonable time'.

Once the investigation was launched, however, Touche Ross, Barlow Clowes's auditors, refused to sign any monitoring returns until it had been completed. There was thus no chance of the Department receiving 'satisfactory' monitoring returns. If it was to renew the Barlow Clowes licence it would have to do so on the basis of unsigned, unaudited returns. This it decided to do. Its decision was not referred back to Frances Maude, the DTI minister who had sanctioned the investigation and given his permission to renew subject to receiving the monitoring returns.

To an outsider the renewal of the licence would seem to support Clowes's contention that the investigation was merely routine. Gordon Petty, one of the financial intermediaries, had been on the point of mailing his investors telling them that he could no longer recommend investing with Barlow Clowes. 'We had the labels prepared to do a mail shot to get our investors out', says Petty. Then the licence renewal came through and Petty cancelled the mail shot.

The DTI inspectors, Hoffman and Ziman, were having difficulty in getting information from Clowes. They particularly wanted to examine what were called the 'old partnership accounts'. When Barlow Clowes was being legitimised by the DTI in 1985, the Department had insisted on it forming itself into a limited company. This company – Barlow Clowes and Partners Ltd – would take in all new money from investors and put it into the custodian bank account with Lloyds Bank. This was the arrangement the Bank of England had insisted upon to get around Barlow Clowes's breach of the Banking Act. Barlow Clowes was also supposed to transfer to the same account all the money it had taken in while operating as a partnership. This had never happened. The inspectors found that £7 million was held by Barlow Clowes with Lloyds, subject to the custodian trustee arrangements. The 'old partnership accounts' – amounting to over £44 million – had never been transferred. So, in effect, the tough new system which the DTI and the Bank of England had insisted upon as a condition of licensing Barlow Clowes applied to only a tiny corner of its business, some £7 million in all.

The inspectors' attempts to probe the old partnership accounts were frustrated by a series of excuses from Clowes; the computer, he said, had been programmed to absorb only 999,999 entries. The millionth entry had been made shortly before the inspectors were appointed, Clowes said, making it impossible to extract information about the old partnership clients' investments. When the inspectors asked to see hard copy information, in the form of computer printouts, Clowes said that he did not keep any. 'Mr Clowes at his first explanation of the system held out to us that his ideal state was to have a "paperless office" ', Hoffman later said.[1] 'As a result the vast majority of the information produced by the client accounting system in the form of either regular print-outs or ad hoc computer print-outs . . . are destroyed "after use". . . . This shredding of "hard copy" data severely hampered our investigation and destroyed any evidence of many of the controls purported to be operated over the system.'

What the inspectors did not realise was that a massive shredding operation was going on under their noses often for fifteen or sixteen hours a day. While they worked in the Poynton offices, files, print-outs, letters and thousands of other documents were being deliberately shredded and stuffed into plastic bin bags. These were then spirited away to an office across the road which the Barlow Clowes inspectors knew nothing about. (Clowes in fact kept a shredding machine in his home at Centre House. When, during the course of an interview with him, the lights fused and I collided in the dark with the shredding machine which he kept in his garage, Clowes laughed: 'That is public exhibit number one,' he said.)

Files were doctored with letters removed and new ones created which pretended that clients had cashed in their investment, whereas in fact they had written asking to be transferred to the Gibraltar operation. Clowes was going to great lengths to ensure the inspectors knew as little as possible about his offshore funds. Staff were instructed not to make any mention of Barlow Clowes International to the inspectors or within their hearing. The existence of the secret office in London Road, where the shredded documents were taken, was covered up; all internal telephone directories were removed as soon as the inspectors arrived and a revised list of numbers prepared which only covered the headquarters building. Staff worked weekends on the shredding, with the window blinds down and under instructions never to refer to the fact that they were working at the weekend. The shredding created an enormous mess which was tidied up to make it look as though the office was functioning normally before the inspectors returned on Monday morning.

Nor was the shredding confined to the Poynton office. Clowes sent a team of employees and others out by private jet to the Gibraltar headquarters. With them on the flight was a shredding machine. Along with computer terminals and desks hired from the nearby Holiday Inn, it was installed on the top floor of the Barlow Clowes office. The 'A-Team', as they were dubbed by the Gibraltar staff, systematically went through every client's file, altering details of their investments, destroying letters and also all the back-up computer tapes. The computerised link between the Poynton and Gibraltar offices was severed, meaning that the inspectors in the UK would not be able to utilise the computer system to obtain information on the overseas funds. By mistake some 2000 client files were overlooked in the doctoring process, as was a single back-up tape which later revealed the discrepancy between the cleaned up records on the computer and the true details.

The wholesale destruction of documents was accompanied by a refusal on Clowes's part to give the inspectors any details of the overseas funds. They were not subject to investigation, Clowes said, and therefore he did not feel obliged to give any information on them. Hoffman and Ziman could only grapple in the dark about the size of these funds and speculate, correctly, that they were far larger than those held in the UK.

Clowes was engaged in another process while the cover-up operation was going on: discovery. He had been so profligate with his investors' money that he had no clear idea how much of it he had diverted, where it had gone or to whom. He engaged John Watton, a self-employed business consultant, to go through all the computer records of the offshore funds and record all the loans and transfers that he, Clowes, had made into assets other than gilts. The process would take Watton several months: Clowes had not drawn up any loan documents or kept any record of the non-gilts investments. There was no written record of where the money had gone. It was a mammoth task because Clowes had bought no gilts for the investors in the offshore funds, Portfolios 28 and 68, for years.

Covering up was just one of the directions in which Clowes was moving. Even after the inspectors moved into Barlow Clowes, he continued his spending spree with a reckless venture into private jets. Clowes had no experience of the private jet business other than as a customer. But he wanted his own company – and his own jet. G-P Jet, a six-seater Lear 35 Jet, arrived on 19 December – slightly more than three weeks after the DTI inspectors had paid their first visit. Clowes put down deposits and guarantees of $1.5 million on the jet. This was not his first aircraft: in September 1987 he had paid £800,000 for a Twin Squirrel helicopter. Despite being in pristine condition, Clowes had the helicopter refurbished, installing a new stereo system, leather seats and changing the design on the exterior of the aircraft. The helicopter and G-P Jet were only the beginning: Clowes had ambitions to become an aircraft dealer, buying and selling Lear Jets in the UK. More deposits followed for other private jets, and another helicopter was purchased for £350,000.

The venture into private jets was a disaster. The first Lear Jet arrived even before Clowes had a pilot to fly it, and waited idly at Manchester airport. Clowes put down deposits to buy two Lear Jets which were not even certified for use in the UK. A team of four pilots was recruited and then sacked. Clowes got the AA to run his private jet business even though he had based it at Manchester airport and the AA offices were in Coventry. Eventually he ended up with the private jet business being run from Manchester airport by his nineteen-year-old stepdaughter Nikki Haydock. Three million pounds of investors' money was poured into the private jet business over a period of only months. Most of it was lost.

Clowes may have been motivated by a subconscious desire to escape, to flee the country, when he invested so much money in private jets. It would have been subconscious because, even when he was covering up, Clowes still believed he could get away undetected. He had managed it for fourteen years, survived threats of closure, investigations by accountants, and other probes. Why should he not manage it again? There was another reason why Clowes would not simply flee. In large part he felt that he had done nothing wrong; everything – the diversion of funds, the property, jewellery, Buckley's Brewery, J. England, Ferguson and now the private jet business – was aimed at securing investment returns for his customers. The inspectors would not see things that way, so he had to cover things up.

Meanwhile, the inspectors were pressing for access to the Barlow Clowes computer, which would allow them to examine the old partnership accounts. Clowes knew that he would eventually have to give them access but first he had to sort out a major problem: there was a shortfall of £10 million in the partnership accounts. The intermingling between the UK and offshore funds, coupled with the diversion of these funds to planes, boats and other 'investments', left a massive gap in the UK funds which had to be plugged.

Once again Clowes resorted to his old trick of teaming and lading. Barlow Clowes International transferred £16 million into the partnership accounts to cover the shortfall. But that alone would not solve the problem. If the inspectors saw from the computer records that a lump sum of £16 million had been suddenly introduced into the UK funds after their appointment, they would obviously suspect malpractice. A history had to be created; gilts had to be bought, they had to be shown to have been acquired over a number of years to make it seem as though these were normal transactions which had been carried out on the investors' behalf. The £16 million needed a history that included dates of purchase and details of the broker through whom the gilts were bought. But inventing a series of gilts deals also meant inventing a stockbroker through whom the gilts had been bought and sold. This was risky: if Clowes used a real broker the inspectors might check with the broker and discover the deals were bogus.

A history was created going back to 1984. A pattern of dealing was created to show that all the gilts had been bought and sold by an overseas firm. Clowes described the 'firm' as 'brokers who do matched bargain business' in gilts. This was a lie. It was simply a front to provide Clowes with the history he wanted.

There remained the Financial Services Act to deal with. It was due to come into effect in April 1988 and Barlow Clowes would have to secure membership of one of the four new self-regulatory organisations (SROs). These were the new investor protection watch-dogs operating under the control of the Securities and Investments Board, the overseer of the new system. Without membership of an SRO Barlow Clowes would have to close down. However, the transitional provisions allowed firms who had merely applied for membership of an SRO – but had not yet been accepted – to continue in business unless and until that application was refused. Clowes therefore applied for membership of IMRO – the Investment Manage-ment Regulatory Organisation – in February 1988.

This was only a temporary solution, however. In due course IMRO would want to process the application and would require full details of the Barlow Clowes business including the offshore funds. The Financial Services Act would effectively require these funds to be closed down and Clowes would have to repay the money to the investors. For years he had had the luxury of taking more money offshore each month than he had to pay out in withdrawals and distributions. Paradoxically, as the investigation into his UK business was reaching a climax, Clowes was taking in record sums offshore. In April 1988 £8.8 million was paid into the offshore portfolios – more than £2 million a week. This was the most Clowes ever took in a single month offshore. Even taking into account the April with-drawals and distributions to investors, Clowes still took in a record £4.7 million net. The investors, like lemmings, continued to pour their money offshore.

The purchase of a bank had been blocked, for the time being, by the Bank of England. So Clowes tried another desperate measure:

he decided to launch a new product, a new portfolio, which would be called Portfolio 90 or the Gemini Trust Fund. This would not invest in gilts. It would, Clowes explained to his staff, be a long-term investment, a small amount of the money being in gilts and the balance being invested in a series of private and public companies. These, Clowes explained, would include investments in Ferguson shares, in yachts, planes, property development and other assets. This would incorporate those loans and other 'investments' in private companies of which John Watton was preparing details for Clowes. Watton was nearing the end of his task, alarmed at what he was discovering but reassured by Clowes that they were all for the benefit of the investors.

The idea was to switch the investors in Portfolios 28 and 68 into Portfolio 90. It was a last-minute attempt to legitimise the diversion of investors' money which Clowes had been perpetrating for years. Clowes flew the intermediaries to Gibraltar for a presentation of the new product. It was a last desperate act which showed how much Clowes had lost touch with reality. He was asking the intermediaries, who for years had invested with him because he offered the ultimate security – investment in British Government stocks – to switch their clients into a hugely speculative capital venture fund. It was not as though Clowes had established any track record as an investor in private companies. Everything he had done in this direction had been effected secretly. The intermediaries did not bite. 'We could not recommend it to our clients because it was not in gilts', says Hyett of Analysis. Clowes had beat one drum for the previous fifteen years – 'invest in gilts, security guaranteed'. He would not be allowed to change his tune now.

But there was at least one exception in the ranks of intermediaries: David Gray of IPAS. Clowes and Gray worked closely on a number of new products which involved investing in gilts and in James Ferguson shares. Clowes wanted Gray to switch IPAS clients out of Portfolio 28 and into these new products. Gray was amenable but events would overtake both men before their plans could be implemented.[2]

Hoffman and Ziman were regularly reporting back to the DTI about what they had found at Barlow Clowes. Early reports focused largely on the frustrating delays they were encountering in prising information out of Clowes. The inspectors had had to pull a team of accountants out of the Poynton office in January because the flow of information to them had dried up. There was literally nothing for them to do.

The inspectors reported on the complete control which Clowes exercised over the computer system and that several breaches of the licensed dealer rules had taken place. But none of them was sufficient to guarantee the DTI success if it moved to wind up Barlow Clowes in the High Court.

Other regulators were notified of the DTI's action: the Department was worried that Barlow Clowes might apply to join an SRO without telling it that it was currently under investigation. The Securities and Investments Board was kept closely informed: the system of licensed dealers administered by the DTI was due to be replaced at the end of April 1988 by the Financial Services Act. The SIB was the overseer of the new investor protection system. If need be it, rather than the DTI, could exercise powers against Barlow Clowes.

Meanwhile Hoffman and Ziman had discovered the gilt deals with the overseas firm and decided they were bogus. Hoffman had also spotted that some £10 million had at some point gone missing from the UK funds. The £16 million infusion seemed like an attempt to replenish the coffers before the inspectors had had a chance to discover the shortfall.

Hoffman prepared a draft report for the DTI, also giving an oral presentation of it to the SIB and IMRO. There had been several factors indicating that the £16 million gilts dealings with the overseas firm were bogus. Perhaps the most potent was the fact that the deals, which ostensibly went back to 1984, had been recorded on Twinlock office paper, marked 'copyright 1986'. Clowes's crude attempt at a cover-up had been exposed.

CHAPTER TWENTY-ONE
•
COUNTDOWN TO DISASTER
•

'This is going to the top. This is not the insolvency of a corner shop. The political side of this is going to get bigger.'

Peter Clowes

At 9.15 p.m. on Friday 27 May 1988 the telephone rang at the desk of John Bell, the City Editor of *The Times*. Bell, unusually, had left for home. I was walking past his desk and took the call. On the other end was Barbara Conway, a director and chief press officer of the Securities and Investments Board. Before joining the SIB Conway had been a tenacious investigative journalist, whose weekly 'Scrutineer' column in the City pages of the *Daily Telegraph* was much respected. 'We've provisionally closed down Barlow Clowes, the gilts fund manager,' Conway said.

'How much is at risk?' I asked.

'Fifty million pounds at least,' Conway replied.

I hung up. I would speak to her another four times before the evening was out.

The Business News section of *The Times* uses a 'late man' system – one person has to stay until 11 p.m. each night to cover any late-breaking stories. That night it was the turn of David Smith – *The Times* economics correspondent. Between us we knew next to nothing about Barlow Clowes. Smith found a woefully thin file of press cuttings on the company in our business news library. These revealed that two days earlier James Ferguson Holdings had asked the Stock Exchange to suspend dealings in its shares. Ferguson's suspension, followed by the closure of Barlow Clowes, meant something was clearly wrong.

'You know Barlow Clowes has its headquarters in Gibraltar?' Smith said, reading aloud from the cuttings file.

I rang Conway while Smith started writing the story, such as it was at the time. 'What's this about a Gibraltar office?' I asked.

Conway wouldn't say anything about Barlow Clowes's Gibraltar offices except to point out that the company run from Gibraltar was called Barlow Clowes International and was not directly affected by the closure order. The only company closed down at this stage, said Conway, was Barlow Clowes's UK company, which was called Barlow Clowes Gilt Managers.

I rang David Brewerton, who was in charge of the Business News section of *The Times*, at his Essex home. It was too late to change the first edition of *The Times*, but there were at least another three editions to go. What did Brewerton want to do with the Barlow Clowes story?

Brewerton was terse and to the point: 'Change the splash,' he said, 'we're leading with Barlow Clowes.'

I sat down at the nearest terminal and started writing. I was joined by Graham Searjeant, the financial editor, who flitted between me and Smith advising. In the background the sub-editors were remodelling the front page of *The Times* Business News section, making space for a 600–word article which appeared in the later editions of *The Times* the following morning, under the banner head-line: 'SIB Acts Against Gilt Fund Manager.'

The story of Barlow Clowes, a company which, until then, few people other than its investors had heard of, had begun. Within a fortnight it would be virtually a household name. The Government would be defending itself in both Houses of Parliament for giving Barlow Clowes a licence to deal with the public, and would be forced to announce an independent enquiry. Clowes would be dramatically arrested and 15,000 investors, mainly retired people, would be devastated by the news that their life savings had disappeared.

On Sunday 29 May Clowes flew in his private jet to Gibraltar for an urgent meeting with his Gibraltar lawyer James Levy and the managing director of the Gibraltar office, John Perez. Levy was frantic with concern. He knew nothing of Clowes's massive diversions. Perez himself had seen isolated examples of money not being put into gilts but had no idea of the full extent of the diversion of investors' money. He was reassured when Clowes told him the offshore portfolios were 'safe'. 'There's nothing to worry about,' Clowes said.

The picture changed dramatically when Levy, Clowes and Perez arrived at Barlow Clowes International's offices to find that the fax machine had been running non-stop since Friday evening, receiving requests from clients and financial intermediaries to return their money immediately. Clowes told the two men that he needed time.

Even the largest bank or building society, he argued, would not be able to repay all its depositors right away. Investors could have their money back in three tranches over a six-month period. He drafted a statement for the staff, assuring them that nothing was wrong.

The next morning, at 7.53 a.m., James Ferguson's new stock-brokers, Charlton Seal, faxed to the Stock Exchange the text of an announcement about the closure of Barlow Clowes. It was immediately released on the Exchange's Company News Service, which flashed it on brokers' screens throughout the country. The announcement presented the background to the SIB's closure of Barlow Clowes and ended on a note of defiance: 'The Board of BGCM [Barlow Clowes Gilt Managers] strongly disputes that SIB is justified in taking this action and is taking urgent advice on how to seek redress.'

The SIB's action against Barlow Clowes had been triggered largely by Hoffman's and Ziman's findings and the SIB's own investigations. On 17 May Hoffman had presented the results of the inspectors' investigation to a meeting of officials from the SIB, IMRO, the Department of Trade and the Treasury. Even at this stage there was some doubt whether a High Court petition to wind up Barlow Clowes would succeed. The SIB officials were prepared to take a chance: 'Investor interests called for something to be done immediately,' an SIB official said.[1] Six days later the SIB served a notice on Barlow Clowes Gilt Managers prohibiting it from taking in any new business. At that stage the SIB's action against Barlow Clowes was kept private.

There then followed four days of frantic negotiations. Clowes offered to pay back all the investors in the UK funds if the SIB would lift its prohibition notice. There was a shortfall of £1.6 million, but Clowes said that he would meet this 'from his own personal resources'. Clowes's offer was made on Tuesday 24 May – the day after the SIB had acted. But SIB officials were worried about how the £1.6 million deficit had arisen in the first place and the possibility that the Gibraltar funds had been intermingled with money in the UK. Clowes went to the the SIB's offices in the City to press for an answer to his repayment proposals. At the same time, the SIB and the DTI were taking legal advice on the chances of actually closing down Barlow Clowes. The prohibition notice from the SIB had merely stopped the company taking in new business. It was only a temporary measure. To close down Barlow Clowes a winding-up petition would have to be presented in the High Court. The legal advice from a senior barrister could be described only as fairly encouraging: 'Although the case was not exceptionally strong, there was a reasonably good chance of securing a winding up of [the company] even if the company opposed,' he said.[2] The SIB decided to go ahead. It rejected Clowes's offer of repayment, and applied to the High Court for a winding-up order. The application was made without giving Barlow Clowes any notice – a standard procedure since the element of surprise is important to minimise the risk of money being siphoned off. The court, largely on the basis of a lengthy document sworn on oath by Hoffman, accepted the petition and granted a provisional winding-up order against Barlow Clowes. This effectively closed down the company. The order was granted in the late afternoon of 27 May. It was this that had triggered Conway's telephone call. Finally, after four years of secret, behind-the-scenes warnings, the public were to be given the first adverse news ever about Barlow Clowes. Its UK operations had been shut down. For the 5500 investors in the UK the news was a bolt from the blue.

From the investors' point of view the SIB could not have chosen a worse time to close down Barlow Clowes. It was a bank holiday weekend and thousands of investors spent three traumatic days trying to discover the fate of their life savings.

'What was the most devastating was the lack of information. Being a bank holiday there was nobody we could get in touch with. It was a nightmare. I pray I will not live through another weekend like that,' one investor wrote in a letter to *The Times*. 'We tried to phone our advisers in Weybridge, they just were not answering the telephone, and what hurts most is the fact that they never did. I tried to telephone the City Editor of the *Telegraph*, was put through to the Sports Editor, who thought it was all frightfully funny; after that I gave up.'

In common with many investors this lady craved anonymity. The reasons varied. In her case she could not face being helped: 'This is a tiny, caring village, very helpful to one another. At this particular time I could not cope with their concern,' she wrote. Some were so ashamed of themselves that they could not face their own family with the news: 'Our children don't know,' one couple told me.

The ten days following the closure of Barlow Clowes in the UK were a kind of phoney war. No one apart from Clowes really knew what had happened. He was still trying to save his company and therefore presenting a version of events which suggested nothing much was wrong. Instead snippets of truth intermingled with lies, half-truths and pure fantasy leaked their way into the national press.

There were fiery words from Clowes. 'We've been treated very badly, in a deplorable manner,' he said. 'We are seriously considering every option, which includes fighting the appointment of the liqui-dator. The business is solvent but if the liquidation goes on for a year, or maybe longer, then by the time the lawyers and accountants put their fees in it won't be any more.'

Clowes put himself forward as a man wronged: 'My paramount concern is to get the money back to the investors as soon as possible,' he said. For months afterwards there were variations on this theme: 'I will move heaven and earth,' he would say; 'I am working 20 hours a day' or 'I have devoted 100 per cent of my time.' And all for the investors whose lives he had, in truth, blighted if not destroyed.

I spoke to Clowes several times during that period of confusion when not even the liquidators really knew what was going on. He focused on the hardship of the investors in a way which suggested that others, such as the SIB or the liquidators, were to blame. 'They have stopped the income payments to our investors even though some people totally relied on them,' he told me on the Tuesday after Barlow Clowes had been shut down.

This of course was true. Many of the investors in Barlow Clowes had chosen the company because it offered to pay them a monthly income. The prospect of a regular cheque each month appealed to them. Stopping the payments was like cutting off a lifeline. 'How do I pay my gas bill?' was a common question.

In the 'phoney war' period Clowes found a plausible role as a man aggrieved and seeking justice. The reason given for the SIB action, at that stage, seemed rather technical. The accounting records of Barlow Clowes were not complete, there was the £1.6 million shortfall in the funds – although even at that stage it was only a rumour which the press had fastened upon. 'That's a complete red herring,' Clowes told me. 'In any event I have offered to pay back the investors every single last penny of their money from my own personal resources.'

Clowes's denials of wrongdoing and expressions of injustice were echoed by his staff. 'Our clients realise that this is all a storm in a teacup,' said Perez, the managing director of Barlow Clowes International, when I rang him in Gibraltar. Perez's public remarks were in stark contrast to his private horror when he had seen the fax machine spewing out demands for repayment from the investors.

Back in the UK a director of James Ferguson whom I spoke to was indignant and virtually on the point of tears. 'Cork Gully made an accusation that James Ferguson had borrowed £150,000 from the clients of Barlow Clowes. We categorically denied it. We refuted it. It's totally and absolutely untrue,' he told me. He was wrong. (Cork Gully had been appointed special managers of Barlow Clowes, a caretaker role they later shared with another accountancy firm, Ernst & Whinney, when one partner from each firm was appointed joint liquidator of Barlow Clowes.)

Ludicrous reasons were suggested for the SIB having acted against Barlow Clowes. It was even suggested that Sir Kenneth Berrill, the SIB chairman, wanted 'to go out with a bang' since he was due to leave the SIB days after it closed down Barlow Clowes. 'Berrill's last days – they were looking for a success story to go out on,' one Ferguson's director claimed.[3]

The financial middlemen who had introduced the vast majority of the investors to Barlow Clowes were also claiming to be completely in the dark. 'I have two views,' said Gray, head of IPAS, who put over £50 million with Barlow Clowes. 'The first is that Peter Clowes is a complete buffoon and charlatan and has stolen a lot of money. The other is that this is all a big mistake by SIB. Either I'll break Clowes's legs or I'll throw a hand grenade into the SIB's offices.'[4]

But in those ten days of uncertainty some concrete events occurred which later made sense in the context of the full story. Clowes resigned from the board of Buckley's Brewery and put his stake up for sale. A couple of days later, his business partner von Cramer resigned from the board of J. England. There was a public rift between the two erstwhile business partners and friends. 'He [Clowes] has got himself in a mess and it is impacting on us unfairly,' von Cramer said after Clowes announced the sale of his Buckley's stake.[5]

In desperation Clowes tried to sell the Barlow Clowes UK operation. No one would touch it. It was completely unrealistic for him to expect that anyone would voluntarily assume the liabilities he had created. But for a few days it provided further nourishment for his fantastical projection of himself as an aggrieved party deserving of rescue. The term used in the City for a company which takes over another which is ailing in some way is 'white knight'. Clowes was anything but the damsel in distress – but it was a role he played well for a short while, until it was no longer available.

On Friday 3 June Clowes admitted that not all the Gibraltar money had been invested in gilts: two-thirds of it was in what he called 'ninety-day commercial paper' – usually a form of lending to public companies. This was followed up on 5 June by the *Sunday Times*, which revealed that at least £40 million of the Barlow Clowes

International money had been lent to what Clowes called 'property development' companies. He admitted to me the same day that Barlow Clowes International money had been put into 'a range of private companies'. 'But it's all asset-backed,' he said. Small chinks of daylight were beginning to emerge in the wall of secrecy and lies which Clowes had built over the previous fifteen years.

These were highly significant admissions. 'All the receipts say that we acknowledge investment in Barlow Clowes for British Government securities,' a confused Denis Wilson said. Clowes himself, when later faced with an angry meeting of financial intermediaries demanding to know why all the money was not in gilts, eventually blurted out: 'I must have gone mad.'

The revelation that not all the money was in gilts was the beginning of the end for Clowes. The mask had slipped a little and within days it would be off completely. Clowes would still maintain that there was a plausible, valid explanation for what he had done. But the shadow of doubt had grown too large by now and was obliterating Clowes's version of the truth, until it was visible only to himself.

On Monday 6 June Clowes attended the first of two meetings with financial intermediaries. It was held at the offices of Cork Gully, the court-appointed receivers of Barlow Clowes. The meeting was intended to brief the financial intermediaries about why the SIB had closed down Barlow Clowes. Clowes did not need to attend, but he did.

There was a hushed air of expectancy. Sober faced and dressed in a very dark suit Clowes entered flanked by his legal advisers. He nodded without speaking to a few of the intermediaries who caught his eye as he walked through the gap between the rows of chairs to the front of the room.

At the meeting Clowes came under tremendous pressure from the intermediaries to explain where the Gibraltar money was and why it was not all in gilts. He changed his story yet again. Instead of one-third of the money being in gilts and two-thirds in commercial paper, it was now one-third in gilts, a third in commercial paper and the balance 'needing to be refinanced'.

Clowes stuck steadfast to generalities. He refused to say exactly what enterprises the money had been invested in. He said that the investors did not care whether their money was in gilts or not; all they wanted was a return on their investment. The way in which that return was generated was of no interest so long as the investors received their monthly income. He stuck to this line even when some of the fifty or so intermediaries at the meeting quoted at him the terms of the application form for investing in the Gibraltar company: 'Absolute security is provided because your portfolio will always be in British Government Stock or on deposit with a Bank, Local Authority or other Corporation.'

The cracks were beginning to appear and grow wider. Evidence was presented to the meeting as to the precise reasons the SIB had acted against the UK operation of Barlow Clowes. It did not bode well for the Gibraltar operation. The evidence revealed that Barlow Clowes had artificially run down the returns that investors were earning on their money, had illegally creamed off excessive management fees from the investors without telling them, had transferred millions of pounds of investors' money between the UK and Gibraltar businesses and had falsified clients' records by backdating entries on the firm's computer.

The following day a court order was obtained appointing two partners in the accountancy firm of Ernst & Whinney provisional liquidators of Barlow Clowes International. The move had been initiated by the Ferguson board, which also announced on the same day that Clowes had 'resigned' as chairman and chief executive of the company. In fact Clowes had refused to resign and had been voted off the board by a show of hands. 'Not even Newman supported me,' Clowes later complained. 'He was too scared when he saw all the others were against me.'[6] Christopher Newman was a director of Ferguson and bought shares for Clowes. He was later charged with several criminal offences and acquitted on all.

Early in June I had a telephone call from a woman who asked whether I knew that Clowes owned a luxury yacht. I did not. 'He has bought a boat down in Gibraltar reputedly belonging to Tina Onassis. It's called *Boukephelas*. He paid about £14 million for it,' the caller said. 'He has a helicopter which he keeps at Manchester airport. He spent about £70,000 having it totally refurbished. He spends literally hundreds of thousands of pounds chartering private jets.'

And so the caller went on. Did I know about the three private jets and helicopter that Clowes ran or the fleet of luxury yachts, known as 'floating palaces', which he claimed he owned? Did I know that he was in the habit of hiring private jets to fly him from Manchester to Marbella for the weekend at a cost of £8000 a time or that he flew his family out to the Caribbean the March before in an HS 125 jet, paying £80,000 for the trip? Was I aware of the 'rumour in the area' that he started in business with a Mrs Barlow selling turf from a caravan?

'Peter Clowes's wife Pamela was married to Eric Haydock, the bass guitarist of the Hollies pop group,' the caller told me. 'Eric is now Mr and Mrs Clowes's chauffeur and general dogsbody.' Did I know that Clowes was currently spending hundreds of thousands of pounds rebuilding a luxury home for his family in Macclesfield and installing a helicopter pad in the grounds? 'The head of customs at Manchester airport has been notified not to let him out of the country,' the caller told me. She told me that two weeks earlier Clowes had been spotted in Périgueux, near Bordeaux, France, and that he was believed to own a château out there.

There was nothing that I could do immediately with this information. There would be enormous problems persuading the newspaper's lawyers to allow any of it into print. The source was someone whom I had never met and the information came solely from her. But it helped build up a picture of whom and what we were dealing with so we set about trying to confirm as much of it as possible. *The Times*'s Gibraltar correspondent quickly located the *Boukephelas* – costing $2.5 million according to public records in Gibraltar, not £14 million.

The caller was able to provide us with the registration numbers of the jets and a vague idea of where they were located. They were found and photographed. The *Sun* cuttings library had a 1966 clipping of Eric Haydock of the Hollies marrying a lady called Pamela Done. The records of Barlow Clowes kept at Companies House showed that Pamela Clowes was at one time known as Pamela Done. We found the floating palaces in the Caribbean, but they were owned by C. H. Bailey. They were the *Welsh Falcon* and the *Welsh Princess*, both of which would later be destroyed by fire in separate incidents. Clowes had a stake in Bailey – but he did not own the yachts themselves.

The next day, 8 June, *The Times* published an article on the bizarre personal life and jet-set lifestyle of Clowes. It was based on the information we had received and illustrated, the following day, with photographs of the jets and *Boukephelas*. It was popular journalism and David Brewerton was convinced we would be sued. I tried, weakly, to cover us in the article: 'How much is fact or local fiction about the man is hard to discern,' I wrote after cataloguing the Cloweses' extravagances, including the suggestion that Clowes had started by selling turf from a caravan.

But the 8 June article was important because it completely changed people's perception of the man. The following day the *Independent*'s front-page splash was 'Luxury yacht investigated in City scandal'. Clowes's image was undergoing a rapid transformation and the story was running away from his control. No one dared say it overtly but the clear implication of the stories was that Clowes had used the money entrusted to him by Barlow Clowes investors to finance his own extravagant lifestyle. And, in a way, we ourselves, the media, were out of control. No one had threatened to sue us and the liquidators were not discouraging the line of attack. Much of it was completely new to them as well. We had *carte blanche* to print more or less what we liked. There were no writs, not even threats of writs or demands for corrections and apologies. Clowes was not going to do anything about it.

The day after Clowes's lifestyle became headline news the story abruptly changed direction. I received a telephone call from a public relations man whom I already knew. Would I like to talk to one of his clients who had information on Barlow Clowes?

'What sort of information?' I asked.

'He wants to tell you about the Government.'

'What about the Government?'

'Meet him and you'll find out.'

At 8 a.m., in the panoramic breakfast room of a West End hotel, I found out how the Government had been warned against licensing Barlow Clowes and yet had given it a licence. 'We warned the Department of Trade several times,' my informant told me. 'We' in his case was Nasdim – the body set up as an alternative to securing a DTI licence. My informant also pointed out that Barlow Clowes had operated for several years without a licence from the DTI – a criminal offence. 'The DTI was aware of this but it turned a blind eye', he told me.

All this was very interesting but my informant had been vague on the warnings that had been given. It was clear that Nasdim had been unhappy about Barlow Clowes – but had had no hard evidence against the firm. My meeting with the informant had been mentioned at the morning editorial conference of *The Times*, and the editor was very keen that we should have a story which attacked the Government. I was nervous – we had so few facts.

'Milk it for what it is worth,' John Bell said to me.

So I did. During the day I managed to speak to other Nasdim officials who more or less confirmed my source's account of events. None of them had anything tangible. The Department of Trade refused to comment.

The next day, Friday 10 June, the front-page headline of *The Times* was 'DTI Ignored Warning over Clowes Deals'. It contained just two significant new facts – both in the first paragraph. 'Top level warnings about the crashed investment company Barlow Clowes were ignored when they were given to the Government at least four years ago – after it had been trading illegally for more than four years.'

The story was incomplete but at the same time sufficient. It only scratched the surface but it transported Barlow Clowes into the political domain for the first time. It was a front-page headline story in a 'serious' newspaper and as such could not be ignored. Three days later a government enquiry would be announced in both Houses of Parliament and gradually the litany of warnings which the Government had received about Barlow Clowes from several different sources began to emerge.

The same day as the 'political' front-page splash appeared the Business News section of *The Times* led with a story about two jewellery companies in which Clowes was involved. 'Interest-free loans made to Clowes firms', the headline read: 'Two Barlow Clowes companies have made interest-free loans of more than £2.4 million to private jewellery companies of which Mr Peter Clowes is a director.' The clear implication was that investors' money had been misused. Not so, said Pamela Clowes, who had been interviewed the same day by a freelance journalist working for *The Times* in Manchester. 'If I told you the truth it is so unscandalous I don't think you would want to print it. Who can prove that any money is misplaced? As far as I am concerned the money is there,' she said. 'Surely if my husband had anything to be guilty about, he would have run away by now?'[7]

All sorts of people were telephoning the newspaper with information. These included 'Edward', who called several times from a coin box in Nice in the South of France. 'I was a courier for Peter Clowes,' Edward said. 'I was given two suitcases, one had £25,000 in it, the other £5000,' Edward said. 'I took them to Antwerp and exchanged them for precious stones.' Edward claimed that he then deposited the stones in a safety deposit box at a bank in Geneva in the name of Pamela Clowes. Edward had a great deal of accurate information about Barlow Clowes – particularly its Geneva operation. And ostensibly he had a motive for talking – Clowes had not paid him: 'He still owes me a thousand pounds.' He wanted me to go with him to the Geneva bank and examine the contents of the safety deposit box – Edward claimed that he had the requisite documentation to do so.

We decided that he was a hoaxer. He certainly wanted money – 'a few hundred to cover my expenses'. Thankfully, John Bell, the

City Editor, stopped my flying to France to meet him. 'We can get together in a hotel in Marseille,' Edward said. 'No chance,' said Bell, 'it's too risky.' Edward later tried selling his story to the *Daily Mail* and to Michael Jordan of Cork Gully – again without success.

On the night of 9 June a lady who wouldn't give her name telephoned *The Times* and said that she had information about documents being secretly destroyed at Barlow Clowes's head office in Poynton. Rodney Hobson, at that time the Business News night editor, took the call. The lady would not leave her number or identify herself in any way, but Hobson arranged for her to call again at 1 p.m. the following day. He telephoned me at home and told me to expect the call. 'It sounds interesting,' he said.

At 1 p.m. on Friday 10 June the lady called. 'I used to work at Barlow Clowes,' she said. She told me how documents were secretly shredded at Barlow Clowes's headquarters after two DTI inspectors started investigating the company:

> Most of it was happening after work and at weekends. Peter Clowes's secretary was making the arrangements. The inspectors used to be going back and forward for coffee while Sandra would be making all the arrangements for people to go over to Gibraltar to shred documents there. I couldn't believe that they didn't know what was going on.
>
> All the files were gone through, papers were gone through. Papers were removed from files. Some were letters about tax returns – they were removed. If people had invested in Portfolio 30 and wanted to move to Portfolio 37, their letters of instruction were removed.

She continued in similar vein: 'Peter Clowes instructed the staff to remove papers from the files and shred them. He didn't want the DTI to know about Megerberry [the private property company run by Clowes]. We were instructed not to mention the company at all.' The Megerberry telephone number was removed from an internal list of telephone numbers, the caller told me.

All this was very exciting, but how could we verify it? I spoke to *The Times* lawyer, Alistair Brett. He advised that the only way we could run the story was if we did not specifically say that Clowes had authorised the shredding. This would of course be implicit, however.

I had arranged for the anonymous caller to ring me back at 5 p.m. Meanwhile I telephoned an official who was involved in the closure of Barlow Clowes. 'I don't know whether it's true or not but it certainly fits in with what we know,' the source said. I called Stanley Wright, the former civil servant and now chairman of James Ferguson. Did he know about shredding? Wright was shocked: 'I have no knowledge of any shredding taking place. I don't live in Poynton; I was a non-executive director. If I was aware of any action of that kind being taken I would not be a member of this board now.'[8]

Some fundamental questions needed to be answered. How could I be sure that the caller was who she said she was? And, even if she was a Barlow Clowes employee who had witnessed the shredding, could it have been routine destruction of documents rather than a deliberate attempt to conceal information?

The caller rang back at 5 p.m. 'It was definitely a panic measure, no question about it,' she said. 'The DTI were working in the top floor conference room and all the shredding was going on on the ground floor. I'm amazed that they didn't know. . . . They [Barlow Clowes] sent about six people at a time out to Gibraltar in the private jets to destroy the documents there.'

The Times ran the story – on the front page. I believed that the caller was genuine so we took a chance on the accuracy of her information. The headline the following day, Saturday 11 June, was: 'Papers were shredded at Clowes HQ'. Above the headline, just beneath *The Times* masthead, were the words, suggested by John Bell: 'Former employee claims that the DTI was working on the top floor while there was shredding on the bottom floor.' We held our breath. If we were wrong we would know soon enough.

At 2 a.m. on Sunday 12 June I received a telephone call at home from a source closely connected with the closure of Barlow Clowes.

'What's going on?' I asked.

The person at the other end could hardly speak: 'Ninety million pounds is missing,' he said, his voice shaking with emotion. 'In madcap ventures associated with Mr Clowes. It's the most monumental fraud that there has ever been in this country. It's hideous. There is huge distress among the investigators. It's like a funeral here.

'We need your help,' the caller said.

'What can I do?'

'Come to the SIB's offices at ten.'

'Why?'

'They want to arrest Peter Clowes – they'll need to know about the shredding.'

The offices of the SIB in Royal Exchange Buildings in the heart of the City were full of people. Most of them were coming to or going from a large conference room in the basement of the building which was often used to hold press conferences. There were SIB officials, Cork Gully staff and a number of other unidentified people whom I saw but was not introduced to.

I gave various people as much information as I had about the shredding, Clowes's jet-set lifestyle and a list of private companies of which he was a director. These included Mekom and Cottrills, both of which were showing enormous losses. Clowes's ambitious expansion plans for the companies had not worked. These, along with others, had been lent money by Clowes interest free. The suspicion – and at that time it could only be a suspicion – was that the loans had been made from money belonging to Barlow Clowes investors.

Later that day I wrote a front-page story for the first edition of *The Times*, headlined: '£90 million from Clowes investors sought by lawyers.' It was a deliberately cautious story, which referred to 'mounting concern' that up to £90 million of investors' money 'may be missing'. We did not have the confidence to accuse Clowes of outright fraud. The headline on the Business News page was: 'Clowes private empire comes under scrutiny.' The article listed several private companies which had received interest-free loans from Barlow Clowes. But we did not say that the money belonged to investors.

That evening I received a telephone call at work to tell me that Clowes had admitted shredding documents: 'He has admitted that he was there when the shredding took place. He has admitted that most of what you said is correct and has named the people involved. The truth is out. I was there when it was confirmed. He may disagree on minor details.' The caller told me that it would be 'worth keeping an eye on Clowes for the next couple of days. They could snatch him at his home tomorrow morning.'

Although I did not know it at the time Clowes had cracked. After a day-long meeting at the Poynton head office, and under repeated questioning from Jordan and David Freeman, the senior partner of D. J. Freeman , the law firm called in to advise Cork Gully, Clowes had admitted his mad diversion of investors' funds into assets other than gilts. Clowes had broken off to make a telephone call. Twenty minutes later a battered old van arrived, driven by one of Clowes's stepsons. It was crammed with documents which would reveal the extent of the diversion of investors' money.

I knew none of this when I rang Clowes's home. His number was listed in the directory. I wanted to run a story saying that he had admitted that the shredding of documents had taken place.

The telephone was answered by Pamela, to whom I had spoken once before. She had told me then that she was 'a family person': 'I just enjoy looking after my children.' Then she had been quite friendly – now she was anything but.

'I don't see why my husband should want to talk to you of all people,' she barked when I asked to speak to Clowes. 'You have given us a very unfair press.'

I probably said something trite such as that I was only doing my job and reporting what I considered was true. Pamela was not taking this. She attacked me for writing about her first husband Eric Haydock and recounting how he still worked for them. This had been part of the 'bizarre personal life of Peter Clowes'.

'What has that got to do with anything? It's totally irrelevant. Yes, Eric does work for us. Peter gave Eric a job when he needed one. I am a very, no fairly, broad-minded person. I like unusual people.'

I apologised to her for mentioning Eric Haydock. 'I'm sorry about that. It wasn't relevant.'

'Thank you for that,' she said.

She then accused me of obtaining information about her and her husband from Robin Cottrill, of J. T. Cottrill & Sons, a man I had never spoken to before. Cottrills was one of the recipients of Barlow Clowes investors' money. 'You've published information which could only have come from him.'

'I've never spoken to him. All the information is publicly available,' I said. 'That's the truth.'

Pamela's tone changed gradually from hostile to aggrieved. We spoke for about half an hour. She clearly wanted to talk.

'There has been a lot of sensational speculation. My husband has not cheated anybody,' she said.

'What about the money that is missing?' I asked.

'Has it gone missing? My husband yesterday told me that all the UK gilts had been sold and all the investors will get their money back. It's all there – it is going to take longer to sort it out. He has made personal pledges with his own money. There are problems but he will sort it out.'

She sounded very genuine. She believed that what she was saying was the truth. 'I have complete faith in my husband,' she said.

'I think he's duping you,' I replied. It was a disgraceful thing for me to say. But I had locked into her desperation. The conversation had become twisted. It was if we were now on the same side and I wanted her to believe my version of the truth, to see things as I saw them, as I thought they really were. Her husband was a conman and I told her so.

'So you think my husband has stolen all the money?' she asked meekly.

'Yes,' I said.

We continued like this for a while. She felt I had been 'unfair' to her and her husband in the way I had covered the story. I countered, saying that her husband was not returning my telephone calls. 'I've got no chance to put his side of the story.' This was true up to a point. But it was not the reason I had taken the line I had. We – I, my editors and all the other newspapers and media – took the view that Clowes was a crook. The fact that he had not been tried or convicted of anything was irrelevant.

Eventually I reached a point with Pamela where I am sure that she started to believe me and to doubt her husband. Or perhaps she simply started to question a little for herself where the trappings of massive wealth which she had enjoyed for several years had come from. I don't think she knew the full extent of the deception Clowes had perpetrated. By the end of our conversation Pamela was no longer saying, 'Peter says all the money is there.' This had changed to: 'I'll get him to phone you when he gets in.' That was what I had wanted.

Half an hour later the telephone rang: 'It's Peter Clowes speaking.'

Clowes had returned from his all-day grilling by Jordan and Freeman. They were a good double act: Freeman played the soft guy, gentle and understanding; Jordan was the tough man. Clowes was exhausted.

'I believe you told my wife that I was a conman,' he said.

I don't know what I replied. It was probably a feeble 'Yes, but . . .' sort of response.

'Do you think that was fair?'

'No, I don't. I should never have sought to come between you and your wife. It's none of my business. I'm sorry. I should never have said it.'

'Thank you', said Clowes. 'Now I'd like you to tell my wife that.'

Pamela came to the telephone and whispered a quiet 'Hello'. Goodness knows what sort of scene she had had with her husband.

I apologised to her: 'I really am very sorry.' She thanked me for my apology and before putting me back to her husband said goodbye.

'Now let's talk,' said Clowes.

I spoke to Clowes for an hour and a half, until well after midnight. John Bell, the City Editor, sat opposite me all that time, pushing handwritten questions across whenever I seemed to be flagging. The key thing was to keep the man on the telephone. At one point I said something which offended Clowes – I suggested that he had personally benefited whenever interest-free loans of investors' money had been made to private companies since he often had shares in those companies. 'I'll put the phone down if you go on talking like that,' he said. I retrieved the situation and he kept talking. We both knew what I wanted: his confession.

Like his wife, Clowes needed to attack me: 'Apart from Patrick Donavan at the *Independent* you have given me the most hostile press,' he said. He then tripped out the usual platitudes which he had used for the past fortnight. 'Let's get things clear,' he said. 'First, I am not running away and, second, I will not rest until they [the investors] get their money back. I admit I have made mistakes. I trusted people I shouldn't have.'

Bell passed me a note: 'Ask him about the shredding, is it true?' I asked him. 'You had a very dramatic article there,' Clowes said. I pressed him: 'Is it true?'

'I have discussed it with Cork Gully,' Clowes said. 'Of course it's true but it's true within a context. We have rightly a duty of confidentiality to our clients.'

I did not challenge this. He was suggesting that his motive in shredding documents was to protect his clients, to keep their details confidential. Clowes was talking and he was beginning to admit things. We talked generalities for the next fifteen minutes. Clowes explained why he thought that his gilts portfolios were incompatible with the Financial Services Act. I was too tired to listen. It was not what I wanted but I did not want to stop him. Somehow we got back to the investors.

'Did you put any of the investors' money into public companies?' I asked him.

Clowes paused for what seemed like a long time, and said: 'I'm not denying that at the moment.' It was almost a confession. Then he said something which just did not make sense: 'There are situations where I have used the money to generate a return under my control rather than going out to the man in the street.'

I don't know why or how but I shouted at him: 'That's meaningless and you know it. You are still making excuses. Did you put the investors' money into Buckley's Brewery?'

'Yes.'

'Into C. H. Bailey?'

'Yes.'

'Into J. England?'

'Yes.'

The private companies had received investors' money too, as had some of the trappings of the jet-set lifestyle. 'I have signed everything over to the special managers [Cork Gully],' said Clowes. 'That includes the yachts, the planes, everything. Very little of the offshore funds are in gilts.' (Only £1.9 million out of £140 million owed to the offshore investors was subsequently found to be invested in gilts.)

Clowes had confessed. I asked the obvious question: 'Why did you do it?'

'To get the greatest return for them [the investors]. If we had just invested in gilts there is no circumstances [sic] we could have got the return.'

Bell pushed over a note: 'Was the Government's abolition of bondwashing a factor?' I asked Clowes. 'Bondwashing is a factor. Of course it is a factor.'

'What about the stockmarket crash?' wrote Bell on another note. 'Yes, the market crash is a factor; everything is a factor,' said Clowes wearily.

Clowes was almost in free fall now: 'I have been in discussions at the most senior government level today. This is going to the top. This is not the insolvency of a corner shop. The political side of this is going to get bigger.'

One thing that Clowes did not do during our conversation was admit that he was a thief. He was far from admitting that he had stolen the investors' money or even that he had taken it for his own use. Everything he had done, he claimed, was to achieve the returns he had promised his investors. They would have had their money back eventually. Even though I challenged this Clowes stood fast. The luxury yacht, the *Boukephelas*, was a charter operation, he said. He would hire it out to people for so many thousand pounds a day. 'Have you hired it out?' I asked him. 'Not yet, we only bought it recently.'

He spun a similar story about the private jets. The company that owned them had been financed with the investors' money: 'We are buying and selling private jets through our own company. Any profits will go to our investors,' Clowes said. There were no profits – 'yet'.

The investments in the private companies were 'venture capital'. The idea was that the companies would expand and then be floated on the stock market or be taken over by other companies. In this way investors could obtain a large capital profit.

It was all fantasy – at best – but in reality blatant lies. Clowes did have visions of himself as an empire builder and scattered investors' money far and wide. But when he took money out of the investors' accounts to pay for his private jet trips, part of him knew this was wrong. When he and his family sunbathed on the deck of the *Boukephelas* he knew the investors, whose money he had used to pay for the boat, were not benefiting.

He could delude himself comfortably when his Barlow Clowes business was thriving, telling himself that the investors would benefit in the long run and that none was losing out. When his empire crashed this delusion became far harder to maintain. Clowes desperately needed it because now that the music had stopped he looked very much like a liar and a thief who had robbed the most vulnerable section of society to feed his fantasies. And he would lose all he had achieved: the power and respectability that he had enjoyed in Gibraltar, the launch party eighteen months earlier, the master plan, the acquisitions he was going to make, the public companies he controlled – all this was about to disappear. To admit that it was his own fault, that his achievements were built on a lie, would probably have been too much for Peter Clowes, the little lad from Lancashire who had started off selling pots and pans in his dad's hardware shop. Clowes never let go of his capacity for self-delusion and probably never will. He twisted and turned it, until it told him that it was all the liquidators' fault, the SIB's, the DTI's, all those who had conspired to close down his business. Had Barlow Clowes not been closed, none of the investors would have lost out, Clowes argued. Any high street bank, if it were closed, could not pay all its depositors back. He was like the high street clearers. He had been unfairly treated – so had his investors. It was not his fault.

'I am not running away. I will not rest until they get their money back,' were his last words to me that night, at 12.45 a.m.

We had to change the front page. 'Clowes admits £100 million diversion' was the headline in *The Times* the following morning. Underneath, in bold letters, was a second headline, known as a strapline:

'Government statement expected today.' The Barlow Clowes empire had fallen apart and was about to be minutely dissected by the national press. In the coming days and weeks thousands of retired people would read to their horror how the money they had accumulated over a lifetime's work had been dissipated in order to feed Clowes's craving for power and respectability.

CHAPTER TWENTY-TWO
·
THE FIGHT FOR COMPENSATION
·

'My methods might have been unconventional but I have not done anything wrong and I have not stolen any money from anybody.'
Peter Clowes

On Monday 13 June the Government had announced that it would hold an independent investigation into the way that the Department of Trade and Industry had handled Barlow Clowes. Simultaneous announcements were made in the House of Lords by Lord Young of Graffham, the Secretary of State for Trade and Industry, and in the Commons by Francis Maude, Lord Young's junior minister at the DTI. 'I shall appoint an independent person of standing to investigate and report to me as soon as possible on the facts of my department's handling of the matter', Lord Young told the Lords. A separate investigation would also be launched into James Ferguson, Young said.

In the Commons, the announcement of an investigation had been welcomed by the Labour Opposition spokesman on City affairs, Tony Blair. But he attacked the Government for its record on investor protection: 'the trenchant action today stands in stark contrast to the years of gullibility and incompetence which preceded it'. Blair's attack made headlines the following morning. The Barlow Clowes affair was now firmly in the political arena; it was no longer a scandal confined to the City and the financial community. The political dimension had put it on the front pages of the national newspapers, where it would stay for weeks to come.

The announcement of the investigation was welcomed by both Houses and the national press. It was followed up the next day with the news that Sir Godfray Le Quesne, a former chairman of the Monopolies and Mergers Commission, would head the investigation. Sir Godfray was a highly respected lawyer who had presided over several controversial Monopolies Commission investigations in the past. These included two investigations several years earlier into the takeover intentions of Tiny Rowland's Lonrho conglomerate towards House of Fraser, owner of the Harrods department store. During the course of his meetings with the Commission Rowland had noticed a hole in one of Sir Godfray's shoes and wondered 'why Lonrho's bid was in the hands of a man who couldn't organise his own shoe repairs'.[1]

Lost among the general air of optimism that followed the announcement of an official enquiry into Barlow Clowes was an astute point Lord Williams of Elvel had made in the House of Lords in response to Lord Young's announcement. Lord Williams, a Labour spokesman on City affairs, has pointed out that the original text of the Barlow Clowes announcement, released to him through the Government Whips Office, had been slightly different. In referring to the intended investigation it had said that the appointed investigator would report 'as soon as possible on the department's handling of the matter'. When Lord Young had read out the announcement he had inserted the words 'the facts' so that the report became a report 'on the facts of my department's handling of the matter'. Why the change? 'My Lords, notwithstanding the advances of modern technology words are occasionally left out,' Lord Young explained.

Lord Williams's point may have seemed to be nitpicking at the time but would eventually prove very important. The issue it addressed was whether the independent investigator would be allowed to make a judgement on the DTI's handling of Barlow Clowes. Or would the investigation be more limited – a purely factual enquiry, to determine what had actually happened. If it was the latter, who would make the judgement on the facts established by the investigator?

Other statements by Lord Young that day seemed to indicate that there would be a wide-ranging investigation: 'This is an enquiry to determine the facts of what actually happened within the department and to determine whether or not the department is to blame in any way.'

Events moved quickly. Clowes was dramatically arrested and held overnight in a cell in Bishopsgate police station in the City. He appeared at Guildhall Magistrates' Court the following morning, charged with perverting the course of justice and released on bail of £300,000. It was a holding charge – relating to the destruction of documents at Barlow Clowes's offices. The police wanted to take steps to ensure Clowes did not leave the country while they collected evidence against him over the coming months for more substantial charges. The bail conditions required Clowes to surrender his pass-port. The same tactic had been used in the Guinness case when Ernest Saunders, the former chairman of the international drinks group, was suddenly arrested at his solicitors' office also for allegedly destroying documents – charges of which he was later acquitted.

Clowes, when released by the magistrate, clutched his wife Pamela's hand and disappeared for a short consultation with his lawyers before emerging to push his way through a throng of reporters and television crews into a waiting taxi. His legal adviser, Charles Buckley – who represented Clowes for a short while – sounded off on the pavement outside the court about the summary manner in which Barlow Clowes had been closed down by the Securities and Investments Board. 'I do not doubt that Mr Clowes is a very honest man and he will be directing his energies first second and third to the recovery of the investors' money,' he said.[2]

Also at the court that day was Edward Dunn, a former British Airways pilot who had driven by motorbike from Farnham in Surrey to watch the hearing. Along with another British Airways pilot Dunn had invested in Barlow Clowes after the idea of investing with the group was raised at a seminar organised by British Airways. He had put £25,000 in Barlow Clowes International, mainly his redundancy payment but also including money on behalf of his mother and mother-in-law. When he heard of the demise of Barlow Clowes in the UK, Dunn and a former colleague at British Airways, James Budd, who had invested £65,000, had flown directly to Gibraltar to get their money back. They met John Perez, the managing director of Barlow Clowes International, who told them they could have 30 per cent of it back within six days. It proved to be a futile trip. 'I waited six days in Gibraltar and went back to Barlow Clowes's office and found it closed,' Dunn told reporters outside the court. He had driven to the court, he said, because he needed to see Clowes in the flesh.

Meanwhile thousands of investors had been telephoning the offices of liquidators Cork Gully and Ernst & Whinney, desperate for help and information. Cork Gully was taking an average of 3000 calls a week from investors.

'They were utterly bemused and shocked that a company of this repute, backed by a government licence, could collapse,' says David Graham, one of the Cork Gully partners handling Barlow Clowes:

They were dumbfounded. We were not dealing with illiter-ate, unsophisticated people. You were dealing with teachers, former civil servants, a fairly representative cross-section of the middle classes, people who were never going to be very rich. The elderly were saying, 'Where's the income going to come from to help us pay for next week's gas bill? I'm going to have to sell and live with my kids. Who do I turn to, what do I do?' They were driven to distraction. These people genuinely had agony. You were not dealing with small amounts, these people had at stake on average something between ten and twenty-five thousand pounds. They were very bitter towards the Government. They were in a state of panic, suffering real hardship. They suffered resignation, hoping, reading the papers for every bit of news. 'We can't take our minds off it; whose fault is it, is it my fault?' they said.

The vast majority of the Barlow Clowes investors were either retired and living off their investment with Barlow Clowes or had intended their investment with the group as a lump sum for their retirement. 'I lost over £40,000, it's my pension. I have got no private pension or anything,' an investor with Barlow Clowes International told me. His was a typical experience. It soon became apparent that most of the investors had put virtually all their money in one basket: Barlow Clowes. To lose it was a life-shattering blow.

The DTI was by no means the only target for the investors' anger and sense of betrayal. They turned on their professional advisers, the financial intermediaries who had recommended that they put their money with Barlow Clowes in the first place. The intermediaries were generally as dumbfounded as the investors to find that only a tiny fraction of the money placed with Barlow Clowes International had been invested in gilts. 'Barlow Clowes has been known to us for the past nine years and in that time we have had no reason to doubt their integrity and honesty,' financial adviser Roger Chapman wrote to Barlow Clowes investors who had invested via his firm Chapman How Financial Management. He pointed out how he and other intermediaries who had invested in Barlow Clowes had found that the firm had always paid out income to investors on time and returned their capital when requested. From their point of view the firm had shown no signs of being shaky. 'We have acted in good faith in recommending these investments and would never have done so if we thought there was any element of risk.'[3]

But the curtain came down on some of the intermediaries very shortly after the demise of Barlow Clowes. FIMBRA, the watchdog over financial intermediaries, suspended IPAS, the Surrey-based intermediary run by David Gray. This effectively closed the business down – almost three years after FIMBRA's predecessor organisation Nasdim had granted Gray and IPAS a reprieve by rejecting a recommendation to expel them from membership. Gray's behaviour had been mercurial to say the least. When the Barlow Clowes scandal broke and thousands of panic-stricken investors were bombarding the IPAS office with telephone calls, Gray took his daughter and went on holiday. The man with 'a strong set of principles' – according to the IPAS literature – simply disappeared for a week, saying that 'he'd had enough'. (Ironically the IPAS promotional literature says: 'Indeed we prefer to think of our customers as clients and actively encourage them to contact us at any time for help or advice'.)

Gray's junior partner, David Myers, was furious. 'I don't know how he could have done this', he said. Later he was to complain bitterly about Gray: 'All that stuff about him being a family man was nonsense', said Myers. 'His personal life is a mess and always has been.'

Some 4500 people had entrusted their money to Gray's business. Gray channelled their money – £56 million – into Barlow Clowes. Most of it – £39 million – went offshore, into Barlow Clowes International where the prospects of investors getting their money back looked very bleak. IPAS clients knew nothing about the secret commission payments which Barlow Clowes paid to the firm in return for putting so much business its way. From early 1986 onwards Barlow Clowes paid IPAS an extra 1 per cent of all the money which was invested in its offshore fund. The payments were made from a secret numbered account in Barlow Clowes's Gibraltar offices to an equally clandestine account for IPAS in Switzerland. From June 1987 onwards the secret commissions were paid into the account of a Panamanian company at Swiss Bank Corporation in Geneva. Gray had purchased the Panamanian company for the specific purpose of receiving the commissions.

More than £500,000 was paid to IPAS in secret commissions. Gray did not pay any tax on this money or disclose its existence on his income tax returns as he should have done. He claimed, in later court proceedings to wind up IPAS, that he had not known that the secret payments were subject to UK income tax. 'I understood that if the commission was not received in the UK it would not be subject to UK tax provided the monies were retained offshore and provided they were not held in my name but in the name of a foreign company of which I was not a director or a signatory to that company's account,' Gray claimed.

The best that can be said for Gray is that he made an error. But it is a surprising one given that he promoted his business to investors as one which took into account taxation matters and could advise on the subject: 'Before selecting any investment, however, you should give careful consideration to your own tax position etc. That is why we provide counselling services on all financial matters.'

The adviser, it appears, could not advise himself.

When the Securities and Investments Board successfully brought High Court proceedings to wind up IPAS the SIB's barrister Philip Heslop recited an amazing story of how Gray had lost two large sums of money. Gray claimed that he had lost a briefcase containing £197,000 in Swiss francs while on a business trip abroad. He also maintained that he had lent £97,500 to an Australian businessman whose address and telephone number he had left in a telephone box. Heslop said that these cases gave rise to 'extraordinary doubts about the man's probity, let alone his competence'.[4]

Soon it was the turn of Denis Wilson, the Cheshire-based financial adviser, to be suspended by FIMBRA. Wilson was the second largest generator of business to Barlow Clowes. 'We have been suspended because FIMBRA says we are over-exposed to Barlow Clowes,' Wilson told me shortly after learning of his suspension:[5]

> We are only over-exposed because we wanted to play safe. We thought the money was in gilts. I've put my ninety-year-old mother-in-law into Barlow Clowes. The thing that grieves us most is that we have never been a commission-hungry type of business. When the stock market crash came we thought how pleased we were that all our dear oldies, our clients, were in British Government securities.

Events moved so quickly in the weeks following the collapse of Barlow Clowes that almost every day bought dramatic new revelations. Clowes's actions, successfully concealed over the past years, were now being forced out into the open, confronting the investors with a reality they had not the slightest inkling of before. James Ferguson collapsed, brought down by the secret loan to the company from Bank of Credit and Commerce International which the bank had now called in. Ferguson owed the Bank £10.6 million. The loan had been supported by an equivalent deposit of funds belonging to Barlow Clowes International investors. This money was now at risk.

Stanley Wright, the Ferguson chairman, declared himself 'appalled and horrified' to discover that the loan was backed by Barlow Clowes investors. Clowes had told the Ferguson board that it was his own money or that of his companies. Within a week Wright resigned as chairman. 'I have learnt a lot, particularly in the last few weeks,' he said. 'I believed in Mr Clowes for a very long time until a very late stage.'

As Ferguson collapsed von Cramer issued a statement denying that he knew that Barlow Clowes investors' money had been used on the corporate forays in which the two men had engaged. Investors now knew that shares in companies such as Buckley's Brewery, C. H. Bailey and quiche-maker J. England had been bought with their money. 'I can categorically confirm that I had no knowledge at any time that these investments may have come from anything other than Mr Clowes's own *bona fide* resources,' he said.

News of the previous police involvement in Barlow Clowes leaked out. Brian Carlton, the airline executive who had kept tabs on Clowes and reported his suspicions about the man's jet-set lifestyle to the police, telephoned me. So did the shredding informant – this time to tell me about the French château. Philip Jacobson, *The Times*'s correspondent in Paris, was dispatched with a photographer to locate Château d'Auros, which he did, tasting the wine to enable him to provide a full report of this bizarre receptacle of investors' money.

David Pine, a partner in the Manchester firm of solicitors Alexander Tatham and Co., had been following the Barlow Clowes developments with interest ever since the firm had been closed down at the end of May. Pine had called me up the week after the closure to discuss the case. He had acted in the past for investors in Farrington Stead, the Manchester-based licensed dealer run by two former Barlow Clowes employees. The collapse of Farrington had brought down Hedderwicks and David Pine had managed to recover 92 per cent of the Farrington investors' money from the liquidator of Hedderwicks. Now he wanted to start an action group for Barlow Clowes investors, to co-ordinate any legal action they might need to take. Other firms of solicitors were also taking an interest, notably Glaisyers, a Birmingham-based firm whose Gibraltar office had already been contacted by several investors. Articles began appearing in the press mentioning the firms and soon they too were being inundated with calls as the investors swarmed to another potential source of help. Fifteen people were employed full time at Alexander Tatham taking calls which never stopped throughout the day. A meeting of investors was called at Manchester Town Hall, for Thursday 23 June.

On the evening of 22 June Antony Gold, a twenty-nine-year-old junior partner at Alexander Tatham, was preparing an address which he would give at the following day's meeting. Sitting on his bed at his home in Wilmslow he hit upon a simple idea which would prove vitally important to future events: the investors has to be organised into a political lobby group. They were united in one thing – they wanted their money back. Why not channel their common aim into a lobby group which would campaign for compensation from the Government? 'I realised that it wasn't sufficient to have 18,000 people sitting in their homes waiting for cheques to come through the door', Gold says. The investors 'needed to be mobilised to raise the profile of their case, to give them a sense of purpose and to make it quite clear to the Government that they were going to be dug in for a long fight.'[6]

Twelve hundred investors travelling from all over the country attended the meeting the following afternoon. They were reluctantly thrust into the limelight because dozens of reporters and television film crews were also there. Many investors were reduced to hiding their faces behind newspapers or notepads which they had brought with them to avoid being identified. They were truly a sorry bunch, many of whom had tragic stories to tell. A Sheffield couple, Anne and Vincent Middleton had invested £200,000 in Barlow Clowes International. 'We sold our house in January and had the solicitors make out the cheque there and then to BCI because our financial adviser told us it was as safe as the pound in our pocket, safer than the building society,' Mrs Middleton said.[7] A disabled man from Nottinghamshire invested £30,000 in Barlow Clowes International one month before the crash. He received his first monthly payment and then persuaded his daughter to invest her £10,000 life savings days before the crash.[8]

Pine, Gold and a representative from Cork Gully, Stephen Hook, all addressed the meeting. There would be two groups – a Legal Action Group, which would co-ordinate the solicitors involved and examine what legal rights the investors had and whom they could sue. The investors were invited to contribute £100 each to put the group in funds. 'I think it is also very important to have an Investors' Group,' Gold told the meeting. 'It is important that investors co-ordinate pressure on MPs and other bodies to try and force the DTI to make compensation payments.' His view was echoed by Pine: 'The maximum amount of political pressure must be applied. If you have not already written to your MP then do so immediately,' he said. The investors were not optimistic. Many were angry and downright suspicious. One investor challenged Pine, claiming, incorrectly, that he had been representing firms of financial intermediaries. Another who had lost money in a previous financial collapse told the meeting: 'We've been through the trauma you are going to go through and we have got exactly nowhere.' Was it worth chipping in £100 each to sue the financial intermediaries, another investor asked. 'If you sue them you would just close them down,' he said. Some were defiant – 'It's going to cost this Government more in social security payments than compensation', one investor claimed – and others were shell-shocked and confused. 'He was such a nice fellow, I have known him for years,' a retired printer said, referring to Denis Wilson, the financial intermediary.

Some investors had already taken a more pragmatic approach to their problems. Elizabeth Nathaniels, a teacher and lecturer, had been persuaded by her financial adviser that it made sense to take out a mortgage on her house and invest the proceeds with Barlow Clowes. She did, putting £27,000 into Barlow Clowes International. 'I am going to go on fighting until I get it back,' she said. When the crisis broke she had started collecting names and addresses of fellow investors. John Dyer, a forty-six-year-old managing director of a Cambridge medical equipment supplier, had also been organising his own small group of investors. 'I knew four or five people who had invested in Barlow Clowes,' says Dyer. 'I made contact with my local paper suggesting that other investors in my area get in touch. Within a few days I had 120 people.' After the meeting Dyer joined forces with Nathaniels to form the nucleus of what would become known as the Barlow Clowes Investors Group. Another investor, Malcolm Rae, had his own mailing company. A newsletter would be printed and investors were asked to contribute what they could afford, preferably at least £3 to cover mailing costs.

In the next few days other meetings of investors were held: in Stockport Town Hall a packed meeting of investors who put their money into Barlow Clowes via local intermediaries such as D. C. Wilson was addressed by local Conservative MP Stephen Day. A meeting was held in Cardiff on 30 June. A week after the Manchester meeting, twenty-six MPs, mainly Tories, signed a motion arguing that if the Le Quesne enquiry revealed errors on the DTI's part then the Government should provide compensation to the investors at the earliest practical date. In the meantime the liquidators had taken action against von Cramer and Naylor, freezing their assets and demanding the return of money allegedly loaned to them. Clowes himself had signed over to the liquidators most of the assets which he regarded as his own – many in fact purchased with investors' money. The agreement with the liquidators had, however, allowed him to draw £1000 a week living expenses – an amount which would infuriate the investors when details of it leaked out several months later.

Dyer was appointed chairman of the Barlow Clowes Investors Group at a small meeting of volunteers held in the offices of Alexander Tatham. Gold regarded Dyer as the natural choice: 'He was a level-headed businessman with a flair for organisation. It was important to have someone as chairman who was making full-time executive decisions.' Dyer was already a wealthy man. The loss of his money, some £70,000, hurt him but was a relatively small percentage of his capital. Indeed he considered himself a lucky man: he had withdrawn £195,000 from Barlow Clowes International a few weeks before the crash.

Dyer's first decision was to divide the country into eleven regions, appointing a regional co-ordinator for each. The regions were then subdivided into areas with area organisers. The idea was to orchestrate support for the Barlow Clowes investors at local, regional and national level. This would involve securing newspaper coverage for the investors' campaign while at the same time ensuring that as many MPs as possible were involved.

Although groups of MPs, sometimes accompanied by Dyer, held meetings with DTI ministers, the Government's line – that it would await the results of the Le Quesne enquiry before making any further comment – held firm. Without the investors' group and its relentless lobbying the Barlow Clowes story might have become a dead issue by the time Le Quesne's report was published in October. Parliament was in recess so the political forum was removed. But in the intervening months more detail emerged of what had gone wrong in the DTI's handling of Barlow Clowes. Details of the Stock Exchange's warnings were revealed, as was the advice from Spicer & Pegler, to Clowes, dating back to 1986, that he should return the money in Barlow Clowes International to UK-based investors. How had the situation been allowed to continue for so long? The *Sunday Times* revealed that the DTI had renewed Barlow Clowes's licence after it had been given details of Clowes's directorship of the Cottrill jewellery shop. The paper also revealed the warnings which Peter Hayes, the Macclesfield-based financial adviser, had given the DTI about Barlow Clowes. Hayes's own informant had been Adrian Collins of

Gartmore. The *Financial Times* revealed the details of the revolt in the Geneva office of Barlow Clowes and how the employees there had forced Clowes and Naylor to sign a letter of comfort. Derek Tree's secret visit to Spicers, Robert Posey's fears, Richard Hooper's memorandum about the chaos in the Geneva office to his partner at Spicers, Julian Pilkington; these and other revelations forced their way to the surface, emerging in black and white newspaper print which kept the Barlow Clowes issue firmly alive.

There was a worry which I, and I am sure other journalists, had at the time when we were publishing revelations which showed clearly that something had gone wrong at Barlow Clowes and that someone had to take the blame. The worry was simply that the revelations would give the investors false hope. That they would still end up with nothing. The Government would dig its heels in and refuse to pay compensation. The chances of legal action against the DTI succeeding were extremely remote. Most of those involved in the Barlow Clowes affair hoped that the political pressure from the investors filtering up through their MPs would, when combined with the newspaper revelations and, hopefully, Sir Godfray's report, force the Government into making a voluntary compensation offer.

A crucial worry for the investors was that if the Government did recommend compensation it would be limited to those investors who had placed their money with Barlow Clowes Gilt Managers, the UK firm, which had been licensed by the DTI, while the Gibraltar arm, Barlow Clowes International was completely unlicensed. Most of the 7000 investors in Barlow Clowes Gilt Managers faced losses of around a third of their money while those in Barlow Clowes International might recover only 30 per cent of their money or in many cases far less than this, perhaps nothing at all. In any event the complications of realising the assets into which Clowes had sunk the Barlow Clowes International investors' money would mean that the 11,000 investors in this fund would have to wait years.

The Le Quesne report was finished in early September 1988. But Lord Young decided to publish it as soon as Parliament had reconvened towards the end of October. This was conveniently after the Tory Party conference in Brighton where Sir Godfray's report, had it been public at the time, would have made the Barlow Clowes affair a disruptive and controversial issue. As it was the conference was picketed by the investors, who handed out leaflets to delegates, arguing that the Government had a moral responsibility to compensate investors. Shortly before the conference began Mrs Thatcher pledged that there would be no 'cover-up' on Barlow Clowes, saying that she found the plight of the investors 'deeply distressing'. Her remarks were contained in a letter to Alf Morris, Labour MP for Wythenshawe, the south Manchester suburb where, ironically, Clowes's father had run his paraffin round almost thirty years earlier.

The Le Quesne report was published on the afternoon of Thursday 20 October and simultaneous statements were made in the Commons and Lords. As had been feared Le Quesne had confined himself to a factual account of what had happened. He had drawn no conclusions. The Government, in contrast, had appended its own conclusions to the report and decided that it was not to blame. 'The facts set out in Sir Godfray's report in the Government's view provide no grounds for concluding that my department's handling of the matter was unreasonable or caused the losses experienced by investors, and therefore provide no justification for using taxpayers' money to fund compensation,' Lord Young told the House of Lords.

The reality was quite different. The Le Quesne report highlighted a catalogue of warnings received by the DTI about Barlow Clowes over a number of years. But more than that, a careful reading of the report – one which would take far longer than the few hours afforded to journalists between the report's publication and their newspaper deadlines – showed clearly that the DTI had made a number of crucial errors. These flatly contradicted some of the conclusions that the Government had itself drawn from the report. MPs from all sides of the Commons refused to accept the Government's conclusions. Tony Blair, the Labour spokesman on City affairs, described the Government's denial of blame as 'so brazen as to be risible'. Within hours of publishing the report Lord Young appeared before the Backbench Trade and Industry Committee. 'I was used to an attendance of about a dozen. This time the Committee room was packed, with at least ninety [MPs] there. I opened with a short statement. The first question was hostile and it went straight downhill from then on. The general line was that the Government should pay. I was given a very stormy ride.'[9] The MPs were angry and dismayed at the way the Government had used the Le Quesne report to justify not paying compensation. After the meeting Nicholas Winterton, MP for Macclesfield, who was in the forefront of the campaign for compensation, said: 'He [Lord Young] got a clear message that what he had done was not good enough. I think he has taken on board the strength of opinion expressed by many members, some in very positive and direct terms.'[10] 'I am sorry I cannot sell this line. I'm not even going to try. Go away and think again,' Michael Latham

MP, a member of the Parliamentary Accounts Committee, told Lord Young.[11]

The pressure for the Government to change its tune subsided a few days later when the Ombudsman, Sir Anthony Richard Barrow-clough, announced that he would investigate the DTI's handling of Barlow Clowes. Known formally as the Parliamentary Commissioner for Administration, he investigated cases referred to him by a member of Parliament which involved potential maladministration by a government department. Maladministration covered a multitude of sins – such as undue delay, incompetence, neglect and ineptitude. It meant that there would be another enquiry into the DTI, immediately after Sir Godfray Le Quesne had reported. There would be a considerable amount of duplication, but the Ombudsman's investigation represented the best chance yet of the investors being compensated.

The statistics showed that in the vast majority of cases the Ombudsman took on he found at least some degree of maladministration in the government department concerned. Moreover, he could, if he considered it appropriate, recommend that the Government compensate the complainant in the particular case. The Government had no obligation to follow his recommendation but in the case of Barlow Clowes, with the investors' group having secured so many MPs to its cause, there would be an enormous political outcry if the Ombudsman's recommendation for compensation was not followed. And there was a precedent too which favoured the Barlow Clowes investors. A few years earlier the Ombudsman had investigated the DTI's handling of another licensed dealer which had collapsed and, finding the DTI to blame, had recommended compensation. The Government had paid. The difference was that in the case of Langford Scott, the dealer concerned, the amounts involved were small – perhaps as little as £60,000 in all.

The Barlow Clowes case was referred to the Ombudsman by Alf Morris MP on behalf of one of his constituents, Leslie Mullard, a seventy-four-year-old retired major in the Royal Engineers. He had invested £56,000 in Barlow Clowes, almost half in the Gibraltar end. The disappearance of his savings had forced him and his wife to sell their cottage and move to a smaller bungalow to raise capital. Although this specific case formally triggered the Ombudsman's investigation, a total of 159 MPs wrote to the Ombudsman on behalf of their constituents. But it was clear that the investors were in for a long wait.

*

In the early hours of Wednesday 7 December von Cramer, Christopher Newman and Naylor were arrested in dawn raids on their homes by police officers acting under the instructions of the Serious Fraud Office. Clowes himself was arrested, this time in less dramatic fashion – he presented himself by prior arrangement at Bishopsgate police station. All four were charged with theft. James Levy, the Gibraltar lawyer whose firm Hassan & Partners acted for Barlow Clowes International, was also arrested – at Gatwick airport – and charged with offences relating to the Hermes false computer income which had been used to inflate the profits of Barlow Clowes. All charges against Levy were later dropped.

There were other casualties as well. FIMBRA, the intermediaries' watchdog, had been embarrassed by the discovery that one of its council members had recommended Barlow Clowes to her clients. Christine Leach stepped down from the council early in 1989, claiming that she felt she had done nothing wrong. Her firm, the Cardiff-based Chris Leach Associates, was one of about twenty-five firms facing disciplinary action mainly for recommending Barlow Clowes International to their clients without having authorisation to do so. She eventually paid a £3000 fine levied by FIMBRA.

The FIMBRA position was complicated: about 160 of its members had dealt with Barlow Clowes over the years, most of them recommending its products to their clients. (A few had put clients into Barlow Clowes only at their clients' insistence.) From FIMBRA's point of view there was nothing wrong with recommending Barlow Clowes – provided members were in the appropriate FIMBRA category of membership. In the case of Barlow Clowes International, because it was an unregulated offshore fund, FIMBRA's rules imposed an additional requirement that permission must be sought by any of its members that wanted to recommend BCI. No firm ever sought permission!

However, FIMBRA's rules only became active in April 1988 when the main provisions of the Financial Services Act came into effect. So the watchdog could only discipline members who had recommended BCI in the narrow period of weeks between the activation of its rules and the closure of Barlow Clowes at the end of May 1988.

But there was a broader point at stake: back in February 1985 FIMBRA's predecessor, Nasdim, had circulated its members warning them not to deal with an unauthorised investment business. Barlow Clowes was not named but the circular had been aimed at it. Once Barlow Clowes had been licensed by the DTI the embargo was lifted. But in reality the licence was blinkered, limited only to Barlow Clowes in the UK. The DTI never knew of the true activities of BCI, so it remained unregulated. Hence, the danger which the Nasdim circular sought to avert had still existed in the ensuing years and FIMBRA, before the Financial Services Act came into effect, blithely allowed its members to recommend to clients that they put their savings squarely in the danger zone.

Meanwhile the Institute of Chartered Accountants launched an enquiry into the role played in the Barlow Clowes affair by Spicer & Pegler (by that time renamed Spicer & Oppenheim), accountants to Barlow Clowes, and Touche Ross, the James Ferguson auditors. The outcome of this enquiry had not been made public at the time of writing.

Some groups of investors did receive part of their money back. When Barlow Clowes Gilt Managers had been closed down the liquidators had found £7 million in the Lloyds custodian bank account which the DTI had insisted that Barlow Clowes establish as a condition of granting the firm a licence in 1985. Some thousand investors whose money was in the custodian account received three-quarters of it back by the end of the year. In January 1989 the High Court approved a distribution of 25p in the pound for some 6000 investors whose money had been invested in Barlow Clowes Gilt Managers in the UK and was held by Midland Bank. Allied Dunbar, the financial services group, and Barclays Bank both made compensation payments to investors who had been introduced to Barlow Clowes through salesmen associated with them.

But the majority of investors – the 19,000 in Barlow Clowes International – received nothing and waited anxiously for the Ombudsman's report. The liquidators sought the advice of the High Court on how they should distribute the little money which they had recovered on behalf of Barlow Clowes International investors. The court's ruling favoured investors whose money had been invested late in the day or could be traced to a specific asset, such as the *Boukephelas* yacht. The effect would be that some investors would recover practically all their money while several thousand would recover little or nothing.

The stress and strain on the investors were beginning to tell. They were dying at the rate of seven a week. One investor told a meeting at Westminster Town Hall how she had been driven to attempt suicide. Many investors needed counselling or tranquillisers to keep them from breaking down. In the long months of 1989 Dyer and his investors' group did as much as they could to keep the momentum going. They kept printing newsletters and holding meetings but for several months the newspaper interest in Barlow Clowes had, not surprisingly, waned. The issue was on hold, awaiting a decision from the Ombudsman to reactivate it.

The political pressure continued. The investors' group prepared a document entitled 'The Case for Compensation', which it sent to investors. They in turn took it to their MPs and in many cases insisted on returning at a later date to discuss it with them. 'It was important to have a well-written document, a product which we could take to MPs', says Dyer. When it became clear that the Ombudsman's report would be published just before Christmas, all 18,000 investors were sent a newsletter urging them to write to their local MP, Mrs Thatcher and the then Trade Secretary Nicholas Ridley, who had replaced Lord Young at the DTI, arguing their case for compensation. Tens of thousands of letters were written as a result.

The Ombudsman's report was finally published six days before Christmas and provided the investors with a Christmas present beyond their wildest dreams. Sir Anthony Barrowclough found five different areas where the DTI had been guilty of maladministration and recommended that all the Barlow Clowes investors should be compensated. The DTI, he said, should have realised that Barlow Clowes had an operation in Jersey marketing to UK investors before it licensed the firm. Had it done so, in the Ombudsman's opinion, the further enquiries which would have resulted made it 'a virtual certainty' that Barlow Clowes would have been shut down. The DTI would have discovered that Barlow Clowes had been expelled from the island and that Clowes had lied when he claimed – in his first meeting with the DTI in December 1984 – that his Jersey funds served expatriates only. Moreover, by that time £3.65 million was already missing from the Jersey funds. This was the Ombudsman's key finding of fault. He also criticised the DTI's 'legitimisation' attitude to Barlow Clowes and its failure to evaluate the Barlow Clowes product properly. Even the mistakes which the Department had made in the 1970s – erroneously advising Barlow Clowes that it did not need a licence – could not be disregarded. In his summary the Ombudsman criticised the DTI for 'the lack of a sufficiently rigorous and enquiring approach'.

The Ombudsman said that no distinction ought to be drawn between the UK and the offshore investors. Nor should there be any difference in treatment between those who had invested before Barlow Clowes had been licensed by the DTI and those who had placed their money with the firm afterwards. Everyone was to be treated in the same way. Everyone was to be compensated.

Nicholas Ridley told the House of Commons that afternoon that the Government disagreed with the Ombudsman's conclusions – indeed the Government published its own observations on the Barlow Clowes case, defending its actions. But, 'out of respect' for the Ombudsman's office, the Government would pay the compensation. The vast majority of the investors would get 90 per cent of their money back from an unprecedented £155 million compensation package which the Government, albeit reluctantly, had put together. Ridley spoke in the House of Commons of 'the large number of investors, many of them elderly' who had 'suffered hardship'. 'Many believed, albeit wrongly, that they were investing in gilts. They were led to believe that their investment was safer than it was.' But Ridley sounded a note of warning for the army of financial intermediaries and professionals involved in the rise of Barlow Clowes. 'The Government believes that there are others whose role in the Barlow Clowes affair deserves close examination and who cannot escape part at least of the blame for what happened. I give notice of our intention to pursue vigorously any claims which show prospects of reducing the cost to the public purse of these payments.' Later the Government would issue over 600 writs against IPAS and its founders, D. C. Wilson, Analysis and a host of other financial intermediaries who had recommended Barlow Clowes. Midland Bank – the bank which received Derek Tree's warning about possible fraud and yet continued to act as banker to Barlow Clowes – would also be sued.[12] These proceedings were launched in the second half of 1990, and their outcome was not determined when this book was finished. Spicers has recently been threatened with a writ unless it contributes towards the money the Government had to pay out.

The payment of compensation to investors signified victory for the unprecedented grassroots campaign they spearheaded and also a just finale for the Government and its appalling record on investor protection. Without Barlow Clowes, the years of gullibility and neglect encapsulated in the pathetic system of licensing at the Department of Trade and Industry would have been known only to those few who operated in the financial arena. Put crudely, the Government would have got away with it. The unprecedented compensation payment for the Barlow Clowes investors was a fitting punishment. It provided an equivalence of sorts, balancing what had gone before.

More than six hundred of the investors died before the Ombudsman's report was published. The trauma undoubtedly speeded, if not caused, the deaths of many of these people, a few of whom committed suicide or died of shock shortly after the Barlow Clowes scandal broke in the newspapers. And many died in the saddest circumstances, such as husbands who thought, in dying, that they had left their wives to live in poverty. But for the vast majority who survived the eighteen months of stress there was a therapeutic neatness in the fact that the body that they most blamed for their woes – the Government – was the source of the compensation.

As for Clowes, he blames the Securities and Investments Board for closing down his business. If the SIB had not intervened, the investors' savings would have remained intact. After all he always paid them their guaranteed return – and gave them their money back if they wanted it. 'My methods might have been unconventional but I have not done anything wrong and I have not stolen money from anybody,' he claims. 'My brother was never a rogue,' says John Clowes. 'He was not bad, just overtaken by events.' This view is at least partly shared by Clowes's first business partner and former mistress Elizabeth Barlow. 'He really didn't have the education to do what he was doing with gilts. It seems to me that he got roped in and things took him over.' Others, many others, see things rather differently.

CHAPTER TWENTY-THREE

·

BREATHTAKING CHEEK

·

The trial of Peter Clowes began on Tuesday 2 July 1991, more than three years after Barlow Clowes had been closed down by the Securities and Investments Board. Clowes faced eleven charges of theft, as well as charges of conspiracy to deceive and of making false statements to persuade people to invest with him. The theft charges amounted to almost £17 million. Other defendants were charged with Clowes. They included Dr Peter Naylor who had joined Barlow Clowes straight from university in 1982 and operated as Clowes's right-hand man for several years; Guy von Cramer, who had partnered Clowes on his major corporate raids, such as the successful takeover bid for Buckley's brewery; and finally Christopher Newman, the former finance director of Barlow Clowes, the man who had done much of Peter Clowes's share dealing for him.

All the men faced theft charges. The trappings of their wealth over the past few years were now paraded before the jury by the prosecution as examples of their dishonesty: Clowes's luxury yacht, the *Boukephelas*, Naylor's magnificent Surrey home, Cramer's Ferrari Testarossa, the French château – all had been purchased with investor's money, the prosecution alleged. Moreover, the defendants had known exactly what they were doing. They had known the money was not theirs. They had been dishonest.

This was 'flagrant fraud conducted on a massive scale,' declared prosecuting counsel Mr Alan Suckling QC in his opening speech to the jury. The scheme was 'simple and as old as the hills. You persuade people to entrust their savings to you by telling them they will be kept in a safe and rock-solid investment but use it to live the life of Reilly. You make good any deficiencies with fresh money from new investors and you lie and cheat to cover your tracks.'

Clowes, said Suckling, had been 'the mastermind of the Barlow Clowes organisation, the instigator and driving force in the fraud'. Naylor had started as a computer analyst but became Clowes's second in command. 'He helped Clowes to milk investors' funds and used them to line his own pocket,' Mr Suckling alleged. Cramer, at twenty-nine the youngest of the defendants, had nevertheless stolen millions of pounds 'used to fund takeovers of private and public companies he and Clowes wished to control'. He had also used investors' money to pay off his overdraft when under pressure from his bank manager.

There were twenty charges in all, each one denied by the defendants. Their defences were not always the same. As the trial progressed Peter Clowes became more and more isolated in his position, each of the defendants denying his version of the truth. The prosecution exploited these differences to portray Clowes, Naylor and Cramer as 'thick as thieves' who had 'fallen out as thieves frequently do'.

The setting for the Barlow Clowes trial had none of the traditional hallmarks of great criminal trials of the past. It took place in an annexe to the Old Bailey, a purpose-built court in London's Chancery Lane. The courtroom itself looked like a vast open-plan office, its low ceiling streaked across with fluorescent lighting, a huge empty space at the rear of the room. The defence teams were each boxed off in a separate rectangle of tables, low metal partitions and cardboard boxes on which rows of files were lined. At the front, on a raised dais, sat Mr Justice Phillips, whose wig and red gown were the most visible evidence of courtroom tradition. Virtually everything else was modern and new: the light brown office furniture, the wall-to-wall pink and blue carpet, and, in particular, the rows of computer terminals.

This was the courtroom of the future. Each juror shared a computer terminal with his neighbour; the prosecution and defence teams were supplied with them, as was the judge. Documents and witnesses were filmed by a video camera and appeared on the computer terminal screens. This made the case for and against the defendants easier to present, as well as giving the jury, who sat at some distance from the witness box, an excellent view of each witness's demeanour as they gave evidence. The most important aspect of this modern courtroom, from the defendants' point of view, was that there was no dock. They did not have to sit day after day next to one another in a separate area of the court. Instead each sat with his team of lawyers, the Clowes team located closest to the jury. Clowes himself was easily visible from the small side area of the court which had been partitioned off for the press.

An air of unreality hung about the court, largely engendered by the temporary nature of all the office furniture and the lack of natural daylight, the fabric blinds being kept permanently shut. One could imagine, when the day's proceedings finished late each afternoon, the court being cleared of all furniture so that it could be used later on for exercise classes or a lecture.

The reality, of course, was very different for everyone directly involved in the case. The Barlow Clowes trial was scheduled to last for as long as eight months and dozens of witnesses would be called. A guilty verdict on any of the charges would mean a prison sentence. The Clowes camp knew their man could go down for ten years. Another of the defendants was pessimistic about his own chances, estimating that he was likely to be imprisoned for as long as seven years.

For Peter Clowes the proceedings must have appeared like a nightmarish version of the television show *This Is Your Life*. Witness after witness was called by the prosecution, people who had known Clowes more than half of his lifetime, such as the intermediary Denis Wilson or Clowes's Manchester solicitor Roger Anders. People who had worked with him, for him or even against him, for years – secretaries, government officials, bankers, accountants – virtually all of them gave evidence which, if accepted, could mean only one thing. Clowes was a liar.

What was the case against Clowes? The prosecution argued that he had systematically deceived investors into putting money with his offshore business on the basis that it would be securely invested in gilts. In fact, very few gilts had been bought, the money instead being used to finance Clowes's corporate raiding, his private company empire, his lifestyle and the expenses of the Barlow Clowes offices, such as rent and wages. When Barlow Clowes International, the offshore side of the business, was closed down by the authorities in June 1988, the cupboard was bare. Investors were owed £140 million, but only £1.8 million worth of gilts had been bought and this was for one of the minor investment products of Barlow Clowes. Investors in the key offshore 'portfolios', Portfolios 28 and 68, had been deceived. There were no gilts for them.

Early on in the case the jury were shown advertisements that Barlow Clowes had produced to attract business from Gibraltar residents. All of them extolled the virtues of Barlow Clowes, the 'gilt specialists', and made out very clearly that the money would go into safe government stock. Then there were the Barlow Clowes brochures, which used phrases such as: 'An international management service providing a high return from British Government Securities'. A brochure which was used by Barlow Clowes until around April 1986 told investors that 'Absolute security is provided because your portfolio will always be in a British Government Stock or cash.' And, when investors sent their money in, Barlow Clowes issued them with receipts saying, '£...... was received and will be managed on a fully discretionary basis in British Government Securities.' Everything made it clear that investors' money would be held in gilts, the prosecution said.

The first stage of the trial was taken up with investors and intermediaries who repeated the same story. They had invested in Barlow Clowes or recommended others to do so on the basis that the company was a specialist in gilt-edged securities. They had no idea that Clowes was scattering money into planes, boats, shares and 'deadbeat jewellery companies', as Mr Suckling put it. They thought that at worst their money might have been on deposit with a bank, either because it was awaiting investment in gilts or because the gilts had been sold and the proceeds were being reinvested in other gilts or about to be returned to the investor. It was gilts or cash. Nothing else.

Clowes sat through all this listening intently, his head bowed as he leant forward, making notes. He was scribbling for his freedom, relaying information to his counsel, Anthony Hacking QC, trying to point out inconsistencies between the evidence that the intermediaries were giving to the court and what they had said in earlier interviews with the Department of Trade inspectors who were investigating Barlow Clowes and its parent company James Ferguson Holdings. The Clowes team scored a few minor points but nothing which removed the clear perception that all the witnesses believed that the money was going into gilts. Some of the intermediaries had not understood the extremely complicated gilts stock-lending scheme which Clowes claimed to be using to make the returns he was promising investors. But this was really a smokescreen thrown up by Clowes to confuse them. They all thought the money was in gilts, or cash.[1]

Clowes's wife, Pamela, often attended in the early stages of the trial, sometimes accompanied by her daughter Nikki. She sat stony-faced and silent, occasionally returning journalists' looks with hostility. The trial had been delayed a few months because Clowes was in hospital with ulcers, most likely brought on by the stress of the pending ordeal. At one stage before the trial he had cut a pathetic figure, visibly aged, using a walking stick, which had gone by the time the trial began.

As is common with major fraud trials, the first few days received heavy newspaper coverage which rapidly tailed off. Mr Suckling's opening address was calculated to grab headlines, and it did: 'Barlow Clowes' only gilt-edged assets were taps, jury told', proclaimed *The*

Times on the third day of the trial. Suckling had shown the jury pictures of Clowes's yacht, the *Boukephelas*. 'If you look very clearly you will see the only gilt-edged objects bought with Mr Clowes's money. Can you guess what they are, members of the jury? The taps.'

One of the most interesting events in the first stage of the trial could not be reported by the press because it occurred in the absence of the jury. It is common for the jury to be sent out while counsel make applications to the judge and on the twenty-seventh day of the trial, Robert Rhodes QC, acting for Guy von Cramer, raised a delicate point. Earlier in the week Doc Naylor's former secretary Shan Swinstead had given evidence. She had made a number of transfers out of bank accounts containing client funds, on the instructions of Clowes, Naylor and others. She had not mentioned Cramer as having authority to give those instructions. Then Mr Justice Phillips intervened: 'Was Mr Cramer someone from whom you would take instructions to make a transfer or not?' he asked.

'Yes,' Miss Swinstead replied; she had forgotten about Cramer, although she could not remember a particular instance when he had given her instructions.

Cramer's defence was that he had never known that Clowes was using investors' money for purposes other than buying gilts. Whenever the two men had engaged in joint ventures together, such as the bid for boardroom control at Belgrave, the hotels and property group, or that for Buckley's brewery, Cramer had assumed that the financing came from Clowes's personal resources. After all, Clowes had presented himself and been portrayed by others as a very wealthy man. David Courtman, the head of the Leeds office of Singer & Friedlander, merchant bank advisers to Clowes, had told Cramer he thought Clowes had £40 million of his own money.

The judge's intervention upset the Cramer team because Swinstead's response could have undermined Cramer's defence. Swinstead regarded Cramer as having authority to tell her to take money out of client accounts and put it in assets other than gilts. Rhodes, although claiming to speak with 'a feeling of diffidence', made his point clear. The judge's intervention 'was not the first time that Your Lordship has intervened, apparently in order to assist the prosecution . . . In my respectful submission, it is not right for Your Lordship to give the prosecution a helping hand: a referee should never kick the ball, let alone kick it towards a particular goal,' Rhodes said. 'If Your Lordship makes further interventions of the nature I have described my client will be bound, rightly or wrongly, to have a perception of partiality towards the prosecution on Your Lordship's part.' 'I will bear your comments in mind,' Mr Justice Phillips said tersely before the case moved on to other matters.

Slowly but surely, the key events in the history of Barlow Clowes were reconstructed for the jury. Richard Syvret, the Jersey Commercial Relations Officer, gave evidence about his decision to move Barlow Clowes off the island in December 1983. Letters from Clowes's solicitors were read out assuring him that the business had been moved and the bank accounts closed. This, as we have seen, was untrue. Syvret admitted under cross-examination that he had not checked independently with the managers of the Midland and Lloyds banks which held the Barlow Clowes accounts. 'I think now, looking back, that would have been a prudent step,' he said.

Former staff from the Geneva office were called to give evidence about the revolt which had taken place in the office in early March 1987. This had culminated in Clowes and Naylor signing letters of comfort, reassuring the staff that the investments which they had processed had been made in the best interests of the investors. The Clowes and Naylor defence teams sought to make out that the revolt was concerned only with fears that the staff might have breached Swiss banking regulations by making the transfers from Geneva. But participants gave evidence against them. Robert Posey, the marketing man in the Geneva office, had written several memos in the days prior to the signing of the letters of comfort, making it clear that his anxiety was that investors were being misled because their money was not going into gilts. He repeated this from the witness box, alleging that he had discussed it with both Clowes and Naylor.

The prosecution called the accountants – Pilkington and Hooper of Spicers, Counsell of Touche Ross – the merchant bank advisers such as Courtman of Singer & Friedlander, and Fleck of lawyers Herbert Smith who had helped Clowes acquire his licence from the DTI back in 1985. One by one they said that they had never known what Clowes was actually doing with investors' money. In most cases the prosecution was able to point to written evidence that Clowes had told them the money was invested in gilts. This was important for they had to prove that not only had investors' money been dissipated into assets other than gilts, but Clowes knew that what he was doing was wrong. The prosecution's case was that he had been dishonest, and, as evidence of his dishonesty, he had lied to his advisers about the true nature of his investment products.

The issue of honesty was vital for Peter Clowes: if he genuinely believed that he was entitled to invest his clients' money in assets other than gilts, he was not guilty of inducing people to invest under false pretences. He was accused of 'making statements as to investment intentions and/or promises which he knew to be misleading, false or deceptive'. His defence was that he believed he was entitled to invest in assets other than gilts. He had what he called an 'investment strategy' whereby he invested money in a wide range of assets to generate the returns he was promising his investors. He argued that although the Barlow Clowes brochures had the word gilts splattered all over them, they actually authorised him to put investors' money 'on deposit', which did not necessarily mean with a bank or building society. The investors' money was on deposit with him, Peter Clowes – or, to be more precise, with his Jersey Partnership. Part of the partnership's function was to act as a bank, taking deposits from investors, paying them returns. And, like a bank, it could invest their money anywhere it liked so long as it paid the returns it promised. In this respect Barlow Clowes was no different from the high-street banks or building societies.

It was a defence, as Alan Suckling later invited the jury to believe, which showed 'breathtaking cheek' on Peter Clowes's part. To sustain it, and to maintain that he was being honest, Clowes had to show that he had told all his advisers what he had been doing. Spicers knew, Singers knew, Touche knew, everyone knew, said the Clowes team. They denied it now because they were protecting their own backs. The government had issued writs to recover the compensation it had paid out to the Barlow Clowes investors. If the advisers, intermediaries and banks admitted that they knew what Clowes was doing they would undermine their defence against the government's lawyers or expose those who had not been sued to legal action by the government. So they were all lying. And on the seventieth day of the trial, when Clowes stepped up to the witness box to begin giving evidence, that is exactly what he said. He maintained this position throughout the nine days that he gave evidence.

In this respect there was a similarity between Peter Clowes's defence and Ernest Saunders's performance in the witness box in the first Guinness trial. Saunders alleged a widespread conspiracy of city advisers, merchant bankers, financiers and stockbrokers to make him the scapegoat for their own actions. Clowes, too, alleged a conspiracy on the part of the professionals, a conspiracy of silence. They had known all along what he was doing with investors' money, had approved it explicitly or implicitly, and were now saying that they had known nothing because they faced writs for negligence from the government. This was Clowes's defence. The intermediaries, the stockbrokers, the accountants from Touche Ross and Spicers, the merchant bankers Singer & Friedlander, the lawyers such as Simpson Curtis were all lying, said Clowes, as one after the other gave evidence on oath that they had believed investors' money was going into gilts or cash. They were lying when they said that they had not known that Clowes was using the investors' money for his corporate raiding, to buy a château, a home for Dr Naylor, a yacht, and so on. They were all liars. Only he was telling the truth. It was a hopeless, desperate defence, one which became less and less credible as Clowes lied his way into corners and tried to lie his way out again.

Clowes, like Saunders, portrayed himself as a victim of the establishment. They had not liked him, said Clowes, ever since the criminal trial which arose from the collapse of the stockbrokers Hedderwick Sterling Grunbar. The Stock Exchange had got it in for him because of the evidence he gave at that trial. The City had not liked him because he had taken away lucrative bondwashing business from them. As in the case of Ernest Saunders, there was some truth in it but, like Saunders, Clowes had brought the anger of what he termed 'the establishment' on himself. The establishment to which both men referred was, in reality, the regulators, institutions such as the Stock Exchange and the Bank of England who had been exasperated by their behaviour. In Saunders's case it was his decision to renege on formal undertakings, given at the time of the Guinness bid for drinks' group Distillers, to move the Guinness headquarters to Scotland and appoint Sir Thomas Risk, governor of the bank of Scotland, as chairman if he won.

Clowes had given evidence at the Hedderwick trial which the Stock Exchange considered plainly dishonest. He ran a business which the Exchange thought could not have a legitimate basis. Both men's actions excited the suspicions of the regulators that something deeper, more sinister was going on beneath the surface. In both cases they were right. Clowes and Saunders were victims only in the sense that they had been caught out.

But what came through from the evidence at the trial given by professionals, bankers, brokers and so on, were the suspicions many harboured that something was wrong but which they had not followed through with effective action leading to the closure of Barlow Clowes. In his opening speech Mr Suckling provided an indication that this was to emerge from the evidence: he claimed that Clowes 'was helped by the reactions of those who strayed dangerously near to discovering the truth. There seems to have been a reluctance in some of them to believe that a fraud of this nature and scale could have been perpetrated.'

It was clear that some of the professionals involved with Barlow Clowes were concerned as to the nature of Clowes's activities but did not penetrate to the core of what he was doing. Spicers had had their doubts about him – the returns on his offshore portfolios were not tax free as Clowes claimed; millions of pounds offshore could not be accounted for by the staff of the Geneva office. Midland Bank had been told of a 'possible fraud' connected with the offshore side of Barlow Clowes. But nobody stood up and openly accused him of stealing tens of millions of pounds of clients' money, because no one knew what he was doing. When they raised questions, Clowes successfully deflected them. He was like an armoured soldier facing a line of archers firing arrows at him. Some bounced off him, many he knocked away with both forearms, others occasionally pierced his skin and may eventually have proved fatal – but none went straight through the heart until the advent of the Securities and Investments Board.

Through his counsel, Clowes tried to twist the meaning of all this. That people had entertained suspicions but not openly accused him of fraud meant that they had 'tacitly encouraged' what Clowes was doing. Tree had warned Midland Bank, but Midland Bank had not stopped Peter Clowes. 'Clearly in our submission the investment strategy was tacitly encouraged by the Midland Bank,' said Mr Anthony Hacking, QC for Clowes. Spicers had received expressions of concern from Tree and Posey. They had not confronted Clowes. Therefore, according to Mr Hacking, 'The investment strategy was tacitly encouraged by Spicers.' When Clowes bid for Buckley's brewery, investors' money coming from clients' accounts had been transferred directly to Singer & Friedlander, the merchant bank advising on the bid. As Mr Hacking put it, 'The bank account in London of Singers had received direct transfers from clients' accounts from the Midland Bank in Jersey and from Barclays Bank in Jersey. There was no criticism by the banking department in London of monies being received in this way in the summer of 1987. No doubt everybody was very excited about a successful bid being made.' His clear implication was that Singers had known that clients' money was being used and yet approved, possibly because they were carried away with making the bid.

This was not true. Courtman of Singers, the executive leading the bid, had no idea that funds from investors were being used. The banking department in London had not told Courtman, who himself headed up Singers' Leeds office. Nor would they be expected to: they were simply a department which processed funds. But Clowes, in his defence, sought to exploit communication breakdowns, imperfections in the system, to his advantage. He turned people's failings or ignorance into a positive, if sometimes tacit, approval of what he was doing. Suckling, for the prosecution, had made clear his belief that the efficiency of some of the professionals could be questioned. 'The vigilance of tenacity of the auditors at a later stage may be thought to have fallen below that which might have been expected of them,' Suckling said. But this did not mean that they had known and approved of what Clowes was doing.

Suckling's point was a very telling one, not for Peter Clowes but for some of the professionals who had been involved with him or his companies. Internal memoranda about Barlow Clowes circulating between various partners of Spicer & Pegler made it absolutely clear that towards the end of 1987 dark suspicions existed as to what Clowes was doing. In one memorandum the fears of Richard Hooper, the partner of the Gibraltar office, were relayed by John Bell, a partner in the Manchester office, to his colleague Allan Pye, who handled Peter Clowes's personal tax affairs. According to Bell, Hooper and the Gibraltar office 'were unhappy about various client account transactions which seem to flit between Gibraltar, Jersey, Switzerland and possibly other jurisdictions and they think it possible [no more] that some of the securities may be used as collateral for some of PC [Peter Clowes] etc's arbitrage deals'. The memo was dated 27 October 1987, several months after the Ferguson deal had gone through, and five months before Barlow Clowes was closed down. Hooper's suspicions were spot on, but he had not known for sure and nothing effective was done about them.[2]

Spicers were not alone. One of the witnesses called in the trial was Roger Fearnley, formerly an executive at NM Rothschild, the merchant bank. Rothschild had provided back-to-back loans for a Clowes computer company called Mekom and for James Ferguson. According to Fearnley, a source outside the bank had told Rothschild to steer clear of James Ferguson, Peter Clowes's master company. This resulted in a memorandum being sent in April 1987 by John Craig, the managing director of Rothschild's banking business, to Charles Price, the head of the bank's Manchester office. Referring to James Ferguson, Craig wrote: 'Could you ensure that we do not have dealings with this company unless and until we have an opportunity to review our relationship.' A copy of the memo was sent to Fearnley who spoke to Craig and told him that the existing back-to-back loans were expected to unwind shortly. Again, there were suspicions. Again they came to nothing.

The day before Clowes took the stand, Mr Justice Phillips had thrown out submissions from the defence teams that they had no case to answer on several of the charges. In the course of his ruling, heard in the absence of the jury and with the press barred from reporting any details, the judge gave an important view on the legal meaning of the Barlow Clowes brochures. As a matter of contract law, there was a contract between Barlow Clowes and the investor to invest their money in gilts. That was the legal meaning of the brochures and other marketing material that Barlow Clowes produced. This did not mean that Peter Clowes was therefore guilty of the charges of deceiving investors. It meant that the way he construed the brochures was wrong under civil, not criminal, law. However, if, despite the breach of contract, he honestly believed he was entitled to invest in non-gilt assets, he was not guilty of these charges.

In his defence Clowes had sought to rely upon a change in the wording of the brochures made around April 1986 as justifying his investment strategy. From this date new brochures had been printed; attached to them was an application form which included what was referred to throughout the trial as the 'investment clause'. It read: 'I enclose my cheque in the sum of £...... payable to Barlow Clowes International Ltd Clients Account and authorise you to buy and sell British Government Stock on my behalf on a fully discretionary basis *and to place any uninvested funds with any bank, local authority corporation or other body on such terms and conditions as you see fit, whether bearing interest or not* [my italics]. I understand that I will receive a guaranteed minimum rate of return each month plus any additional gains as indicated on the monthly statement.'

Clowes argued that this clause meant that there was a contract to pay the investor the guaranteed rate of return. It also authorised him to put the clients' money into anything he chose. This argument got very short shrift from the judge, who had also quoted several of the references in the brochures to investment in gilts. 'The wording of the brochure is only consistent with an agreement on the part of Barlow Clowes to hold investors' funds in trust and to manage their funds by investment in gilt-edged securities.' The investment clause, he said, 'has to be construed having regard to its context. It does not give Barlow Clowes a mandate to invest clients' funds in alternative investments to gilts . . . The authority to place funds with the specified bodies "whether bearing interest or not" cannot be read as giving a power to make such placements by way of alternative investment to gilt-edged securities. The authority is only given to make such placements as action ancillary to using the funds to buy and sell gilts.'

Some witnesses gave evidence in the course of the trial that they had raised the investment clause with Clowes or his staff and been told that it did not mean Barlow Clowes could invest in assets other than gilts. One junior member of the Geneva staff had thought that the clause could cover non-gilt investments, but the general view was that it referred to situations such as the short period when investors' money had been received but not yet invested ('uninvested funds'). At that point, the money would be put on deposit. The Clowes team saw it differently: 'any . . . other body' in the investment clause included Peter Clowes, he argued. But the judge, in his ruling, made it clear that he did not agree. It had to be gilts.

It was against this background that Clowes took the stand in the afternoon of Monday 18 November. He had a comfortable ride at first as he responded to questions from his own counsel. What was his investment strategy, Hacking asked. Clowes replied with confidence: 'The investment strategy was to act like a mini merchant bank . . . and to invest the fund in interest-bearing situations like . . . back-to-back loans . . . which would generate a higher rate of return without deduction of tax than could have been obtained by simply placing the money on the money market in Jersey.'

Clowes had to maintain this position even though Naylor and Cramer both disagreed. Both thought that the investors' money was supposed to go into gilts. Naylor and his advisers made it clear that they did not think that a French château was an acceptable use for investors' money, any more than the jewellery companies or shares in Buckley's Brewery and Belgrave. Naylor claimed that he believed Clowes had been using his own money even though Naylor had, in many cases, transferred the cash for Clowes to make these purchases out of clients' accounts. Naylor's defence was that he thought that Clowes was a client himself, had his own money invested with Barlow Clowes and that it was Clowes's own cash he had believed he was transferring. He believed, also, that some of the money was fees which were owed to Clowes for managing the investors' money. This had been left in the clients' accounts.

The differences between Clowes and Naylor were particularly clear when it came to the Surrey home, Send Barns, which had been purchased for Naylor out of a bank account containing investors' funds. It had cost £365,000. Clowes maintained that this had been

241

an interest free loan to enable Naylor to buy a home. Naylor's version was that it was a bonus he had earned over a two-year period. Clowes had given him the money as a reward for his services. However, in addition, Naylor had withdrawn more than £430,000 from a clients' account for extensive renovations to the house; Naylor said that this money had been an agreed loan from Clowes. Clowes, in the witness box, angrily denied this. He knew nothing about this withdrawal: Naylor had done it entirely on his own authority. He had not been entitled to the money. Here, Clowes seemed to have a good point. Some of the withdrawals Naylor had made to fund the renovations had been entered in Barlow Clowes's computer records as having been made for completely different purposes. One entry was for a private jet trip, another claimed the money had been withdrawn to pay for losses on gilt deals. These entries were bogus: the money had gone on Naylor's home. Clowes's angry response to Naylor's renovations money was out of character with his normal behaviour in the witness box. He typically gave his answers in a completely unemotional way, appearing tired as he was asked the same questions that a series of investigators including his own lawyers, the liquidators, the DTI inspectors and journalists had been asking him over the past few years. Clowes's answers were often robotic, as if the questions triggered a pre-programmed response in his mind.

But Clowes's troubles really began during his cross-examination by the prosecutor Alan Suckling. The five days embracing Suckling's examination were the climax to the decade of deception Clowes had practised on thousands of people: his lies over these years were exposed and thrown back at him by Suckling. He had nowhere to hide. He could no longer tell one story to X, another to Y, yet another to Z, and rely on the fact that X, Y and Z never spoke to one another. He could not compartmentalise the truth. Suckling stood in front of Clowes with all the evidence in his grasp. It was as if Clowes had been forced into a room with all the people to whom he had told different stories over the years standing there, angry, demanding an explanation – only here Suckling was pulling the strings, orchestrating an orderly confrontation, one that took Clowes coldly through each lie, exposed it, and watched while Clowes sank deeper and deeper into his guilt. Sometimes Clowes agreed, yes, he had lied. He was cornered: this time there was no way out – no communication breakdowns, no bureaucratic timidity, no trusting advisers to see Clowes through. Suckling had him.

Time and time again Suckling highlighted Clowes's lies. For example, Clowes's defence maintained that the purchase and sale of a share stake in hotel and property group Belgrave Holdings had been part of his investment strategy. It was clients' money, he had made a £2 million profit on it and, in line with the strategy, he was entitled to keep the profit, because the investors were entitled only to their guaranteed return.[3]

Suckling then referred to a meeting Clowes had held with the Inland Revenue. Clowes's personal accountant, who attended the meeting, had noted Clowes as telling the Revenue that the stake in Belgrave Holdings had been bought by solicitors acting for a syndicate of Swiss and Australian clients. He did not know who they were. The shares were not his. This was an important lie, because Clowes did not want to pay tax on the Belgrave deal. 'It is a lie, is it not, Mr Clowes?' Suckling said.

Clowes admitted it. 'Okay,'he said, after Suckling had repeatedly pressed him.

Suckling was not finished. Clowes had given a third version of the Belgrave share dealings to the DTI inspectors. He told them that he had been acting for an investment 'syndicate' to whom he suggested buying the Belgrave stake. The syndicate had come back to him and said that it was 'very interested' in the deal. The 'syndicate' and Clowes had agreed on a split of any profits. Clowes went ahead and bought the stake. It was another lie.

Suckling read out an interview Clowes had had with the DTI inspectors in which he told them that his Jersey partnership acted for only a handful of overseas clients on a personal basis and probably controlled less than £200,000. The truth, as Suckling pointed out, was that it controlled the entire offshore operation of Barlow Clowes and had over £100 million from investors, almost all resident in the UK.

The inspectors had noticed, moreover, that Barlow Clowes had been receiving a large fee income from the offshore fund, suggesting there was a lot of money under management: '. . . most of those funds have been lost in the last few months,' Clowes told the inspectors, blaming the fall-out of clients on the new investor protection law which was about to come into effect. 'That was completely untrue, was it not?' Suckling said.

Clowes was forced to agree: 'Untrue, yes,' he replied.

Suckling challenged Clowes on his 'investment strategy'. He started by showing him a brochure for Portfolio 28 and made him read aloud the wording describing Barlow Clowes as 'gilt-edged specialists'. 'You had never been known as someone to go to buy a deadbeat company and revive it, had you?' said Suckling. 'You did not describe yourself in there as a mini merchant bank, did you?'

Suckling continued in the same vein, quoting from the brochure himself: ' "The perfect service for security." ' Then, turning to Clowes, he asked, 'What is so secure about putting money in a deadbeat jewellery company?'

'Because the investor was not the beneficial owner of a deadbeat jewellery company as you put it,' Clowes responded. The investors, said Clowes, owned a deposit.

Suckling quoted again: ' "A high guaranteed return from gilt-edged securities",' and added, 'You do not say a high guaranteed return from deadbeat jewellery companies . . . or loss-making châteaux.' Again he returned to the brochure. ' "Absolute security is provided because your portfolio will always be in a British Government stock or cash." You do not think for a moment, Mr Clowes, that it is rather misleading, to say the least, to say your portfolio will always be in a British Government stock or cash when you have every intention of using it for other purposes such as buying a château?'

Clowes: 'I don't believe it is misleading.'

Suckling: 'Mr Clowes, they would not have invested with you, would they, if you told them what you were going to do with the money?'

Clowes: 'They invested with us because we told them their capital would not fluctuate. If they simply wanted a gilt they could have trotted along to the local post office and bought the gilt. But they didn't want that because there they knew that their money – their capital value – could and probably would fluctuate.' No matter what the question, Clowes always proffered an answer.

Clowes also had another problem. He had taken millions of pounds out of the investors' accounts for personal expenditure, his yacht the *Boukephelas*, a Bentley Turbo costing over £70,000 for himself, a Porsche for his wife, not to mention nearly £1 million for his trips by private jet, £243,000 for a temporary home for him and his family in Prestbury, near Manchester, and a host of other things. Suckling calculated that altogether he had taken over £5 million out of the investors' bank accounts for personal expenditure, which even Clowes could not claim was part of his 'investment strategy'. So what was it? Clowes claimed that it represented fees due to him for managing and investing his clients' money. Even though none of the Barlow Clowes brochures or other literature made any mention of it, he claimed that he was entitled to deduct a 3.5 per cent charge on all the money coming into the offshore funds. There was no evidence that he or anyone else had tried to calculate this 3.5 per cent entitlement, no document that he could point to saying that he could take it. In fact, the brochures suggested precisely the opposite: 'Your capital is 100% invested because there is no initial fee or bid/offer spread.' An *aide memoire* which Barlow Clowes sent to investors and intermediaries for Portfolio 68 made the same point even clearer: Clowes was not entitled to a 3.5 per cent fee. It read, 'The capital is 100% invested because there is no initial fee or bid/offer spread. We are able to achieve these high rates from gilts because of our computer-controlled anomaly switching system.' That was an impossible statement since Clowes himself admitted that virtually no gilts had been bought for the offshore portfolios.

Suckling continued with his demolition of the 3.5 per cent fees to which Clowes claimed he was entitled. When Clowes was frantically trying to draw up a record of what he had spent investors' money on, these 'fees' were documented in what was termed by him as a 'loan book' and referred to as loans. His own solicitors had at one point written to the solicitors acting for the liquidators relaying Clowes's view that the £243,000 he had withdrawn to pay for the Prestbury home was a loan to him.

'You have invented that [the 3.5 per cent fee] to justify putting your hand in the till,' Suckling said.

'Absolutely not,' Clowes replied.

'Why is it not there then?

Clowes used his standard reply. The investors were guaranteed their money from making a deposit with him. So long as he paid them out the rate he was promising, he was entitled to withdraw his 3.5 per cent. Moreover, Clowes said, there were two sides to the Jersey partnership – in effect Clowes himself – which managed the funds. There was the manager who was entitled to take an annual fee which was stipulated in early brochures as 0.5 per cent. From 1986 this was increased to 1.5 per cent. But there was also the investment banking side, which invested the money in shares and jewellery companies, etc. This banking side earned the 3.5 per cent.

Clowes used the same argument when Suckling pointed out that when the accounts of the Jersey partnership were sent to the Inland Revenue they made no mention whatsoever of earning a 3.5 per cent fee. Clowes had told the Revenue only about the 0.5 per cent fee. This, said Clowes, was because the accounts submitted only covered the management side of the Jersey partnership. He had not yet provided accounts for the investment banking side.

Clowes had an explanation for everything; he had constructed a scenario which flew in the face of conventional reality. His passionate belief in his own isolated world amounted to intense self-delusion. He clung to it as his only hope of persuading the jury that his intentions were honest. When Suckling referred to Clowes and his associates as a 'team of thieves', Clowes angrily refuted it. 'I find that objectionable, sir, there has been no thieving in this case whatsoever. I have never stolen one penny of anybody's money and I think you should take that back.' Not one person who gave evidence throughout more than one hundred days of the trial supported him in the sense that they could fully confirm his version of reality. None of them saw the same world as Peter Clowes. He was truly isolated just as surely as years earlier, as a child, he had played for hours alone constructing railway fencing out of matchsticks. It was not hard to see how Clowes had reached the point of refuting the usual definitions of words, twisting them into meanings they could not bear. He was a loner who throughout his business life had set all the rules. He had run his own company, no one had been in a superior position to him, he had never had any formal training. Indeed the only financial services house where he had received training – International Life – was renowned for its swashbuckling style and the hidden charges of its main UK product, the Dover Plan. Clowes had made the rules and bent them to suit his purposes. The more he went on, the more bending he had to do, until what he was doing was completely upside down.

This side of Peter Clowes probably explains why he generally delivered his evidence well, even under cross-examination, never completely floundering, always having an answer, no matter how preposterous. The other side of Clowes, the one which had dealt with the real world, which knew what was expected of people entrusted with other people's money, that side of him was a barefaced liar. But now, with many people to whom he had lied individually brought before him to present their version of events, along with all the contradictory statements he had made or approved ranged against him, Clowes was completely exposed.

One might wonder why Clowes chose to give evidence. He did not need to. Neither Cramer nor Newman, the finance director, did. The answer was that the charges against Clowes were so serious, and the evidence to support them so telling, that Clowes had to appear in the box to provide an explanation. This was the view of Clowes's advisers, and Clowes, with no enthusiasm for the task, agreed with them.

Nowhere was Clowes more exposed than when he was cross-examined on the cover-up operation he had orchestrated to deceive the DTI inspectors. A fortnight before he took the stand the court had been told in graphic detail how Clowes had instructed his staff at the Poynton headquarters to shred masses of documents under the nose of the inspectors.

The same operation was carried out in Gibraltar. And, crucially, it was clear that the instructions had come from Peter Clowes. The shredding in Poynton had taken place in the ground floor general office, an area Clowes rarely visited under normal circumstances. According to Anthony Joannou, a junior employee at Barlow Clowes who gave evidence at the trial, he was a fairly regular visitor once the shredding began.

What could Peter Clowes say about this? Anthony Hacking QC provided the answer in his opening speech for his client on the seventieth day of the trial. 'Mr Clowes will tell you that he authorised the shredding of non-UK documents at Poynton to protect the interests of those who had invested offshore.' But in what way did the offshore investors need protecting? Apparently, from the Inland Revenue. The DTI inspectors, said Peter Clowes, had refused to assure him that the results of their enquiries would not be relayed to the Inland Revenue. His clients expected their affairs to be kept confidential, so he was simply following a 'banker's duty of confidentiality' in shredding and falsifying all records within the inspectors' reach which referred to the offshore funds.

'I was concerned for the confidentiality in respect of fiscal matters concerning our investors who were investing overseas,' Clowes told Suckling under cross-examination. This was vintage Clowes, resorting to ridiculously formal language when lying, as if that would give an air of legitimacy to what he was doing, and obscure the underlying dishonesty.

Suckling carefully dissected Clowes's justification for the shredding. If the purpose had been to prevent the Revenue from getting details of the offshore funds then why had he given instructions for all letters of complaint to be destroyed which had nothing to do with offshore investors? 'I believe it was a duplication,' said Clowes. 'We had a complaint book which was maintained on the top floor. There was also a complaint book in Gibraltar with BCI, and I believe that these complaints had been duplicated in the client files as well.'

'Why have them destroyed?' asked Suckling. 'Why go to the extent of having people working in the evenings and weekends tidying up, amongst other things, letters of complaint?'

'It seemed reasonable to do it as the exercise was being done at the same time,' said Clowes.

Another part of the cover-up operation had been the sudden infusion of £16 million from the offshore side to cover up a £10 million shortfall which had arisen in the UK funds due to losses on gilts and illegal transfers. The infusion had taken place early in 1988 after the inspectors had moved in to Barlow Clowes. To disguise it, Clowes had purchased gilts with the money and invented a history of contract notes going back to 1984. The inspectors had easily discovered that the contract notes were bogus and that the money had suddenly come in after their investigation. Again, how could Clowes explain this away?

Clowes said that the money he had repatriated was 'a contingency fund' made up of three main elements. It included £2.5 million to £3.5 million from old investment portfolios and almost £10 million which, Clowes said, had been erroneously credited to the offshore bank accounts but belonged instead to the UK funds. The final element, Clowes said, was £6 million of profits on share dealings which he had made on the money erroneously transferred overseas. To ensure no tax was payable on these deals, Clowes and his associate had made several verbal agreements to buy and sell gilts in such a way as to shelter the profit. Yes, 119 contract notes for these deals had been prepared after the event and backdated to 1984. But they merely recorded the deals he had verbally agreed with his overseas associate at the relevant times in the past. The backdated contract notes, he said, accurately reflected the dates and times the deals had been carried out. The explanation reeked of dishonesty.

'It would not be, Mr Clowes, that you are trying to pull the wool over the eyes of the DTI inspectors and accountants of the onshore companies, would it?' Suckling asked Clowes.

'Absolutely not,' replied Clowes.

Suckling returned to the cover-up operation in his closing speech to the jury: 'It really is fictional paperwork, is it not?' he said, referring to the backdated contract notes. 'Can there be any honest explanation for creating that kind of document?' Clowes had also recorded the deals on the computer system for the offshore company, again making it look as if they stretched back to 1984. These were 'phoney' deals, said Suckling. It was 'straightforward stealing' by Clowes from the offshore investors, because 'the heat was on, the DTI was there, and he had to fill the gap'.

By the time the judge came to sum up the case, Clowes's thefts, his cavalier treatment of the offshore funds as his own pot of money, had been exposed. In the witness box Clowes had sought to cover up his actions with convoluted and barely credible explanations. The sheer weight of factual evidence – the bank records showing massive diversions of investors' funds into the bank accounts of Clowes and his associates – meant Clowes could not deny what he had actually done. He could only put a different gloss on it, claim that he genuinely believed that he had been acting in the investors' best interests, he had believed that he had been entitled to do what he had done with their money, he had not been dishonest.

So, for instance, Clowes freely admitted to robbing Peter to pay Paul, in other words to paying out to investors who wanted their money back with money belonging to new investors.

'You were paying for the investors' withdrawals and their yields out of fresh investors' money?' Suckling had asked Clowes.

'Absolutely,' Clowes replied. 'If I went and invested £350,000 with Barclays Bank or the Halifax Building Society, say five years ago, and they had lent that on to somebody else to buy a house . . . and then subsequently another investor came along . . . and invested funds, if I then wanted to withdraw my funds they would simply pay my withdrawal out of new investors' monies.'

The truth, as Suckling pointed out, was that investors would never have entrusted their money to Clowes had they known what he was doing with it. His final question to the jury asked them to consider who Peter Clowes really was.' Do you have the picture of someone who was honestly running an investment strategy with the interests of the investors at heart, who has done it quite openly but has been deserted by the people he told about it – co-defendants, intermediaries, lawyers and so on; or do you have the picture of someone who was cheating the public with the brochures, using the money as he thought fit to benefit himself and his team of cronies, getting away with it for far too long and lying about it at various stages until it finally comes out in June 1988?'

What of Guy von Cramer, the whiz-kid who had been one of Britain's youngest ever chief-executives of a public company? Robert Rhodes QC described the prosecution of his client as 'blinkered and obsessive'. He pointed out that von Cramer had no authority to make transfers from Barlow Clowes accounts. Moreover, he had never given instructions to Barlow Clowes staff to make transfers from client accounts and where clients' money had been transferred to him there was absolutely no indication on his bank statements to show that the money came from a Barlow Clowes client account. All the transfers of client monies had come from the Jersey Partnership of Barlow Clowes, the von Cramer camp said. Clowes had given assurances that the Jersey partnership would not obtain client funds. This was an important point. Von Cramer said neither he nor his companies ever received transfers of client funds direct from Barlow Clowes International in Gibraltar which was known to handle clients' funds. Instead Peter Clowes would route the transfers through his Jersey partnership – the vehicle he claimed housed only his own money. Despite this, and the fact that there was no documentary evidence to show that von Cramer knew what Clowes was really doing, the prosecution had 'almost a knee jerk reaction', Mr Rhodes said, when it saw clients' funds transferred to von Cramer: 'Barlow Clowes, money, Cramer, fraud.' This, said Mr Rhodes, was simply not sustainable on the evidence. He also pointed out that his client had initially been reluctant to team up with Clowes and resented him for muscling in and taking control of Ferguson. Von Cramer had sought legal advice over whether he could block Clowes from becoming a director of James Ferguson in 1986 but Clowes had too much support. He succeeded in getting on to the board and later, according to von Cramer, elbowed him off it.

Mr Rhodes pointed out that his client played no part in marketing the offshore portfolios of Barlow Clowes and that his previous business experience was unrelated to gilts. He had been reassured by the DTI licences granted to the UK side of Barlow Clowes. Perhaps most importantly, as Mr Justice Phillips would say in summing up von Cramer's case: 'Neither Mr Cramer nor anyone in his orbit ever saw a document which indicated that any of the transfers with which he was concerned emanated from a clients' account.'

At the early stage of the trial, when witness after witness was called to say that they had assumed money was going into gilts, Mr Rhodes would pop up and ask whether they had had any dealings with von Cramer. Time and again the answer came back that they had little or no contact with him. It was clear, early on, that the prosecution allegation that von Cramer had been part of a conspiracy with Clowes and Naylor, to deceive investors by falsely claiming their money was in gilts, could not be sustained against him. He had had no official standing at Barlow Clowes, had not been a signatory to any of its bank accounts, held no directorships in the company. At one point, during cross-examination, Rhodes had asked Peter Clowes whether in his opinion von Cramer knew that offshore investors' money was not going into gilts. 'He probably knew,' Clowes initially said. This was a very important response for the Cramer camp, as Rhodes pointed out in his summing up. This, said Rhodes, was Clowes's 'initial reaction'. 'It was not "Of course Guy Cramer knew." It was a pause and "He probably knew." And that, members of the jury, is why I asked you to write down a while ago "Probably is not enough." ' It was not sufficient for the jury to think that his client was guilty. They had to be sure he was.

Von Cramer was not the only one who asserted his belief that investors' money was going into gilts. Chris Newman and Doc Naylor said the same. Naylor gave evidence in person. 'I believed the money was in a gilt, perhaps on its way to be lent but if not it was in a cash deposit with a bank as secure as that could be,' he said. It appeared from the evidence that Peter Clowes had, at least to some extent, bamboozled Naylor with his supposed gilts stock lending scheme, claiming that he was using the Barlow Clowes computer, combined with nominee companies, to buy and lend gilts so as to generate tax free returns. Naylor did not really understand how the scheme worked but had not wanted to admit this to Clowes, he said, for fear of appearing stupid. The reality was that Clowes's version of stock lending existed more in his mind than anywhere else. Very little stock was bought, no actual stock was lent, and the computer entries, which in Peter Clowes's mind supposedly reflected the lending of stock, were often never made. It was a classic case of seeking to use complexity as a weapon of deception. The question was, in Doc Naylor's case, had he been fooled? He said that he had.

Doc Naylor's counsel, Anthony Hacking, described the 'total control' that Clowes had exercised over the company. Naylor, he said, had been taken in. 'They are the men surrounded with the trappings of wealth, a number of homes, cars and jets. They are very generous with money which later turns out not to be theirs . . . such a man was Peter Clowes.' In the last year or so Clowes had begun to cold-shoulder Naylor, relegating him to an inferior office. He had not been paid compensation when he resigned. These factors said Mr Glass, meant it was 'inconceivable' that Naylor was involved in a criminal conspiracy to deceive investors.

Mr Glass also made another key point in Naylor's favour concerning the money used to renovate the home in which he and his wife lived. It appeared that some of the entries made on the computer which disguised the use of the money had been made after Naylor had left Barlow Clowes. This was an important point since it suggested that Clowes and not Naylor had been concerned to conceal the fact that the money had come from investors. And another incorrect entry on the computer which had been made while Naylor still worked at Barlow Clowes, was he said, a mistake. Perhaps it was

Clowes, and not Naylor, who had been dishonest over the money spent on renovations.

Mr Justice Phillips took a few days off to prepare his summing up. He began on Wednesday 29 January, the 104th day of what he described as 'one of the longest trials in the history of English criminal law. We have heard evidence from 168 witnesses, and we have looked at hundreds of documentary exhibits,' he said. 'But at the end of the day, one vital question arises in respect of each defendant: was he dishonest?'

The day had begun in a buzz of excitement because the judge had decided to withdraw the bail of all four defendants before beginning his summing up. This meant that from then on they would all be kept in custody, at least until the jury's verdict. However, after submissions from the defence at the lunchtime interval, Mr Justice Phillips changed his mind. There was a chance that the jury would learn of the defendants being kept in custody, perhaps from the jurors in the Blue Arrow trial going on in the courtroom below, and draw adverse inferences. The defendants were spared the indignity of being led to and from the court in handcuffs.

The style of Mr Justice Phillips's summing up was to pose questions to the jury. They were often semi-rhetorical, appearing to steer the jury towards a particular line of thought. Only on rare occasions did he voice his own opinion clearly. In a sense it was the questions he posed about the involvement of defendants other than Clowes that were the more interesting. By the end of the trial Clowes appeared to be a doomed man. But Naylor, Cramer and Newman all had a fighting chance. 'It is Dr Naylor's case that Mr Clowes was conning him, was deliberately keeping him in the dark about the fact that gilts were not being bought for P28 and P68,' the judge said. But was this true? Referring to a time when Clowes had sent Naylor to Gibraltar to allocate gilt purchases, he asked, 'You might think, might you not, that this was almost certain to lead Dr Naylor to discover there were no gilts?'

The judge took the jury through Guy von Cramer's involvement in Clowes's 'investment strategy'. He had been involved in the bid for Buckleys which used up £17 million of investors' funds, the bid for Belgrave, utilising £4 million, the £12.5 million back-to-back loan provided to James Ferguson and a number of other, smaller transactions. And von Cramer had personally benefited in some cases as the judge pointed out: 'The agreed facts . . . suggest that Mr Cramer benefited from the various transactions to the extent of something like, perhaps, £3 million.' The Cramer camp maintained that any payments to their client were rightfully his. Some of the money represented part payment for the sale of his shares in Ferguson to Clowes, they argued. Their client had not received the full payment due. More importantly, von Cramer had never for a moment suspected that the money paid to him originated from Barlow Clowes investors.

Mr Justice Phillips's account of von Cramer's involvement was interrupted several times by his counsel, Robert Rhodes QC. Mr Rhodes felt it was unfair for the judge to be drawing the attention of the jury to evidence which seemed to be adverse to von Cramer, if the prosecution themselves had not highlighted it. In particular the judge had pointed to sections of von Cramer's interviews with the DTI inspectors, which might be regarded as inconsistent with the position he was maintaining now.

'I must say, with the utmost respect, that I do protest at Your Lordship making fresh points in favour of the prosecution,' Mr Rhodes said. 'It was difficult enough making a speech in this very long trial dealing with the case that the prosecution had made, without having to gaze into a crystal and deal with the points which the prosecution had not made but Your Lordship had made.'

'You dealt with an awful lot in your seven days' worth of final speech,' the judge rejoined, 'compared to the points which the prosecution made in their final speech.'

According to prosecuting counsel Alan Suckling, the legal position was that the judge was free to draw the jury's attention to any points, provided they had been put in evidence to the jury. Von Cramer's evidence to the inspectors had been read out to the court; if Suckling had not highlighted particular passages, the judge could nevertheless do so in his summing up. The judge appeared to accept this view, although Rhodes's interruptions did his client no harm.

Rhodes, a specialist in fraud and tax fraud cases, was scrupulously polite whenever he protested at the treatment of his client. Before becoming a Queen's Counsel he had spent ten years as prosecuting counsel for the Inland Revenue acting for both the Revenue and for taxpayers. In the Barlow Clowes trial he had indeed spent a long time summing up for his client, 'Bored us to tears,' one of the prosecution team complained, but Rhodes had been very thorough and effective.

The jury retired to consider its verdict on the morning of Wednesday 5 February, the 109th day of the trial. At one point it seemed they would reach a verdict before the weekend. They sent a note to the judge late on Friday afternoon asking for an extra hour which they thought would be sufficient to reach decisions on all twenty charges. The press rushed down to the court, camera crews and photographers waited outside and Clowes sauntered into and out of courtroom 22 appearing quite calm. In the event the jury needed more time and were packed off for a weekend's isolation in a country hotel.

On Monday morning they were back, with verdicts. The foreman, a young man dressed in a suit and tie, stood up, took a few folded sheets out of his pocket and prepared to read the verdicts.

Peter Clowes would be the first to know his fate. He faced nineteen charges in all, far more than any other defendant. The first charge was conspiracy to mislead investors. Was he guilty or not guilty, the court clerk asked.

'Not guilty,' the young man replied.

There was an audible gasp. Would Clowes get away with it after all? The next eight charges concerned misleading individual investors. And, unlike the conspiracy charge where there had to be more than one person involved for the offence to be proved, the involvement of Clowes alone was sufficient.

'Guilty,' the foreman announced for each charge, and continued doing so through all the theft charges Clowes faced. He was convicted of eighteen out of the nineteen charges he faced. He sat at the rear of the makeshift court with the other three defendants in a line of four chairs. His wife, Pamela, and two of her daughters by her first marriage sat immediately in front of the press section.

Just before the jury had come in she had held both Clowes's hands and whispered what appeared to be words of reassurance. Now she was crying. Naylor's wife had also attended court, with her mother, to hear the verdict on her husband.

He faced five charges in all. These encompassed the purchase and renovation of his home, Send Barns. 'Not guilty,' the foreman said to the first two charges, and to the last two. But the jury found him guilty of the most minor charge he faced, the theft of £19,000 from investors which he had disguised with the name of a fictitious client, Dr Patel.

It was von Cramer's turn next. One by one the foreman declared him not guilty on all counts. Chris Newman was similarly acquitted.

Clowes and Naylor were handcuffed together and led out of court by three prison officers. Clowes looked straight ahead of him until just before the door of the court, when he turned his head to look across at the press box. It is impossible to know what he was thinking of in that brief moment when all eyes were upon him. He may have felt that the image of him in the press as a national villain had coloured the jury's judgement. Pamela Clowes, followed by her daughters, had long since run out of the court in tears.

It was a poignant moment, seeing Clowes and Naylor led out of the court bound together by handcuffs. The two men had done their best to damn each other in the witness box, they hated each other and had, in the end, helped to drag each other down. Now united, they were silently led through the waiting camera crews and photographers into a waiting police van. What on earth could they say to one another as the van drove them off, hand in hand, for their first night in custody?

Von Cramer emerged from court to attack the Serious Fraud Office for pursuing a case against him which he said was tantamount to 'guilt by association'. Newman, appearing to be fighting back tears, thanked his lawyers and family for their support.

The indication from the jury's verdict was that they were not satisfied that Clowes had involved others in his fraudulent schemes. The implication was that he had deceived those who had worked closest to him as well as the investing public and the government officials who sought to regulate him. He had not corrupted others. Clowes was convicted for thefts relating to the purchase and renovation of Naylor's home. Naylor was acquitted. The jury had sufficient doubt to accept Naylor's view that he had believed the money had come from Clowes's own resources.

Clowes and Naylor were due to be sentenced the next day. The Old Bailey, the real court rather than the annexe in Chancery Lane, was to be the venue. Pamela Clowes did not appear; instead Clowes's two stepsons, James and Robert Haydock, came to give him support. Eleven of the twelve jurors came to witness the final dénouement, at the invitation of the judge. The foreman alone was absent.

Clowes and Naylor sat in the dock, separated by a prison officer. There was little that could be said in mitigation for Clowes, nevertheless his counsel asked for a single-figure prison sentence. He had signed over his assets, he had co-operated with the liquidators, his counsel said, and he had not profited from the fraud. His was a rags-to-riches-to-rags story.

Mr Justice Phillips retired for a few minutes to consider his sentence. When he came back, Clowes stood, swaying slightly, impassive. 'I do not believe any judge in this country has been called upon to sentence a worse case of fraud than yours,' Mr Justice Phillips said. Referring to him by his surname, he said that Clowes had deliberately picked on small investors who were interested in security, many of them retired people investing their savings. 'It was your intention to help yourself to those monies and to use them for schemes, some of them highly speculative, which you hoped would make you rich.' What Clowes was doing was, in effect, gambling the money dishonestly, he said.

'Anyone who deliberately carries out the kind of massive fraud you have perpetrated must face the fact that if he is caught he must go to prison for a very long time.' The stress, anxiety and anguish caused to investors by what Clowes had done was incalculable.

Very little stood to Clowes's credit, the judge said, and he had shown no contrition. 'Before this story you had a good character but that counts for little in a case such as this,' said the judge. He sentenced him to ten years' imprisonment, the maximum punishment for theft.

At one point Clowes looked as if he might faint. He swayed backwards and forwards continually but his face remained impassive. He stared straight ahead, not changing expression in the face of the judge's rebukes.

It was as if he was not really there, had perhaps moved on from this scene. He knew everyone else thought he was a villain, had long since reconciled himself to the likelihood of a prison sentence. What difference if one more person, the judge, thought he was a crook? Clowes alone knew what had happened.

Naylor was sentenced to eighteen months in prison, a sentence which his wife, who was in court with her daughter, labelled too severe. The judge said the theft Naylor committed was 'an abuse of your position and a serious breach of trust. You had no excuse of any kind for stealing the money of investors whose interests you should have been protecting.'

The two men were led away to begin their sentences. Clowes, a ruined man, disqualified from being a director for fifteen years, his reputation damaged beyond repair. The duality of the Barlow Clowes story was over. No more were there two versions of Peter Clowes, the reputable financial chief with a successful business versus the crook stealing investors' money. There was no doubt now of who he was. Because of his actions up to £90 million owed to investors had been lost.

But there is a postscript to Peter Clowes's disgrace. It dates back to 1984 when about £3 million of investors' money disappeared from a bank account with Midland, in three separate branches. The liquidators have tried for over two years to find out what happened to it, the bank statements giving no indication as to where it went. The entries on the statements referring to the transfers simply state: 'As advised'. Some of the liquidators believe that Clowes has salted this money away: it is his rainy day fund, his protection, his insulation against a world which has cast him as a villain. They may well be right.

EPILOGUE

·

IS ANYONE'S MONEY SAFE?

·

The collapse of Barlow Clowes in May 1988 was a fitting testimony to the deficiencies of the old Department of Trade licensing system. It also came shortly after the introduction of a new system of investor protection aimed at providing ordinary investors with far better safeguards than ever before.

The new system was created by the Financial Services Act, which largely came into force in April 1988. It was the culmination of Professor Gower's Review of Investor Protection. The Act aimed to ensure that investment advisers and managers were 'fit and proper' which in essence meant honest, competent and solvent. It enshrined in statute law what had long been regarded as 'good practice' and was already imposed on certain professional groups such as lawyers and accountants. This included the need for investment businesses to be sufficiently capitalised, to tailor their advice to suit their customers and to acquaint the customers with the risks involved. The Act also contained provisions making it easier to prosecute people who made false or misleading statements to persuade people to invest with them. And it introduced the principle of restitution: instead of investors having to sue a firm that had deceived them to get their money back, the Securities and Investments Board, the new investor watchdog, would do it on their behalf.

The Act replaced the old DTI licensing system with a much tougher entry procedure, one which required firms to provide more information, and be subjected to more external scrutiny, such as spot-checks, than before. Instead of having a licence, every investment business had to be 'authorised'. To gain authorisation they had to be accepted as a member of one of four new regulatory bodies. FIMBRA, the Financial Intermediaries, Managers and Brokers Regulatory Association, generally covered the smaller firms who advised people on their finances or who invested money on their behalf. Larger firms of investment managers joined IMRO, the Investment Management Regulatory Organisation. Futures brokers and dealers joined the AFBD, while the Securities Association covered stockbroking firms. There was a fifth organisation, LAUTRO, the life assurance and until trust regulatory organisation, which laid down rules governing the way that unit trust and life assurance products should be sold. 'The Government's objective is to create a system of regulation which is both flexible and inspires confidence in investors that the financial services sector is a clean place to do business,' declared the then Trade and Industry Secretary, Leon Brittan, when the Financial Services Bill was published.

The idea was to exercise far more control over investment businesses while still allowing them to remain competitive and flexible. The Act would curb the activities of fringe operators, one-man bands that set themselves up offering advice but lacking expertise, high-pressure sales firms, share pushers and so on. Many of the more reputable outfits had already imposed the same or similar controls over themselves, long before the Act came into effect. Some, such as the stockbroking firms, had already been subject to the rules and regulations of the Stock Exchange, which provided protection for their clients. But there had never before been a central system of control, imposed on the investment market as a whole.

A crucial new element in the system was a compensation scheme: if an investment firm collapsed, or stole its clients' money, the Financial Services Act decreed that there must be a safety net to compensate the victims. The safety net was set at a maximum of £48,000 per victim – investors who lost more than this amount could not look to the central compensation scheme to recoup the difference. In some areas this was a distinct improvement: there had never been a compensation scheme for the thousands of firms which had been DTI-licensed or members of Nasdim. But the new scheme did not match that previously operated by the Stock Exchange for its members, which had provided limitless compensation, which, although discretionary, had always been paid out.

It was not surprising that one effect of the Financial Services Act was to weed out thousands of firms who could not be relied on to advise investors or handle their money. FIMBRA, which covered the sharp end of the market, rejected 3000 firms which applied for membership. Share pushers such as Harvard Securities and high-pressure futures company DPR Futures were not admitted into the new system laid down by the Act. Barlow Clowes was also weeded out – it was closed down by the Securities and Investments Board using its new powers under the Act. It was the first major firm closed down by the SIB and its closure illustrated some of the differences between the old and new systems. 'SIB had the Barlow Clowes file for about ten days before the decision was finally made that it was necessary to apply to the courts to wind it up,' explained Barbara Conway, Director of Information at the SIB, in an interview with me recorded a few months before she died.[1] 'Now I think it's fair to make a contrast here with the fact that you had this new body with completely untried powers, which was battling very much like a speeded-up film over that ten days in order to get something done, with the fact that the DTI had known that something was drastically wrong for, certainly at the most charitable estimate, the best part of a year previously. And they did have powers to take action against it, but what I think happened, frankly, was, they wanted to drop it in somebody else's lap.'

This highlights another difference between the old and new systems. The DTI system was manned by civil servants who had no experience of the markets they were supposed to police. They barely had a mandate to police it – staffing levels were pathetically low, resources woefully inadequate, fear of making a mistake was prominent. The new system had a political and financial will behind it, and employed more people who had closer knowledge or direct experience of the markets they were regulating.

Paradoxically the new system of investor protection has been greeted with a proliferation of city scandals and investment frauds or collapses. Since Barlow Clowes there has been an average of at least one major city scandal a year, including the collapse of the Polly Peck empire, the closure of the Bank of Credit and Commerce International – and, most recently, the Maxwell saga. This last case directly involved the new city regulators since Maxwell used one of his companies, which was authorised by IMRO, to help him plunder hundreds of millions of pounds from the pension funds of Mirror Group Newspapers and Maxwell Communications Corporation. All these cases, and several other high profile scandals, have involved financially unsophisticated people losing money, either as shareholders, pensioners or bank depositors.

But the real surprise is in the level of collapses in the investment arena, the territory which the new style regulators were supposed to police. Dozens of investment firms – advisers, managers, brokers – have collapsed. Thousands of investors have lost over £50 million between them before taking into account what they might receive under compensation arrangements.

Dunsdale Securities was another deliberate fraud, similar in many respects to Barlow Clowes. It was a firm controlled by one man, Robert Miller, who offered the alluring combination of high rates of interest and security. Investors' money, he said, would all be put in gilts. In fact the money went to finance Mr Miller's lavish lifestyle and he speculated wildly with it on the stockmarket to try to produce the returns he had promised. When his largest speculation, a £2 million gamble on Reuters shares, went badly wrong, Miller was unable to pay out three investors who wanted to withdraw their money. With insufficient funds coming in from other investors to meet the withdrawals the game was up. Miller was sentenced to six years imprisonment in June 1991.

Miller's case highlights an essential ingredient of most investment frauds – perpetual motion. There needs to be more money coming in than is being paid out to investors, otherwise the fraud will be detected. Miller was able to keep going for ten years largely because he always had a positive flow of new client money coming in. His business was bust in 1980 when he only had four clients but each year he gained new clients, offering above average returns, feigning reluctance to take clients' money thereby making them more keen to give it to him. And, just as in the case of Barlow Clowes, each year the gulf between what Miller had promised investors and what he actually achieved with their money grew wider and wider. Miller was caught out when the money ran out. Clowes was caught out when the Securities and Investments Board brought down an iron curtain which halted his business and led to a totting-up process revealing a massive shortfall on client funds.

In this respect the victims of many investment scams are like participants in a chain letter. If they are one of the early participants they profit. But if they come later and are caught when the chain snaps, they lose everything. Some investors in Dunsdale and Barlow Clowes got in and out and did well. The vast majority got caught.

It is ironic that the Financial Services Act came into effect almost at the peak of the boom period of the 1980s, when confidence was high and money was easy. It was this period which allowed time bombs like Barlow Clowes, Dunsdale and many others to be set. When money is easy it allows people like Clowes and von Cramer to flourish: advisers want them to do takeover deals, banks want to lend money, they become vehicles for the money available. This is not to say that they are not scrutinised, simply that their need to keep going, to do deals, never to stop long enough to allow a proper reckoning, is facilitated by the confidence and optimism of the period. People like Clowes and Miller, unable to distinguish between having control of other people's money and actually owning it themselves, are given more and more of other people's money to manage.

But when money is less easily obtainable, when times are bad, people become more cautious about to whom they lend money or whom they trust with it. It becomes harder to do deals, to keep going, obscuring the true position, and the scandals emerge. This partly explains why there have been so many investment scandals despite the introduction of the Financial Services Act. 'In good times people are relaxed, more trusting and money is plentiful,' J. K. Galbraith wrote in *The Great Crash of 1929*. 'But even though money is plentiful there are always people who need more. Under these circumstances the rate of embezzlement grows, the rate of discovery falls off and the "bezzle" increases rapidly.' The 'bezzle', according to Galbraith, means embezzlement which has not yet been discovered. He continues: 'In depression all this is reversed. Money is watched with a narrow suspicious eye. The man who handles it is assumed to be dishonest until he proves otherwise. Audits are penetrating and meticulous. Commercial morality enormously improves. The bezzle shrinks.'

The Dunsdale case also illustrates another problem which few people anticipated. The deficiencies of the old licensing system of regulation have filtered through to the new investor-protection regime. Firms which were rotten to the core – but nevertheless got a licence from the DTI – were not always weeded out in the mad rush to process applications for the new system. Dunsdale had been licensed by the DTI since 1977. From 1983 onwards, when the DTI required licensed dealers to submit annual monitoring returns, Dunsdale supplied 'clean' returns, signed by its auditors. Its application for FIMBRA membership was processed and accepted. On the face of it Dunsdale was a model company. And yet it had been insolvent and a fraud since 1980.

But there are other financial scams which predated the Financial Services Act and would not have survived it had the large insurance companies properly vetted and monitored the people whom they allowed to sell their products. Under the Act the insurance companies have responsibility for these people. They could be direct employees, self-employed consultants who work from the insurance company's offices, or agents who have a separate business which sells one company's products. However they operate, it was clear before the Act came into force that a large number of them were at best incompetent and at worst crooked. Many of them slipped through the net.

The problem is sometimes known as the 'errant tied agent'. This involves a financial adviser, tied to one insurance group, who uses the cloak of respectability afforded by his link with the group to offer bogus deposit-account schemes or other fraudulent ventures. Garston Amhurst was a London-based tied agent of National Financial Management Corporation and ran an illegal deposit-account scheme alongside its legitimate business. It collapsed in early 1990 and investors' losses, before the TSB stepped in to offer many of them compensation, came to £4.5 million. Many people had thought the deposit scheme was an NFMC product.

In February 1991 around three hundred investors with a Norfolk-based financial adviser, Jake Reynolds, were horrified to discover that as much as £8 million of their money was missing. Reynolds, who was a tied agent of insurance giant Guardian Royal Exchange, callously used his investors to finance his ill-fated business ventures. He offered many of them ludicrously high rates of return if they invested with him, employing four couriers who collected the money in carrier bags. On the morning of 25 February, the day before he was due to meet City regulators, Reynolds tried to draw £25,000 belonging to a client out of a London bank account. He failed and has not been seen or heard of since. Guardian Royal Exchange is offering compensation to some investors who had GRE policies but not to the victims of the illegal deposit scheme.

There have been many other errant tied-agent cases, several where the agent has persuaded people to remortgage their homes to raise cash for him to invest on their behalf. The investors subsequently lose their cash and with it the ability to keep up with the mortgage payments on their homes. LAUTRO has successfully leaned on many of the insurance companies who employed the tied agent to come up with compensation. Some have done so voluntarily. And, after warning its members over their failure to monitor their salespeople properly, LAUTRO has introduced new rules aimed at ensuring companies clarify what the agent is authorised to do in their name, making it more difficult for dubious salesmen to whitewash their own dodgy schemes.

Many of the schemes where investors lost money were offering an above average rate of return. 'I have thought very carefully about why I am in this situation,' says one investor who was consistently offered interest rates of around 20 per cent by Dunsdale Securities and ended up losing £200,000. 'It was simple, naked greed.' Others have been caught out where the rates of interest offered should have been sufficient to warn people off.

No system of investor protection can cater for people who succumb to offers of excessively high rates of return. As Professor Gower said in his review: 'Regulation should be no greater than is necessary to protect reasonable people from being made fools of.'[2]

Also there are many people in the market who should never be entrusted with the management of other people's money; they do not have the discipline, training, self-control to be investment managers. Clowes was a classic case, as were Miller and Maxwell. The Financial Services Act has got rid of many of these people, but many others still remain.

An unfortunate effect of the Act is that it drove the fringe operators into areas into which the new investor protection regime does not extend, such as offering investment in diamonds, certain property development schemes, and mortgage lending. It has converted the shady share pusher into a timeshare tout or an advance-fee fraudster, offering to arrange mortgages which never materialise but in the meantime pocketing an upfront fee. New laws either have been or are being introduced to fill in the gaps, to regulate timeshare operators and estate agents, recognising that specific legislation is necessary to improve standards and safeguard consumers.

Could there be another Barlow Clowes? Virtually everyone to whom I put this question in the course of preparing this book said there could. Antony Gold, of Manchester solicitors Alexander Tatham which successfully represented investors in Barlow Clowes and other collapsed firms, says: 'The fact is no amount of regulation will stop plausible fraudsters telling stories which induce investors to invest with them. You can't license or scrutinise every transaction with every investor.'

Geoffrey Pointon, the man who nearly closed IPAS, the financial intermediary which was so vital to Peter Clowes, says: 'Fraud will always be with us. The character of fraud is that it's already happened when you find out. And if you give a criminal a rulebook, it's rather like giving a blueprint of the bank to a bank robber. They will find a way. The Financial Services Act has done a terrific job: it's improved standards, identified people who shouldn't be in the industry, so on and so forth. But it can never be an absolute one hundred per cent. People who have got money to invest must understand that it is their final decision. And they must take responsibility for what they do.'

Bob Wilkinson, former head of enforcement at the Securities Association, says: 'The thing about fraud is that new generations come along and think that they've found something that nobody's ever thought of, so I suspect that pruning of clients' money – robbing Peter to pay Paul – and so on could happen again, but I think it would be rumbled a damned sight quicker than it was with Barlow Clowes because they would be member of an SRO like the Securities Association. Had they been able to go in and take Barlow Clowes's books to pieces, they would have been brought to book far quicker than they actually were. So I think there could be a Barlow Clowes, but I think the damage would be limited, because they'd be discovered far far earlier.'

The Financial Services Act cannot cure greed, or the desperate steps people like Clowes, Maxwell or Miller take when their business is going wrong. It cannot stop someone who is determined to cheat from doing so. What it does do, however, is make it harder for him to cheat systematically on a large scale. If he does then he will be caught sooner under the new system than under the old. But sooner could still mean years.

What is also clear is that investors cannot rely on auditors to detect their clients' financial frauds. A domineering, manipulative businessman such as Clowes can fool his auditors for years. Maxwell shifted the accounting year-end of a few of his companies to give himself more time to borrow from the pension funds. Auditors have failed to spot fraud or alleged fraud in several companies or investment firms which have collapsed since the Financial Services Act came into effect. Barlow Clowes also highlights how inadequate communication between professionals or between regulators can allow frauds to flourish. Gradually this is being changed. Regulators in Britain have opened up formal and informal channels of communication with their counterparts in other countries.

None of the compensation systems for investors provides a blanket insurance for all of their money. If an individual loses money through the collapse of a UK licensed bank, the Deposit Protection Board will pay compensation of 75 per cent of the first £20,000 deposited, so the maximum you can get from this compensation scheme is £15,000. If a building society collapses, savers will get back 90 per cent of the first £20,000, in other words a maximum of £18,000. And if you lose money through the collapse of a UK authorised insurance company policyholders get back 90 per cent of the value of the policies they had taken out with the collapsed company.

In practice no one has lost money through the collapse of a building society since before the Second World War. The societies, like the banks and insurance groups, are tightly monitored. But recently the collapse of three banks, and in particular British & Commonwealth Merchant Bank, which was caught out by the failure of its parent group, has caused depositors a few anxious moments.

In the BCMB case, depositors received payment under the central compensation scheme and are expected, eventually, to get all their money back once the administration process is completed. This might, however, mean a two-year wait for the complete return of their funds.

If there is a lesson for investors to learn from the demise of Barlow Clowes, it is that a guarantee is only as good as the guarantor, namely the institution offering it. So it is with investment generally. Your money is safest if you spread it around so that no one financial institution has more than would be covered under the compensation scheme to which it subscribes. Following this policy would mean that you put no more than £50,000 with an authorised investment firm (fund manager, financial adviser, stockbroker, etc.) and no more than £20,000 with a UK bank or building society. This is the closest that you can get to a guarantee that most of your funds are protected. While this would be adequate for many people, those with larger amounts of savings would find it very inconvenient and costly to split their money up into so many different parcels. So they could step up to the next layer of risk – investing in sums larger than the compensation limits but sticking to well-known names such as the high street banks and the largest building societies. Your money is then more or less safe.

Even if you spread your money around to bring yourself under the compensation umbrella, you could still lose out. After all, investment advisers can still give bad advice but unless the advice was misleading, or the investment was wholly inappropriate, or some other rule of the self-regulating organisation to which the adviser belongs was breached, you will simply have to swallow the loss.

There are still gaps in the system of protecting investors which are only plugged after a financial crisis in which people lose money. The inadequacy of the rules protecting pensioners in company schemes has been exposed by the ease with which Robert Maxwell plundered the funds. The errant tied agent exposed the shortcomings in the way insurance companies were vetting and monitoring people authorised to sell in their name. Many life-assurance salesmen, allowed to sell to the public after the briefest of training, and under pressure to produce results, mislead investors into signing up for products they do not need. Given the size of the industry and the huge turnover in staff – in 1990 43 per cent of the salesmen employed by the top twenty-two companies changed jobs – there are bound to be irresponsible salesmen deceiving investors. From 1993 LAUTRO will impose far tougher training requirements on these companies.

The Financial Services Act is only four years old; many of its provisions, such as restitution for investors or punishment for making false investment promises, have barely been tested. There will always be guinea pigs whose misfortune leads to an improvement in the rules.

The regulators could seek to head off more investment losses by introducing a system of bank custodians for the small firms of investment advisers and managers. Under this system, popular in the US and obligatory for all UK units trusts, the investors' money is always held by the bank. It carries out the investment instructions of an adviser who never holds clients' money. The investor would make out his cheque directly to the bank, not to the adviser. It is worth remembering that the only section of clients' money found intact when Barlow Clowes collapsed was the £7 million held in a custodian account which the Government insisted Clowes set up with Lloyds Bank. Even Clowes dared not touch it.

NOTES

•

PROLOGUE

1. Buckley was subsequently discharged from bankruptcy and regained his solicitor's practising certificate.

1: EARLY DAYS

1. Information taken from *Kelly's Directory*, 1951 and onwards.
2. This and subsequent quotations are taken from an interview with John Clowes in September 1990.
3. Taken from *Do You Sincerely Want to Be Rich?* (Andre Deutsch) by Charles Rae, Bruce Page and Godfrey Hodgson.
4. James Wright is not his real name. This man, a director of a company taken over by Clowes, has asked for his identity to be kept secret.
5. Interview with Paul Wood, 1990.
6. Interview between Per-Eric Hawthorne and John Bird, February 1990.

2: THE PARTNERSHIP

1. These and subsequent quotations taken from interview with Elizabeth Barlow in September 1990.
2. These and subsequent quotations taken from interview with Peter Clowes in August 1988.
3. Interview with Pamela Clowes, August 1988.

3: ROBBING PETER TO PAY PAUL

1. Interview with Denis Wilson, June 1990.
2. *Barlow Clowes: Report of Sir Godfray Le Quesne* (the Le Quesne report), p. 22.

4: A NARROW ESCAPE

1. Interview with Peter Clowes, August 1988.
2. Ibid.
3. *Financial Times*, 30 April 1981.

5: THE TURNING POINT

1. Interview with Professor Gower, March 1990.
2. Interview with Peter Clowes, August 1988.
3. Figures taken from the affidavit of Walter Hoffman, May 1988.

6: THE ADVERTISING CAMPAIGN

1. Interview with one of the Barlow Clowes Liquidators.
2. Interview with Pamela Clowes, June 1988.
3. The name of the Moorgate executive has been changed at his request.
4. Interview with Peter Clowes, August 1988.
5. Peter Clowes always overplayed the efficiency of his computer system. When Doc Naylor joined in 1982 the system being used was little more than a computer game. Despite spending millions on new equipment and computer programming the system never worked properly. It allocated gilts to the investors who had come into Barlow Clowes early on but not to those who had joined later. 'The net effect of that was that some people got an awful lot of gilts allocated and others got nothing,' says Stephen Hook, of Barlow Clowes' liquidators Cork Gully. Hook quotes an example of one client who put £300,000 into Barlow Clowes and six months later the computer showed him as having £800,000 worth of gilts.

7: A LITANY OF WARNINGS

1. Clowes had, in all probability, been deceiving the Jersey authorities for several years by doing more than he was allowed on the island. Barlow Clowes had been accepted in Jersey on the basis that it would merely be an accommodation office, with no staff of its own, and that any administrative work could be handled by Anders & Whitehead as incidental to its business as local solicitors. But Clowes had installed a computer and, crucially, investors' money was held in two bank accounts on the island.
2. Letter from Richard Syvret to Anders & Whitehead, 11 June 1984.

8: JEWELLERY, LIES AND THE DEPARTMENT OF TRADE

1. At the trial of Peter Clowes, Richard Syvret said that it would have been 'prudent' to obtain independent verification that Barlow Clowes had closed its bank accounts. 'Perhaps we were not as forthright as we would have been knowing the press comment that has occurred since,' Syvret said.
2. Report of the Parliamentary Commissioner for Administration: *The Barlow Clowes Affair* (the Ombudsman's Report), p. 45.
3. Letter from Roger Louth of the DTI to Herbert Smith, solicitors, April 1985.
4. Ombudsman's Report, p. 51.

9: THE TIME BOMB

1. Ombudsman's Report, p. 57.
2. Ibid.
3. Ibid., p. 58.
4. Ibid., p. 57.
5. Interview with Derek Tree, July 1988.
6. Ombudsman's Report, p. 74.
7. Ibid.
8. Ibid., p. 76.
9. This was classic Peter Clowes deception. Clowes had always maintained to Pilkington that the overseas operations of Barlow Clowes were kept entirely separate from the UK funds and had been physically managed from Jersey. Had Spicers known there was no separate operation for the overseas funds then it would have insisted on inspecting them before providing the DTI audit – almost certainly a fatal blow to Clowes getting his licence.
10. Interview with Geoffrey Farrington, June 1990.
11. Ombudsman's Report, p. 88.
12. Ibid., p. 79.

10: CORPORATE FORAYS

1. The description of the château is largely drawn from an article in *The Times*, 15 June 1988, by Lawrence Lever and Philip Jacobson.
2. The name of the female director at Mekom has been changed at her request.

11: THE MAN WITH THE 'VON' IN THE MIDDLE

1. The airline executive's name has been changed at his request.
2. *Birmingham Post*, 14 January 1986.
3. *Yorkshire Post*, 14 January 1986.
4. In December 1990 the Department of Trade and Industry, as part of its attempt to recoup compensation paid to Barlow Clowes investors, issued a writ for damages against several of the advisers involved in the Ferguson acquisition of the Futurist Complex, including Touche Ross, Ferguson's accountants and Rensburg, the brokers.
5. *Birmingham Post*, 29 May 1986.

12: HELLO GIBRALTAR

1. Tree's account of Clowes's reaction is taken from his evidence at Peter Clowes's trial.
2. Ombudsman's Report, p. 102.
3. Ibid.

13: A DARK DAY IN AUGUST

1. Quotations taken from a Midland Bank note dated 18 August 1986, prepared by Derek Sinstead and read out at the Barlow Clowes trial. Tree's motives in going to see Sinstead were mixed. He wanted a second opinion which he thought Midland would be able to provide because he assumed (incorrectly) that Sinstead had previously been involved in discussions with the Bank of England about Barlow Clowes. At one point in their meetings, Tree mentioned that he might want to rejoin Midland. But he was concerned also that the authorities had been reassured by his decision to join Barlow Clowes in 1985 and now wanted to get across the message that they should no longer construe his presence at Barlow Clowes as reassuring.

2. Tree was certainly worried about his own position within Barlow Clowes and the potential damage to his reputation, should there be fraud. Although not involved himself, his career prospects could suffer from association with a fraudulent firm. Under cross-examination in the Barlow Clowes trial he said: 'I wasn't going to see Mr Pilkington to allege fraud, I was going to ask [him] to do some more fact finding, also to inform him that I was intending to leave.' This makes sense. Tree himself knew little about the offshore operations; he did not know where the funds were based or where the supposed gilt dealings for offshore investors were carried out.

3. The issue of how much the professional advisers knew about the source of the funding for the Belgrave stake came up at the Barlow Clowes trial. The Belgrave circular containing the reference to 'expatriate discretionary investment clients of Barlow Clowes Limited' was found in one of the files of Simpson Curtis – the firm of solicitors advising Clowes and Cramer on the boardroom bid. At the trial, Andrew Walker of Simpson Curtis said that he could not recall seeing the circular himself and in any event it never occurred to him that it was gilt investors' funds being used to buy shares in Belgrave. 'I did not make any enquiry as to the source of the funds,' Walker said at the trial. 'I didn't see that as my function at all.'

    Stuart Counsell of Touche Ross said in court that he attended the Belgrave extraordinary general meeting with Clowes. Touche was accountant to James Ferguson Holdings where Clowes was chairman. 'I would have thought I would have read the circular, yes,' he said at the trial.

4. There appears to have been a misunderstanding between Sinstead and Tree which may explain why Midland did not notify its Jersey branch. Sinstead understood that Tree's warning of possible fraud did not involve any Barlow Clowes accounts administered by the Midland. However Tree only said that he did not think there was any problem with the Barlow Clowes accounts at the Threadneedle Street branch of Midland.

5. Derek Tree in an interview on 14 December 1988 with the Department of Trade inspectors appointed to investigate Barlow Clowes.

6. At the trial of Peter Clowes, Midland made it clear that it did not see its

role as requiring it to monitor movements out of the Barlow Clowes client accounts. When it was put to Derek Denton, Manager of Midland St Helier, that he would not allow client funds to be misapplied, he replied 'I don't know that we see ourselves in that role, in terms of an account, as monitoring it and acting as trustees. As a clearing bank that would be too onerous a role, I think.' Later he said: 'I think we would not expect to see a client account on its own become overdrawn, but we wouldn't look deeper than that in terms of actual transactions on the account.' This view was reiterated by Colin Cook, another Midland manager at the trial.

14: IN THE KINGDOM OF THE BLIND

1. It emerged at the Barlow Clowes trial that money from clients' accounts had been used to fund Temple Bar, although none of the intermediaries involved knew this.
2. At the Barlow Clowes trial Hooper also said that he wanted to reconcile the offshore investors' funds as a prelude to the 1987 audit of Barlow Clowes International. 'I was looking to the 1987 audit of BCI. I was aware that these client funds had never been subject to audit previously.'
3. Quotation taken from Posey's evidence at the trial of Peter Clowes.

15: THE FARCE CONTINUES

1. At the Barlow Clowes trial, Hooper said that after writing the memo he 'put it on one side awaiting the receipt of the reconciliation we had been promised.' He discussed the memo with Pilkingon over the phone in October. 'The important point was that this was based on such a superficial review of a limited amount of information that we didn't put that amount of importance on it at that time, we assumed there would be a proper explanation for it,' Hooper said at the trial.
2. Quotation taken from Pilkington's evidence at the Barlow Clowes trial.
3. The Revenue's main concern had been to establish exactly whether Barlow Clowes should be liable to UK income tax on the management fees that it was earning from the overseas businesses.

16: THE HERMES FIDDLE

1. The key point here is that the professional advisers do not appear to have grasped fully what Clowes was doing. The offshore funds were controlled by the Jersey partnership which, in turn, was a mere front for Peter Clowes. He was the Jersey partnership; he controlled the funds. He lied about the size of the funds, the Ferguson takeover document, after stating in various drafts that the Barlow Clowes businesses being acquired had first £350 million under management, then £150 million, ended up being completely silent on the subject when the final document was put out.

As for Spicers, Clowes had been stringing them along. Touche and Singer had been told as long ago as November 1986 that the Jersey partnership was not part of the deal. When Clowes finally broke the news to Pilkington the Ferguson transaction was already well advanced and there was little he could do. Hooper was put under great pressure by Barlow Clowes executives to sign the accounts of BCI, which he did with some reluctance.

Pilkington said at the Barlow Clowes trial that he settled for a written assurance from Clowes that the offshore funds would be transferred to Ferguson by 31 May 1987 because this meant that they would ultimately be subject to an audit when the accounts for Ferguson had to be prepared. This never happened – the crash intervened.

Herbert Smith, who had also insisted on a reconciliation of the offshore funds as a precondition of working on the Ferguson deal, had maintained its position and not been closely involved with the deal. It effectively dropped Barlow Clowes as a client early in 1987 after a row between Fleck and Chris Newman, the Barlow Clowes finance director, over late delivery of monitoring returns to the DTI.

2. The events in the Geneva office have largely been reconstructed from the evidence of Robert Posey and Geoffrey Richardson, another member of staff, presented at the Barlow Clowes trial.

3. Counsell claimed at the Barlow Clowes trial that he did not know there had never been an audit of the offshore funds. He said that the Hooper memorandum, combined with the lack of audit, made reconciliation of the Barlow Clowes funds worldwide essential. But he maintained that the onus would have been on Spicers to do the reconciliation, to check that there was no teaming and lading going on between funds. Touche, he said, could and did protect Ferguson, by seeking appropriate warranties from Peter Clowes.

Although Clowes deceived both Spicers and Touche, neither firm can be proud of the job they did on the Ferguson acquisition of Barlow Clowes: the deal went through with no one taking a proper look at the offshore client funds. This should never have happened. According to Counsell, Touche earned about £150,000 in fees for its work between July 1986 and March 1987.

17: THE MOLE

1. While Varney was beavering away at Barlow Clowes from the Stock Exchange's Surveillance Division, a separate section of the Exchange was approving the Ferguson acquisition of Barlow Clowes. Although each section had different considerations to take into account, it is obvious that Varney's work and information were important to the Quotations Division given the previous involvement with Clowes. The Quotations Division had originally insisted on the suspension of Ferguson's shares because it suspected they were being ramped. Once again, Clowes benefited from inadequate communication within a regulatory authority.

There is strong evidence to suggest that Varney did not even know that Ferguson was going to get its share quotation restored which it did following the acquisition of Barlow Clowes.

18: OUT OF CONTROL

1. Taken from an interview with *Money Magazine*.
2. *Financial Times*, 2 March 1987.
3. Clowes often used the tactic of ringing up in the afternoon just before the deadline for making telegraphic transfers expired and asking for a transfer from clients' accounts to be made urgently.
4. Swinstead's quotation and the account of her transferring the money comes from the evidence she gave at the Barlow Clowes trial. It is interesting that £500,000 of the money came from the account at Midland Threadneedle Street which Midland Bank was monitoring following Derek Tree's warning.
5. *Financial Times*, 28 July 1988.
6. *The Times*, 10 July 1987.
7. *Daily Telegraph*, 13 July 1987.

19: THE SECRET INVESTIGATION

1. Ombudsman's Report, p. 123.
2. Ibid., p. 120.
3. Interview with Julian Varney, June 1989.
4. Interview with Peter Clowes, August 1988.

20: THE COVER-UP OPERATION

1. Taken from the affidavit of Walter Hoffman, May 1988.
2. Clowes had been working on new products for a long time, certainly as far back as 1986. The main ones were portfolios 88 and 90, and their key characteristic was that they would openly state that not all money was invested in gilts. Both were attempts to legitimise the past diversion of investors' money and neither got off the ground.

21: COUNTDOWN TO DISASTER

1. Ombudsman's Report, p. 157.
2. Ibid., p. 160.
3. Interview, June 1988.
4. Interview with David Gray, June 1988.
5. Interview with Guy von Cramer, June 1988.
6. Interview with Peter Clowes, August 1988.
7. *The Times*, 10 June 1988.
8. Interview with Stanley Wright, June 1988.

22: THE FIGHT FOR COMPENSATION

1. Tiny Rowland, in *A Hero from Zero*, published by Lonrho.
2. *Daily Telegraph*, 16 June 1988.
3. Letter from Chapman How Financial Management, 9 June 1988.
4. *Financial Times*, 30 October 1989.
5. *The Times*, 24 June 1988.
6. *Mail on Sunday*, December 1989.
7. *Daily Telegraph*, 24 June 1988.
8. *Guardian*, 24 June 1988.
9. *The Enterprise Years*, by Lord Young (Headline), p. 278.
10. *The Times*, 21 October 1988.
11. Ibid. Lord Young subsequently conceded, in an interview for the Channel 4 documentary on Barlow Clowes, that the Government was probably to blame for licensing the UK side of Barlow Clowes. However, the Government did not want to admit this as such, he said, for fear of creating a tidal wave of claims whenever it made a mistake. 'The problem about this really was that the Government couldn't voluntarily admit that it was wrong and pay the money. That would set a precedent which would lead down a very undesirable course for the whole nation. Because once a Government admitted it was wrong, the next time anything went wrong, the Government would be pushed to do so. And then you go down a whole series of transactions in which the Government becomes insurance company of last resort. And that quite frankly would mean that bad money would drive out good . . .' Young, who pointed out that the mistakes all predated his arrival as head of the DTI, said the better solution was for the Government to pay out as a result of a ruling from the Ombudsman to whom he passed the Le Quesne report. 'I suspect he [the Ombudsman] was right when it came to the United Kingdom. I have slightly more doubts about the Gibraltar company.'
12. All four clearing banks are being sued by the DTI in its quest to recoup the money it paid out in compensation to Barlow Clowes investors. Midland is being sued in its capacity as banker to the accounts where money went missing, the DTI arguing that it was in effect a trustee of those accounts and should have taken more care monitoring them. Midland denies this and claims that the DTI was itself negligent. The other banks are being sued for recommending Barlow Clowes to investors and are defending their claims. In February 1991 the Government won its first case, recovering £500,000 in a judgment against a firm of chartered accountants who had put their clients into Barlow Clowes. One of the DTI's legal arguments is that intermediaries were negligent for recommending clients to invest in Barlow Clowes International because it was not licensed by the DTI and therefore subject to no external safeguards. However, at least one firm of intermediaries being sued – Chittington – is counterclaiming against the DTI for negligence. Most intermediaries are likely to follow suit.

23: BREATHTAKING CHEEK

1. Ross Hyett of Analysis Holdings, one of the most important intermediaries to Clowes, said that he thought that the money could also be invested in local authority bonds which he regarded as providing equivalent security to gilts.

2. This was not the only memorandum which highlighted Spicers' concerns. Earlier in the year, on 8 April 1987, Bell had written a memo to Pilkington about Spicers' resignation as auditors following the Ferguson takeover. Bell's memo made it clear that Barlow Clowes was viewed as a 'high risk client'. According to Pilkington this partly referred to the risk of Barlow Clowes causing the firm embarrassment in the future. As Pilkington also pointed out to the senior partner of Spicers, Barlow Clowes had a high political profile and a large number of small investors. Clowes himself, said Pilkington, was something of a 'fringe operator'.

   What is interesting is that there is no evidence in either of the government reports on Barlow Clowes that any of these new concerns which Spicers had were relayed back to the Department of Trade and Industry. This may be because by the time these memoranda were circulating, Spicers were no longer responsible for preparing monitoring returns for Barlow Clowes, the job being taken over by the new auditors, Touche Ross. They had no obligation to tell the DTI about their concerns. However, the previous year Pilkington had spoken with Laurence Green of the DTI's licensing section about Derek Tree's own concerns. Pilkington had promised that Spicers would look thoroughly at Barlow Clowes's clients' accounts in the forthcoming audit. Moreover, Spicers were fully aware of the background to the licensing of the Barlow Clowes business – such as the DTI's own concerns and the considerable amount of verification work that the DTI had insisted upon before being prepared to grant the licence.

3. None of any profits from Clowes's illicit share deals went back to the investors, even though they unwittingly financed them, Suckling said at the trial.

EPILOGUE

1. The interview with Barbara Conway was recorded shortly before she died, following a brave struggle against cancer, in 1991.

2. It is neither fair nor accurate to say that investors in Barlow Clowes got a higher return than available elsewhere and therefore should have been on their guard. In fact the rates offered by the Post Office Investment Account often bettered those Barlow Clowes was offering on its offshore funds. The difference was that Barlow Clowes was offering its returns as tax free capital gain while the Post Office returns were taxable in the hands of a UK taxpayer. It was the bogus tax free claim by Clowes which meant that his returns were the best in the market. Most investors put their money with Barlow Clowes through financial intermediaries, who

advised them to do so. The investors were not financially sophisticated and it was reasonable for them to rely on their advisers. I would not classify the Barlow Clowes investors as greedy or stupid. Professor Gower's quotation applies more easily to the financial intermediaries than to the Barlow Clowes investors.

PICTURE ACKNOWLEDGEMENTS

•

The author and publishers would like to thank the following who have kindly given permission for the use of photographs:

The Reverend John Clowes: page 1 above, page 2 below; *Daily Mail:* page 5 below, page 6 below, page 8 above: Barry Greenwood: page 3 below; *The Independent*/David Rose: page 8 below; National News: page 6 above; Press Association: page 5 above, page 7; Simon Preston: page 3 above; Stockport News Service: page 2 below; Times Newspapers Ltd: page 4 above and below.